P9-BZX-934

PACIFIC OCEAN

Equator

INDIAN OCEAN

THE

SYRAH, GRENACHE & MOURVÈDRE

GRAPES

SYRAH, GRENACHE AND MOURVÈDRE

Giles MacDonogh

Series editor: Harry Eyres

VIKING

For Margaux Johnston,
whose father introduced me
to the great wines
of the Rhône Valley

VIKING

Published by the Penguin Group
Penguin Books Ltd, 27 Wrights Lane, London W8 5TZ, England
Penguin Books USA Inc., 375 Hudson Street, New York, New York 10014, USA
Penguin Books Australia Ltd, Ringwood, Victoria, Australia
Penguin Books Canada Ltd, 10 Alcorn Avenue, Toronto, Ontario, Canada M4V 3B2
Penguin Books (NZ) Ltd, 182–190 Wairau Road, Auckland 10, New Zealand

Penguin Books Ltd, Registered Offices: Harmondsworth, Middlesex, England

First published 1992
1 3 5 7 9 10 8 6 4 2

Copyright © Giles MacDonogh, 1992
Foreword copyright © Harry Eyres, 1992
All maps in the series by Andrew Farmer

The moral right of the author has been asserted

All rights reserved.
Without limiting the rights under copyright
reserved above, no part of this publication may be
reproduced, stored in or introduced into a retrieval system,
or transmitted, in any form or by any means (electronic, mechanical,
photocopying, recording or otherwise), without the prior
written permission of both the copyright owner and
the above publisher of this book

Set in 9/12 Linotron Janson Text 55 by Wyvern Typesetting Ltd, Bristol
Printed in Great Britain by Butler & Tanner Ltd, Frome and London

A CIP catalogue record for this book is available from the British Library

ISBN 0–670–82588–3

CONTENTS

MAPS

ACKNOWLEDGEMENTS

A great many people have helped in the preparations for this book. Wine-makers who have welcomed me into their homes and cellars are too numerous to mention here; many are profiled in the following pages, and it is to them above all that I owe the greatest debt of gratitude. I have also relied on wine authorities both in Britain and abroad during the course of writing. I should in particular like to thank Hazel Murphy, Vicky Bishop and Scott Gold Blyth Ltd for facilitating my journey to Australia. In Australia itself I received considerable assistance from James and Suzanne Halliday and Len Evans; while in London I learned much from Stephen Walker of Gullin and from Craig Smith and his staff at the Australian Wine Centre in the Strand.

For France I am indebted to Catherine Manac'h, Gabrielle Allen and Sophie Valléjo in London; Tim Johnston and Mark Williamson in Paris; and to Bruno Prats and the late Martin Bamford MW in Bordeaux. Specific help in the regions came from Jean Gabert, Robin Yapp, Hew Blair, Nick Clarke MW, Helen Thompson, Guy Bizot, Simon Farr, Willy Lebus, Sophie Nicolas, Jaquie Kay, Anthony and Novella Lacey, Alain Bochnakian, Louis Bronzo, Gérard Dufour, Christine Behuey, André Brugirard, Jean Rière, Pierre Torrès, Anne Seguin, Christine Ontivero, Christine Campadieu, Alain Halma and Jean-Luc Colombo.

Both David Gleave MW and Paul Merritt were informative about Italy; Rupert Ponsonby, Cessa Beckett and Angela Lloyd gave me help on South Africa; Jeremy Watson, Manuel Moreno and Catherine Scott talked to me about Spain; and Jasper Morris MW, Mel Knox and Dick Ward were kind enough to speak to me about California.

I should also like to thank my fellow writers on this series –

Tim Atkin, Andrew Barr, Stephen Brook, Harry Eyres and Stuart Pigott – for providing me with so many authoritative tips and gleanings.

Giles MacDonogh

FOREWORD

Syrah, or Shiraz, may be one of the oldest grape varieties in the world. Shiraz is the name of an ancient Persian city, suggesting that the grape made its way to France – now its homeland – from the Middle East, cradle of vinous as well as other kinds of civilization. Others say the name comes from the Greek city of Syracuse, the vines having been taken there from the Levant. Whatever its origins, Syrah is indisputably one of the most noble of red wine grapes. If it is not as celebrated as Cabernet Sauvignon or Pinot Noir, that reflects not so much the quality of the grape as the relative economic backwardness of the northern Rhône Valley, where most of the great Syrah wines are made. Tain-l'Hermitage, headquarters of the firms of Paul Jaboulet Aîné, Chapoutier and Delas Frères, is one of the duller towns in southern France – as I should know, because I once spent a summer there assembling wine cases.

Wine-making in the northern Rhône, and in all probability the cultivation of Syrah, goes back to the Romans and very likely the Greeks. The great granite hill of Hermitage is possibly the oldest vineyard site in France. But the top northern-Rhône wines have not enjoyed anything like such consistent fame as those of Burgundy (since the Middle Ages) or Bordeaux (since the late seventeenth century). Indeed the powerful, though not coarse, and reliably full-bodied wines of Hermitage were regularly cut with claret in the nineteenth century, producing such to us sacrilegious hybrids as Lafite Hermitagé. Having said 'sacrilegious', one thinks not only of the popular and successful Cabernet-Sauvignon/Shiraz blends of Australia, but also of the new wave of Cabernet/Syrah crosses pioneered by Château Vignelaure and Domaine de Trévallon in Provence. But the pure-Syrah (we can conveniently disregard small additions of the white grapes Roussanne and Marsanne) wines of Hermitage, Côte Rôtie and Cornas were just beginning to enjoy the renown they deserved in the late nineteenth century when phylloxera struck. It is only really in the last fifteen years or so that the regions have enjoyed a boom, which few would grudge them.

What a boom it has been, though! Touched by the Midas pen of Robert Parker, the American wine journalist who has done so much to promote the cause of Rhône wines in the last decade, prices of the top northern-Rhône wines, and especially Côte Rôtie, have, as Ronald Reagan put it in a different context, 'broken the surly bonds of earth' and risen skywards. Those of us who can no longer even think of buying these wines may maliciously hope that (like the Space Shuttle to which Reagan was referring) they crash earthwards once more. In 1949, after all, a litre of Côte Rôtie cost one franc. In the mid 1970s, at the beginning of my wine-drinking days, I remember buying bottles of Auguste Clape's Cornas from Steven Spurrier's original Caves de la Madeleine shop in Paris for less than twenty francs. Now Marcel Guigal's single-*cru* Côte Rôties cost even more than Château Pétrus (perhaps only a matter of academic concern to most of us). The Hermitages of Chave and Paul Jaboulet cost about the same as super-second growth Médocs – and fair enough, I would say, for these are superb and inimitable wines, with a pungent, yet flowery intensity which is uniquely Syrah.

It is undoubtedly the success of these Syrah-based wines that has led to a minor but interesting Syrah expansion into wine regions which have no Syrah tradition, such as California and Tuscany. The Californian Rhône Ranger school, of which Randall Grahm is the spokesman (but Qupé the most exciting producer), may look like a typically Californian publicity stunt, but the results are exciting. Whether anyone will follow the example of Paolo de Marchi in planting Syrah at Isole e Olena in Chianti Classico is more of a moot point. De Marchi's wine is pretty good, but perhaps the best place for Syrah in Italy might be further south, or on the islands.

For a reason I do not fully understand, Australia persistently undervalues its magnificent Shiraz wines. Perhaps the chilly glitter of Bordeaux persuades wine-growers on the other side of the planet that Cabernet Sauvignon is the classy grape while Shiraz is somehow less noble. I would say that just as many great wines are made from Shiraz as from Cabernet Sauvignon in Australia. Few Australian Shirazes taste even vaguely like the great northern-Rhône wines: the grape tastes very different when grown in different regions and climates. Some of the cool-climate Shirazes of Victoria or Coonawarra have a strongly pepperminty edge. The great old Shirazes of the Hunter (preserved like some national monument – which they are – by Lindemans) have the famous 'sweaty saddle' character and suggest cowboy country. And Australia's greatest red wine, Grange Hermitage, tastes to me (though not to Giles Mac-Donogh) like a bigger, warmer Pomerol – more clarety than Rhôney.

Shiraz is also important in Australia as a partner with Cabernet in blends which combine the elegant but sometimes bony structure of Cabernet Sauvignon with the greater warmth of Shiraz. The best of these, from Yalumba, Penfolds, Wolf Blass and others, together with the Cabernet/Syrah crosses of Provence, show how harmoniously these two great grapes can blend.

Grenache and Mourvèdre, despite the French style they are given here, are grapes of Spanish origin, only introduced to France in important quantities after phylloxera. But even a Hispanophile like myself has to admit that the finest wines from both grapes are currently being made in southern France. Châteauneuf-du-Pape, as Giles MacDonogh points out, is more of a Grenache wine than most Médocs are Cabernet Sauvignon wines; but the appellation makes more play with the fact that thirteen grape varieties are allowed than with the reality that nearly 80 per cent of the vineyard area is given over to Grenache. Forgetting the dubious papal associations, and the sadly substandard wines called Châteauneuf which used to be prevalent, we can appreciate Châteauneuf-du-Pape as the greatest wine of France's deep south. Its roasted, gamy, rich yet still floral character is a perfect expression of the hot, scented Provençal landscape. The large appellation still has its problems, but there are several high-quality estates making excellent wine which is underpriced compared to claret, Burgundy or the northern-Rhône wines.

There is more Garnacha Negra (the grape's original name) in Spain than there is in France, but sadly little wine of any distinction is made from it. Certainly the greatest Spanish Garnachas are the wildly alcoholic, fruit-cake-rich wines made under the rock palisades of Montsant at Priorato, inland from Tarragona. Miguel Torres makes a very plausible Châteauneuf substitute in the form of his Gran Sangredetoro. These are big, solid reds. But Garnacha in Navarra makes some delectable dry *rosés* which go superbly with the tapas of Pamplona and are still a great bargain. Unfortunately, people are foolishly prejudiced against good dry *rosé*.

Grenache is now being grown in California, especially by Randall Grahm at Bonny Doon, and is making some deliciously quaffable light reds and *rosés*. So far it is little used in other New World countries, or born-again European regions.

Mourvèdre is another Spanish grape which crept over the border into southern France. Under its Spanish, or Catalan, names of Monastrell and Mataró, the grape planted over vast areas produces nothing of any great note, though research on this and other old Catalan grape varieties being conducted by Miguel Torres should surely yield interesting results soon. The solitary vineyard producing quality Mourvèdre is Bandol, above the Côte d'Azur. This is one of Robert Parker's favourite wines. Randall Grahm has already had some success with Mourvèdre at Bonny Doon, and this seems to be a minor grape with a future. We should be grateful for all signs of life beyond Cabernet Sauvignon and Chardonnay.

Harry Eyres

INTRODUCTION

History

Syrah, Grenache and Mourvèdre are three grapes which epitomize the hot south. They grow in the land of olives, of lavender-scented hillsides dotted with fig and lemon trees and above all vines – strung across rocky cliffs in terraces, or planted in stubby 'goblets' on stone-strewn slopes unsuitable for any other branch of agriculture or endeavour. With the exception of some of Italy's best grapes, such as the Sangiovese Grosso, Syrah, Grenache and Mourvèdre represent the best of the Mediterranean tradition which began on Spain's eastern seaboard and spread up to the north and east across France's southern littoral before sweeping into the southern half of the Rhône Valley. From Spain the grapes also took off to Sardinia and North Africa.

All three are hardy cultivars which are well adapted to their scorched hillsides. The Spanish took them with them to the New World, and before the end of the seventeenth century French Huguenots had taken Syrah cuttings out to the Cape of Good Hope. More than a century later, Australian viticultural pioneers were adapting Syrah, Grenache and Mourvèdre to the arid beds of the Hunter, Barossa and Clare Valleys. Argentinian colonists later planted Syrah vines on the eastern flanks of the Andes.

After a period during which they fell from favour, our own generation has rediscovered Syrah, Grenache and Mourvèdre, and these three varieties are once again on the move. New World wine-makers are planting them in California, Australia and South Africa in areas where experience tells them they will get the best results. Back in the Old World, countries such as

Switzerland, Austria and Italy have begun to examine the potential of these dark-skinned varieties to see if they could not add a little southern spice to their own array of flavours.

Of the three grapes, Syrah is the noblest. Its origins are open to dispute. Some have said that it was first grown in Persia around the ancient city of Shiraz, by which name it is known in Australia and South Africa, while others claim that the name is a corruption of that of the city of Syracuse in Sicily. In the northern Rhône, where most of the greatest Syrah wine is made, experts advance the view that the Syrah was originally a wild vine indigenous to those parts and they cite the evidence of fossilized pips and leaves to prove it.

It is possible that the original table wines of the Roman colony of Vienna (the modern Vienne, which is less than three miles from the slopes of Côte Rôtie) were made from the Syrah grape; writers seem to agree that they were marked by a tarry aroma which is one of the characters of Syrah wines to this day. Naturally, however, assertions of this sort are hard to prove. What does seem clear, though, is that the style of red wine-making in the northern Rhône remained localized until recent times, and that its big, deep-coloured red wines remained the speciality of the great granite hillsides where they were tasted and appreciated by countless travellers who used the Rhône roads and waterways as they proceeded towards Italy and the South.

The wines of the northern Rhône began to achieve a repu-tation in Paris and abroad only from the seventeenth century. One of the first literary references to Hermitage comes from the satirist Nicolas Boileau, the third of whose *Satires*, *Le Repas ridicule*, contains a reference to a *nouveau riche* trying to pass off inferior wine as Hermitage. Boileau's satire is dated 1665. We know that this was the precise date of Louis XIV's present of some bottles of Hermitage to his cousin, King Charles II of England; possibly it was the French court's use of Hermitage which made it so attractive to the hero of *Le Repas ridicule*.

In 1678 the English philosopher John Locke passed by the great hill on his way to a cure at the French medical university of Montpellier. Locke, who was later to write the first ever oenological study, was not slow to express his enthusiasm for the 'excellent Hermitage wine'. Nearly a century later the novelist Tobias Smollett passed through Tain on his way to Montpellier. At first the old misanthrope (and Scotsman) quailed at the thought of paying three livres for a bottle of the wine. On his return from Italy, however, Smollett joined in the chorus of praise.

John Hervey, the first Earl of Bristol, possessed wines from Hermitage in his capacious cellar as early as 1690, and Côte Rôtie in 1736. Hervey even had some 'white Condrieu' in his cellar in 1714. In the first years of the nineteenth century, the 'Father of the Table' Grimod de La Reynière advocated drinking 'red Condrieu', by which he possibly meant Côte Rôtie. Anthelme Brillat-Savarin, who, coming from the Bugey, was rather more familiar with the wines of the Dauphiné, mentions Hermitage several times in his *Physiologie du goût* of 1825 and even celebrated his being called to the local bar in 1778 by a lavish feast moistened with bottles of Hermitage.

The northern Rhône's best-known vineyard has always been shrouded in legend; far more so than either Côte Rôtie or Cornas. In his 1831 novella *Crotchet Castle*, Thomas Love Peacock has his gourmand clergyman the Revd Dr Folliott exclaim of Hermitage, 'Nothing better, sir. The father who first chose the solitude of that vineyard, knew well how to cultivate his spirit in retirement.' Folliott was alluding to the legendary hermit who is supposed to have planted the vines on the exposed outcrop of the Massif Central. One story tells us that Saint Patrick, the celebrated killer of snakes and toads and converter of the Irish, planted the vines on his way to the old monastery of Lérins in the harbour by Cannes. Another says that one Gaspard de Stérimberg planted them on his return from the crusades. The only evidence of any hermit living on the hill comes from sixteenth-century records, although the vines must have existed there much earlier.

The quality of the wines of Hermitage and Côte Rôtie was well known by the beginning of the nineteenth century, at precisely the moment when the vineyards went into decline. Part of the reason for the fall lies in the use of Hermitage as a *vin médecin* for the lighter but more famous wines of Burgundy and Bordeaux. The fraud originated during the Napoleonic Wars, when the British blockade made the inky wines of Beni Carlo and Alicante temporarily unavailable. The discovery of Hermitage by the merchants made the fortune of the Calvet family of Tain, who bought into the shipping business in both Beaune and Bordeaux, on the basis of their contacts with growers in Hermitage. The plantation-Irish Johnston family, who had traded from Bordeaux since the mid eighteenth century, also seized on the opportunities created by using Hermitage in the Bordeaux blend and actually bought a vineyard in Tain to ensure their supplies of wine.

The 'Hermitaged' wines of Bordeaux created a style which is today more familiar to Australians than to Frenchmen, although the Provençal wines of Domaine de Trévallon and Château Vignelaure continue to blend Cabernet and Syrah to good effect. In order to beat the merchants at their own game, Bordeaux growers began to plant Syrah in their own vineyards. The first vineyards at Cos d'Estournel in St-Estèphe were planted at the very beginning of the nineteenth century, and d'Estournel was careful to include some rows of Syrah. In 1820 there was Syrah planted at Château Lafite (where there was more Petit Verdot than Cabernet Sauvignon for the time being). Syrah was still being planted at Château Latour as late as 1838–40.

Given the popularity of Syrah, it should come as no surprise that it was planted in the first Australian vineyards, which were being mapped out at precisely this time. Vines were being planted in the Hunter Valley in New South Wales as early as the 1820s, and in Mudgee by 1858. Cabernet Sauvignon would have been largely unknown to the Australians. (In 1840 it still accounted for less than 30 per cent of the vineyard area at Latour.) The first man to plant in the Hunter was James Busby, who installed his brother-in-law William Kelman as manager. In 1848 Kelman provided an 1845 Hermitage for the inaugural meeting of the Viticultural Association. In the Barossa Valley, Silesian German settlers were planting Syrah (Shiraz) vines soon after their arrival in the 1840s. The oldest Shiraz vines in the valley date from the 1880s. At Château Tahbilk in Victoria there is still a plot of 1860 Shiraz vines. I can think of no vines any older than these in France; indeed few Syrah vines in the Rhône Valley can have survived the phylloxera scourge which ravaged the vineyards of France during the last third of the nineteenth century, so the earliest there would date from the 1890s.

Phylloxera altered the course of history as far as Syrah was concerned. The progress that Syrah was making in the Médoc was halted, and when the Bordelais came to replant it was Cabernet Sauvignon which became the favoured grape. The consequent slump in wine prices for the Rhône Valley meant that many growers failed to replant after the passing of the scourge. The position of the great northern-Rhône wines remained bad until well after the Second World War, when prices began to rise once again. Much of the credit for this revival must go to the big *négociant* houses in Tain, who kept the vineyards going throughout the difficult years. Real revival came about only in the 1970s, when prices began to rocket. In the last few years we have even seen two Côte Rôtie single *crus* fetch prices superior even to Château Pétrus; nor did the grower, Guigal, have any problem disposing of them. To a large degree the fashionableness of Rhône wines was brought about by the first new books to be written on the subject: John Livingstone-Learmonth and Melvyn Master's *The Wines of the Rhône* (Faber, 1978; revised 1992) and Robert Parker's *The Wines of the Rhône Valley and Provence* (Dorling Kindersley, 1988).

Ironically, the revival of Syrah in the Rhône coincided with the 'puritan' revolution in Australian wine-making (see page 26). Shiraz had been playing virtually every role on the Australian wine stage for a century: claret, Burgundy, Hermitage, sparkling red Burgundy, port and Beaujolais. Once the news of California's successful adaptation of Cabernet Sauvignon and Chardonnay vines reached Australia, the younger generation there wanted nothing more to do with Shiraz. Fortunately in the last ten years there has been a limited revival in Shiraz's fortunes – not least because it has become abundantly clear that areas like the Barossa and the Hunter are unsuitable for Cabernet vines.

Grenache and Mourvèdre both come from Spain. Grenache Noir or Garnacha Tinta probably originated on the east coast of Aragon or Catalonia, where it was perfectly well adapted to the hot, dry climate. Until the seventeenth century, Spanish Catalonia ran right the way up to the Corbières, and the entire eastern half of the Pyrenees lay within Spain. The Roussillon was annexed by France in 1659, but the Spanish were slow to accept the loss: during the French Revolution, Collioure was for a time reoccupied by Spanish troops.

The border may now run between the peaks of the Pyrenees, but a similarity in language, customs and wine remains on both sides. Grenache or Garnacha is the *fond de sauce* for red wines on both sides of the Pyrenees, either in the form of wines made with the addition of some must from the Carignan grape to prevent them from oxidizing or as fortified wines made by stopping the wines' fermentation by adding neutral spirits. Some wines, fortified or not, were made from pure Grenache and kept for years in big old tuns where they progressively oxidized and lost colour. These old wines were said to develop a *'rancio'* character with age: a flavour which used to be much in demand for travellers in the region who savoured that blend of fig, coffee and leather which was thrown off by the wine. The *Guide pittoresque du voyageur en France* of 1836 gives a description of the wines grown on the schisty soils of Banyuls-sur-Mer, in French Catalonia, which were particularly appreciated at the time:

> The area around Banyuls-sur-Mer produces wines of a very deep colour, full-bodied and strong, with a silky texture and an excellent taste. As they get older, these wines acquire finesse and bouquet, and when they are ten years old or more they go a golden colour and develop an old taste which is called *'rancio'* because at this stage they begin to resemble those so designated in Spain.
>
> They get better up to the age of thirty years and may be kept for fifty without going off when they come from a

vintage where the climate has been favourable to the vines; in this case they resemble the wines of Alicante, of which they have all the virtues and all the pleasant characteristics.

Banyuls also makes liqueur wines called Grenache wines, the name of which derives from their grape variety; they are red but not so deep in colour as the other wines of the area. As they grow older, their colour goes: they become light and fine; their pleasant taste begins to resemble the wines of Rota or, even more, the wines of the island of Cyprus.

Grenache had spread from Spain into France before the end of the Middle Ages. There is evidence that it had reached the southern Rhône before the sixteenth century, when it was already giving character to the wines of Châteauneuf-du-Pape. These days growers in the southern Rhône like to play down the importance of Grenache in their wines and will tell you that the grape variety was forced on them after the Second World War by unscrupulous Burgundian merchants who wanted big, strapping brews to give strength to weedy Burgundies. I suspect that the character of Châteauneuf and the southern Rhône villages has been dictated by the Grenache grape for rather longer. In Marcel Rouff's novella *La vie et la passion de Dodin-Bouffant*, written in 1921 (and therefore before the planting of the plateau of Mont-Redon, which gives so much character to the better Châteauneufs), the Prince of Eurasia conducts his gastronomic experiments:

> his mind avid for discovery as a result of a marvellous Châteauneuf-du-Pape, which filled his imagination like a powerful ocean wind fills a sail; all the sun that it had concealed within it, all the vigour of the hot soils of the Rhône Valley, the land which endowed its soul and which, while the waves of raspberry fruit mingled with the tannins, brought a superb lucidity to his brain . . .

By the late nineteenth century, Grenache plantations together with Mourvèdre had begun to give good results in the

torrid vineyards of North Africa. In 1909 the British wine merchant Sir Walter Gilbey noted in the diary he kept at Château
Loudenne in the Médoc:

> The splendid quality and extremely low price of the wines
> of Algeria although of a different character [to the wines of
> Bordeaux] is a topic of daily conversation in Bordeaux, and
> would it is felt with the gigantic quantity approaching 200
> millions of gallons annually, completely revolutionize the
> French wine trade; its suitability for the daily beverage of
> *vin ordinaire* being far superior to anything now produced
> in the Midi, the Hérault and other parts of France.

After the independence of the three westernmost states of
North Africa, the Muslim governments pulled up the vast
majority of the vines which had been owned by the French and
Spanish colonists – the famous *pieds noirs*.

Although one of the world's most widely planted grape
varieties, Grenache elsewhere fell a victim to vineyard fashions.
In Australia, much of the Grenache was pulled up with the first
waves of the Cabernet/Chardonnay revolution; so far there are
few people in the country who regret its passing. But across the
Pacific, in California, growers of the new Rhône Ranger school
can't get enough Grenache to make their southern-Rhône-style
blends and are now obliged to travel up to the states to the
north of California to ensure adequate quantities.

The last of our players, Mourvèdre, is known as Monastrell
in Spain and Mataró in Catalonia, California and Australia. Its
homeland is Murcia and Valencia on the east coast of Spain,
where it has long produced inky wines of no great distinction. It
appeared in Châteauneuf towards the end of the seventeenth
century and was also planted in the Rhône delta around the
village of Lirac. By the eighteenth century it had been widely
planted on the Provençal coast at Bandol, as Lucien Peyraud
was able to glean from historic texts such as those by the *abbé*
Rozier and by Dr Guyot. In the closing years of the last century, phylloxera wiped out the Mourvèdre in Bandol and the
growers chose to replant with Alicante Bouschet and Aramon.

Lucien Peyraud is the re-creator of the Mourvèdre vineyards of Bandol. Since 1941 he has struggled to see the grape variety achieve a 60 per cent share of the vines. His efforts have paid off in that Bandol has become the most interesting *cru* of the southern coast. In Collioure, too, at the other end of the French south coast, Mourvèdre is being seen as the grape to revive the fortunes of viticulture on the slopes of the littoral. Between the two, in Fitou and the coastal Corbières, Mourvèdre is helping to improve the quality of the wines.

Mourvèdre is also currently one of the most fashionable grapes in California, where it has become one of the building blocks for wine-makers of the Rhône Ranger school. One wonders how long it will be before Australians take an interest in the grape, which still exists in fairly large amounts in South Australia and on the Murray River. Already Charlie Melton has started adding some to his 'Nine Popes' Châteauneuf-style blend.

Cépages Améliorateurs

Neither Syrah, Grenache or Mourvèdre is used 100 per cent pure in the vast majority of its incarnations. Syrah exists pure largely in a stretch of the Rhône running from Valence to Vienne, but in both Hermitage and Côte Rôtie small amounts of white grapes are permitted and frequently used to give extra aromas. There are a handful of other pure Syrah wines in France, but other than these you will find 100 per cent Syrah wines only in California, Argentina, South Africa and Australia, barring a few experimental wines made elsewhere; only on mean soils and on exposed hillsides will Syrah give the depths of flavour to make a truly great wine, and the world possesses few enough suitable sites.

Likewise Grenache is rarely used without being cut with other grapes. Apart from Château Rayas in Châteauneuf-du-

Pape, some fruity *rosés* and some Spanish reds, only fortified wines are ever made from 100 per cent Grenache fruit. Grenache has the disadvantage of being a poor resister to oxygen, and so will age quickly, and only with very small yields and extremely old vines can you make a pure Grenache wine. The usual solution is to add one of the better oxygen-resisting grape varieties. Cinsault and Carignan are popular for this; Syrah is better; possibly the best of all is Mourvèdre.

There is more pure Mourvèdre around than 100 per cent Syrah or Grenache. In Spain there are over 250,000 acres of Monastrell, producing wines of deep colour but little distinction. In California there are a handful of Rhône Ranger producers making Mourvèdre wines, and now in Bandol there are perhaps as many as eight growers who regularly produce wines made from 95 to 100 per cent Mourvèdre.

Syrah, Grenache and Mourvèdre may be blended together, and such a blend is generally the successful formula in Châteauneuf-du-Pape. For some growers the combination of Syrah and Mourvèdre is seen as a mistake, as both perform the same role in preventing the Grenache from oxidizing. The Syrah tends to have greater aromatic intensity than the Mourvèdre, but the Mourvèdre gives bigger, firmer tannins. I know of only one Syrah/Mourvèdre blend and that is the Penfolds Bin 2. It is an eccentric combination, but a very decent wine.

Syrah, Grenache and Mourvèdre are all considered to be *cépages nobles*, and their nobility is regarded as a factor for the improvement of lesser grape varieties such as Cinsault or Carignan; in these cases the French refer to the grapes as *cépages améliorateurs* or 'improving varieties'.

The use of *cépages améliorateurs* was particularly important in the Midi and the Pyrénées Orientales. The first task was to remove the '*cépages ignobles*' such as the Aramon and the Alicante Bouschet. The next was to pull up the Cinsault and Carignan, which had been planted in flat sites where they gave too much thin juice; good Carignan may be obtained, but only from old vines on hillside slopes. Once the Carignan had been reduced to only the best vines, the musts were 'improved' by the addition of 20 or 30 per cent Syrah or Mourvèdre to provide better tannins and aromas. This process has been completed in certain areas of the south of France, where the basic wines are likely to be something like 60 per cent Carignan with the rest made up of Syrah or Mourvèdre. In other areas Grenache has replaced the Carignan altogether, so that the wines are now made from Grenache with a certain amount of Syrah or Mourvèdre or both.

Apart from enhancing a typically southern-French palette of flavours, Syrah has been discovered to have other uses when it comes to combining grape varieties. The use of Syrah with Cabernet Sauvignon has already been mentioned; in Australia the two grapes are often blended either with a majority of Syrah or with the mainstay in Cabernet. The effect is to eliminate some of the drawbacks of the 'hollow' Cabernet. Not everyone approves of these blends, however; Bailey Carrodus of Yarra Yering is particularly scathing about the combination.

In Spain, many wines are a combination of Monastrell and Garnacha, the Garnacha having the advantage of softening the tannic Monastrell. In California, Syrah, Grenache and Mourvèdre have been successfully blended with Zinfandel.

Soils and Training

The classic Syrah soils are the great granite rocks of the northern Rhône, which used to form the last outposts of the Massif Central. Hermitage ended up on the eastern bank of the river after the Rhône formed a new passage to the west of the hill, but it is essentially part of the same chain as Côte Rôtie, St-Joseph and Cornas. Elsewhere in the northern Rhône the best Syrah soil is limestone. Syrah also performs well on schists.

The quality of the grape is also determined by the topsoil. In Côte Rôtie the Côte Blonde comes from sandy soils, while the tougher, less perfumed, wines of the Côte Brune come from more clayey soils containing a fair amount of ferrous oxide. In Hermitage the topsoil changes three times as you travel from west to east, starting with fractured granite and ending with limestone. The best soils in Crozes-Hermitage are limestone; the worst (and they are bad) are alluvial clay.

Visiting Australia, it is rare that one gets the impression that wine-makers have actively sought the best soils for their vines. Many of the leading figures in Australian viticulture like to deny the importance of soil factors; some of the more enlightened wine-makers, however, agree that Australia has probably yet to discover the best sites for its vines. It is unlikely, for example, that any wine-maker today would choose to plant in the Hunter were it not for the convenience of an area which has been dedicated to wine production for 150 years and more. The release of the first Shiraz from Knight's Granite Hills – granite-grown wines from high-altitude sites – was a revelation to the Australian wine press in the late 1970s. Up till then climate had been the determining factor and not soil, and to some extent this remains the case. One notable exception, however, is the great *terra rosa* belt of Coonawarra, most of which has been turned over to the creation of Bordeaux blends.

Traditionally Syrah is trained high on posts and is exposed to both sun and wind. In Hermitage and Cornas one stake is used. In Côte Rôtie, four stakes support the vine. Among some growers there is a move towards trellising the vines on wire. The traditionalists in the northern Rhône do not approve of this, but wire-trained Syrah is a common sight in the Midi. Naturally in the New World wire is far more common, and growers are experimenting with new mini-climate-inducing lyre training, which gives the grape more protection from the sun. Michel Chapoutier in Hermitage believes that too strong a sunlight gives the Syrah a chocolatey character which he per-sonally dislikes. The solution is to allow for more leaf cover.

Grenache is generally grown in the stubby 'goblet' with three short shoots. The perfect terrain for the Grenache is arid, stony hillsides providing a maximum of heat. In Châteauneuf the best Grenache soils are on the high plateau, where the famous *galets* (smooth pebbles the size of ostrich eggs) heat up during the day and retain their heat during the night. This baking heat is a factor inducing the tobacco/cigarette character found in the best Châteauneuf.

Growers will often tell you that the best Mourvèdre should have 'its feet in water and its head in the air'. Good Mourvèdre should, we are told, see the sea. Naturally this is stretching a point in Châteauneuf or Lirac, and indeed there are very few of Bandol's vineyards which are within sight of the sea with the exception of the Château de Pibarnon or the Château de La Rouvière. Still, it is clear that good results are probable only in seaside vineyards, and this has given hope to producers in the maritime parts of Fitou, Corbières and Collioure. Mourvèdre is also trained in a high goblet, but there are some growers who have gone over to wire training for the sake of convenience.

Making the Wines

There are naturally as many theories of wine-making as there are wine-makers. There are few, if any, hard and fast rules. Some growers consciously imitate the methods of Bordeaux, while others look to Burgundy for inspiration. The amount of extraction sought from the musts naturally depends on the sort of wine to be made. Syrah, for example, can make virtually every style from a gluggable summer 'Beaujolais' all the way through to some great bruiser which takes years for its tannins to soften sufficiently to let you get at the fruit.

In the northern Rhône the wines tend to be extractive and tannic. Growers feel that their wines should be laid down and savoured after ten years or so. The current feeling is that the musts should be worked to get the maximum extract. One method advanced by Jean-Luc Colombo in Cornas is *pigeage*, or the plunging of the solid cap of the fermenting must with a vertical action, often automatic. In the more modern, forward-thinking estates in the Rhône, this method has replaced submerging the cap and pumping the juice over it. In one or two places (notably the co-operative at St-Désirat in St-Joseph) carbonic maceration is practised. By this method the grapes are macerated whole under a cover of nitrogen so that the fermentation starts within the berries themselves. It is a variation on the Beaujolais method and makes wines which are aromatic but lack body. One or two growers in Châteauneuf-du-Pape use this process, and some Australian estates favour 'cab mac' (as they call it) for a summer wine; Mitchelton's Cab Mac is one of the most famous.

The longer the maceration, the denser and more extractive the wine; but long fermentations also invite difficulties which can lead to tainted wine and vinegary, volatile acidity. Only talented, confident wine-makers attempt fermentations of three weeks and more.

Today, the sort of wood used to age Syrah wines in particular is a controversial issue. Before the 1970s, most Syrah, Grenache and Mourvèdre matured in big, old tuns. Small oak casks (*barriques*) were rare; new small oak unheard of. There is evidence to show, however, that Hermitage wines before phylloxera were generaly aged in small, new oak barrels. The Hermitage grower M. Rey, writing in his *Coteau de l'Ermitage* of 1861, say: 'Hermitage is never put into old casks', attributing the superiority of the new cask to the gallic acid contained in the wood. The current new oak craze is however, a product of the winds of change from California which have resulted in new oak being used as a flavouring ingredient quite distinct from the original purpose of the wooden cask: the gradual oxidation of the wine to bring out secondary fruit aromas. At first, new oak was reserved for the estate's top wines; so new-oak tastes could be virtually guaranteed with every purchase of a bottle of Californian and Australian Chardonnay or Cabernet Sauvignon. Then the public began to appreciate the oaky, vanilla flavours on a wider range of wines; growers felt that the only way they could express their sophistication was by coating the fruit with new-oak tastes.

Growers in the New World experimented with different woods to see which would suit Shiraz the best. Most came to the conclusion that Shiraz did not require the subtler aromas of French oak from Nevers or Allier, but could take the more blatant spicy aromas to be had from Kentucky oak. Personally I feel this was a mistake; Kentucky oak is fine for Bourbon whiskey, where it gives a big sweet, spicy, vanilla flavouring to the spirit; on wine, on the other hand, the flavours seem too big and obvious – almost synthetic.

Some Australian growers use American oak in such a way as to mask its drawbacks: Grange Hermitage is the obvious example here. Other Australian viticulturalists continue to use French oak: Bailey Carrodus at Yarra Yering springs to mind – he told me that he had never been tempted by American oak.

In the Old World, new-oak barrels have contributed to the vicious circle of rising prices. Jean-Luc Colombo recommends them for northern-Rhône Syrah wines, Noël Rabot advocates their use in Châteauneuf (although only for Syrah and Mourvèdre); few apart from Marcel Guigal (for his top *crus*) and Colombo have gone to 100 per cent new oak, and most of Colombo's disciples restrain themselves at 33 per cent or less per annum. Again, some of the more notable growers remain unconvinced: Gérard Chave resists new-oak flavours, and both of Cornas's top men – Clape and Michel – preside over batteries of old wood. In Hermitage, new wood merely seems to add to the indomitable tannins of the wine; so far Côte Rôtie has shown the best results with new oak, possibly because the wines have more elegance than those of Hermitage or Cornas.

In general, Mourvèdre producers are shy of new oak, as most believe that the wines are tannic enough to start with and need no additional wood tannins. One or two growers, however, have used new oak to good effect: Achille Pascal in Bandol is one; the Clos des Paulilles in Collioure is another.

The Wines in Bottle

Hermitage is the longest-living wine of the northern Rhône, although some of the bigger Côtes Brunes from Côte Rôtie may approach it. Domaine-bottled Cornases have only existed since the late 1960s, but one imagines that the wines would hold almost as long as the top Hermitages when properly made.

The Russians used to have a soft spot for very old Hermitage wines, and visitors to the hillside used to enthuse over vintages forty or fifty years old. I have never drunk a Hermitage of anything like this age, the oldest I've tasted being the La Chapelle 1961, which was showing no signs of tiring in 1988. In general, correctly made Hermitage should be drunk at twelve years and more, with lesser vintages (1984, 1986, 1987) requiring only five or six years before they come round.

In Côte Rôtie, the Côtes Blondes drink before the Côtes Brunes, and this is generally also true of the more prevalent blends of Brune et Blonde. A good Côte Blonde is drinkable at five or six years, while a Côte Brune might require ten. Cornas goes through a difficult and dumb stage between the ages of two and eight years. The best Cornas may require ten years. Nearly all the top Rhône wines have, however, been consumed by impatient Frenchmen long before they were ready to drink.

The minor wines of the northern Rhône, such as Crozes-Hermitage and St-Joseph, will be good at three years, although some top producers such as Émile Florentin make long-ageing wines.

The southern-Rhône wines are generally ready earlier. Good Châteauneufs are often ready at five years, and the best will pull round by their eighth birthday. The better wines of Gigondas are drinkable at four or five years. Bandol needs more time if made with a high proportion of Mourvèdre; eight years is a reliable guide in a good year, less in a poor one.

Top vintage-style wines from Banyuls require six or more years. The traditional wines are ready on release.

Most South African Shiraz seems to be ready at five years and unreliable at eight. In Australia, basic Shiraz is drinkable at three or four years but will last rather longer than ten. The most carefully made wines will easily keep for twenty. Grange Hermitage is a special case: in off years some wines are ready at eight years, though most require ten. The best Grange, vintages such as the 1976 and the 1971, needed fifteen years to bring them round.

The history of California Rhône styles is fairly recent. Joseph Phelps's wines develop a strong gaminess at ten years which some people won't like. A Qupé or Ojai Syrah is perfectly pleasant at three or four years.

Flavours

Grapes taste of grapes and wine smells like wine; that's what the man on the Clapham omnibus will tell you. But anyone who is prepared to pay for a wine book is doubtless aware that wines vary in flavours and that the reason for this is largely to do with grapes.

Good wine is not made from the sweet, juicy grapes you buy at the greengrocer, but from thick-skinned, tooth-staining berries full of hard pips and tannins. Each variety tastes different when plucked from the vine, and each variety has a range of flavours when it is vinified. These are the primary flavours of the wine. Secondary aromas derive from ageing in cask or barrel. Then, as the wine matures in bottle, new flavours are thrown off and the differences between wines become more abstract and less tangible.

Syrah's flavours vary according to the potential alcohol levels of the grapes (this is best measured on a Baumé or Brix scale, where the level comes nearest to the alcoholic degree in the finished wine). Picked at a low potential alcohol (10–12° Baumé), Syrah exudes lentilly, peppery aromas. At higher levels

(12–13.5°) Syrah is fruitier, tending to give off the aromas of raspberries, blackberries or blackcurrants.

In the northern Rhône the soil character contributes to the flavours of the wine. Young Syrah often smells of flowers – peonies, carnations and violets – and fruits such as raspberries and blackcurrants. Sometimes the wines are enhanced by a wood-smoke, even sometimes smoky-bacon-like, aroma which is one of the hallmarks of the younger wines. In Australia, where the soil factor is deemed less important, the wines are more one-dimensional and the ample sun gives a more powerful fruit character. Simple modern Shiraz tastes of raspberries or, in its most banal form, raspberry cordial. In the best Barossa, such as St Hallet's Old Block or Henschke's Hill of Grace, the flavour is of creamy blackcurrants and violets.

In the northern Rhône, Syrah vines go through a dumb stage when they shed part of their primary fruit. During this time a dense Côte Brune, Hermitage or Cornas will give off slight tobacco/cereal notes. Australian and South African wines tend to miss out on this difficult period, although Grange can be mute and brooding, hiding behind its immense tannins.

When the Rhône Syrahs come round again, after eight years or more, some of the blackcurrant fruitiness returns with a sweet, almost buttery character and a haunting smell of violets. Some wines also take on a gamy side, when they can smell of Russian leather, tobacco or old meat; even of drains. Australians tend to associate this character with the Hunter Valley and take positive steps to avoid it developing. Some people associate this 'sweaty saddle' character with poor wine-making, but in truth it must be a character derived from the grape: examples of it are legion in the northern Rhône, California, South Africa and Australia.

When young, Grenache wines have a pronounced raspberry character which becomes increasingly enhanced by the smell of cigarettes, cigar boxes or even Virginia tobacco (which I personally associate with Woodbines, the first cigarettes I ever smoked). In a great year in Châteauneuf-du-Pape it is not unusual to encounter blackcurrant tastes in mature wine.

Generally, however, the older the wine the more the tendency towards *rancio* character: leather and spices, particularly cinnamon, gingerbread and honey. Mature Châteauneuf tastes also of liquorice and black olives.

Picked at low yields, a pure Mourvèdre wine gives off an aroma of blackberries and bilberries, occasionally reminiscent of winegums. Like both Syrah and Grenache, it can develop some powerful leathery/gamy characters as it ages. The oldest Mourvèdres I have tasted have been notably spicy, with strong, sweet gingerbread aromas.

The Range of Wines

Sparkling

It may come as a surprise to some to hear that Australia's best known *rosé brut* – Angas – is made from a high proportion of Shiraz. Another Australian speciality is sparkling red Burgundy, which is often made from 100 per cent Shiraz. Seppelt is the leader in this field. A newcomer is Rocky O'Callaghan of Rockford's Wines in the Barossa.

Rosé

Grenache is responsible for almost all the best *rosados* of Navarra, Rioja and Penedès, but it tends to discolour after a year or two and in the wrong circumstances it can develop oniony notes which are unattractive. Likewise much Grenache is vinified as *rosé* in the Midi of France and in Tavel, where it is often blended with Mourvèdre. In Australia, Geoff Merrill makes a rather sweet Grenache *rosé*.

Young Mourvèdre in Bandol is fed into the *rosé*, but the colourless juice is useless by itself and some Cinsault or Grenache is generally required to give colour and taste. Some excellent *rosés* are made from Syrah. One such is Raymond Laporte's fresh wine from the Château de Roussillon in the Pyrénées Orientales.

Light reds

Syrah, Grenache and Mourvèdre are famed for big wines and not for 'easy-drinking' Beaujolais-style wines. Carbonic maceration, however, can be used to make fresh, light wines which concentrate on aromas at the expense of body. Recently Georges Dubœuf of Beaujolais has been travelling up and down the Rhône, vinifying his wines after this manner. The wines will appeal to some more than they do to me personally. The co-operative at St-Désirat has also specialized in this sort of wine. In Australia, Mitchelton makes a Cab Mac from both Shiraz and Grenache.

Another area where carbonic maceration has been attempted is in Châteauneuf-du-Pape, where the specialists are the Domaine de Nalys and the Domaine de Beaurenard. I'm not passionate about this sort of Châteauneuf. Carbonic maceration is popular with some of the big co-operatives in the Midi. Generally, however, it is the Carignan which is given the treatment and not Syrah, Grenache or Mourvèdre.

Full-bodied reds

This is the field in which our heroes really excel: Syrah, Grenache and Mourvèdre all make big *vins de garde*. Representative examples of Syrah's most powerful long-living reds would be an Hermitage from either Sorrel, Chave, Jaboulet or Chapoutier; a Côte-Brune-dominated Côte Rôtie from Guigal, Jasmin or Gentaz; or a Cornas from Clape or Michel. In Australia, Grange makes the biggest wines, but representative styles would be Hunters from McWilliam's or Tyrrell's; Barossas from Henschke or St Hallet's; Clare Valley wines from Tim Adams or Taylor's. In South Africa I'd choose wine from Klein Constantia; in California, from Joseph Phelps or Bonny Doon; in Italy, Isole e Olena – all these give benchmark Syrah styles.

The longest-lasting and most classic Châteauneufs are Les Clefs d'Or, Château Rayas, Domaine du Grand Tinel and Clos des Papes. The classic full-bodied Mourvèdre is possibly the huge wine of Domaine du Ray Jane, although Le Galantin also makes big wines. More elegant wines come from Château de Pibarnon and the Domaine Tempier. In Collioure, the Clos des Paulilles has joined the new classic wines from the Domaine du Mas Blanc and the Domaine de la Rectorie.

Fortified wines

The best fortified Syrahs are Australian vintage ports. Peter Lehmann has led this field since the mid 1980s. Seppelt and Yalumba make top wines in the Barossa, and All Saints and Stanton and Killeen are among the most typical in Rutherglen. Grenache and Mataró (Mourvèdre) are only used for inferior tawny ports in Australia.

The best Grenache-based wines are Prioratos, Banyuls and Maurys from Spanish and French Catalonia. Representative Prioratos come from De Muller, Scala Dei and Barril. Classic Banyuls comes from the Cave de l'Étoile, but look out too for Banyuls from the G.I.V.B. and the Domaines of Mas Blanc, La Rectorie, Casa Blanca and La Tour Vieille. Classic Maury is made by the Vignerons de Maury and Mas Amiel. Most of the better Rivesaltes is made from Grenaches Blanc and Gris and lies outside the scope of this book.

Lastly, Syrah, Grenache and Mourvèdre musts may be distilled to make decent *marc* brandy. Vidal-Fleury in Côte Rôtie makes a delicious *marc*; Père Anselme in Châteauneuf-du-Pape and the Mas de la Rouvière in Bandol all make representative *marcs*.

Wine and Food

When your sources of sustenance have lain cheek by jowl with your vineyards for ten generations or more, you rarely err when it comes to putting the two together. As the future wine-maker learns his skill at the hands of his father and grandfather, he learns too from his mother how to combine the wine with the food on the table. In our own time it has become increasingly fashionable to seek out 'revolutionary' ways of combining new-style dishes with wine. Most of the time I remain unconvinced by these.

Syrah, Grenache and Mourvèdre all originate from the Mediterranean, and their ideal partners in the kitchen are the traditional foods of the Mediterranean countries. On the coast, Bandol *rosés* combine admirably with spicy fish dishes such as *bouillabaisse* or *bourride*, where the saffron would assassinate a red or white wine. At Christmas in Provence it is traditional to cook salt cod with red wine, and this can take on even the biggest red wines of the region – something which was admirably demonstrated to me by the Bérards at the Hostellerie Bérard in La Cadière d'Azur.

Provençal lamb has a strong, almost goaty taste which makes it an admirable match for the old wines of Bandol and Châteauneuf. The subtler, more elegant, wines of the northern Rhône lend their fruit to dishes of roast game and combine with hare and well-hung grouse better than any other. Also, the cheese of the Rhône, being mostly goat, can take only the bigger reds. Lighter Syrahs would be fine with poultry or veal.

The raspberry-cordial-style wines of Australia are more of a problem with food, but Australians seem to know how to serve them with barbecued meat. Naturally, bigger Shiraz wines are as good with red meat, cheese and game as any from the northern Rhône.

Australian vintage port is excellent with blue cheese, and fortified Grenache wines are possibly the only thing to drink with chocolate.

GAZETTEER

KEY TO RATING SYSTEM

Quality

☙ indifferent

☙☙ average

☙☙☙ good

☙☙☙☙ very good

☙☙☙☙☙ outstanding

Price

★ cheap

★★ average

★★★ expensive

★★★★ very expensive

★★★★★ luxury

NOTE ON VINTAGE RECOMMENDATIONS

In most cases these are given only when the wine has been tasted. Only occasionally have I departed from this rule, and then only when I have received what I believed to be a wholly trustworthy report.

ARGENTINA

| Production: no figures available for individual varieties

Syrah is grown in the provinces of Mendoza, San Juan, Rio Negro, Neuquén, La Rioja, Catamarca, and Córdoba and around the Upper Colorado and Calchaquí. It seems highly unlikely that Grenache is not grown too given the extraordinary number of grapes which abound in what *should* be a winemaker's paradise.

I have only come across an Argentinian Syrah once, and this was a very cheap and reasonably good wine which I used to buy from a South London wine shop called Bernardi's Vineyard. There were no Syrahs shown at a tasting of Argentinian wines organized by the Argentinian embassy in London in the spring of 1991, and given the overall quality of the wines on that occasion I doubt very much that they would have been anything to write home about. The problem facing Argentinian wines is enormous yields which leave the red wines in particular tasting like slightly bitter, rust-flavoured water.

It is likely that the impulse for reform will come from the other side of the Andes, where the wines have improved of late. But if the Argentinians do follow the Chilean lead we cannot hope for decent Syrahs: the Chileans make their wines only to please Western wine-drinkers, and the word in Chile is that we in the West won't drink anything other than Chardonnay and Cabernet Sauvignon.

AUSTRALIA

Shiraz

The history of Australian wine is closely bound up with Shiraz. Until twenty years ago the Shiraz or Hermitage grape was required to perform the roles of virtually every European black grape variety from the Gamay in Beaujolais, the Pinot Noir in Burgundy and the Cabernet Sauvignon in claret, to the Touriga Nacional in port. What was remarkable was that Shiraz rose to the challenge: it performed all the roles and achieved styles of wine unheard of within the narrow purlieus of the Rhône Valley.

During the 1970s, however, Shiraz fell into disrepute. New wisdom had flown in from California: wines had to be made from the grapes designed for a particular purpose: Cabernet for claret, Pinot for Burgundy, Gamay for Beaujolais, even Touriga for port. Shiraz looked set to lose its role.

The Californians were right, of course, and the result of their work has been a revolution in Australian wine-making which has resulted in Australia entering the club of the world's great wine-making countries. However, there remained the question of what to do with the Shiraz. The Rhône Valley and its wines were comparatively unknown in Australian wine-loving circles, and even to this day knowledge of the great wines of Côte Rôtie, Hermitage and Cornas is not widespread in the Antipodes. One solution was to vinify the Shiraz as cleanly as possible by bringing down the pH to avoid the 'bacterial' character associated with the Hunter Valley. As much as possible, wine-makers tried to make a pure-fruit 'raspberry-cordial-style' wine: good for the 'barbie', but hardly the sort of wine which merited serious consideration.

Another solution was that first aired at Knight's Granite Hills and other pioneering estates in Victoria: this was to pick the grapes at a much lower degree Baumé than before, indeed in some cases picking underripe grapes. This produced the so-called 'pepper-spice' character of Shiraz which reminded some commentators of Rhône Valley wines. The new school was an instant success with Australian wine writers; pepper-spice had come to the rescue of Australia's historic grape variety.

Next came the discovery that not all the traditional wine-growing areas were in fact suitable for the new gods: Cabernet, Chardonnay and Pinot Noir. The Hunter injected its weird character even into the Bordeaux grape, most of the Barossa was too hot and the same drawbacks applied to Clare or Rutherglen. In those areas it was best to come to terms with the Shiraz. In two or three cases there has even been a reappraisal of Grenache.

And then there was port. Although Wolf Blass tried making his port from Cabernet as early as the 1970s, he eventually came to realize that Shiraz was responsible for the quality of the best Australian vintage wines. Australian port remains something of an unsung hero even in the country itself. Anyone who has doubts about the ability of Shiraz to make first-class vintage port should try Peter Lehmann's latest vintages.

Shiraz was also kept alive by the cool-headed traditionalists of Australian wine, from huge firms like Penfolds in the Barossa to individual craftsmen like Bailey Carrodus in the Yarra, Murray and Bruce Tyrrell in the Hunter, the Purbricks at Château Tahbilk and Stephen Henschke in the Adelaide Hills. To a great degree the success of their endeavours has stayed the hands of those who might otherwise have ripped up or grafted over their vines to whatever grape happened to be fetching the highest prices at the time. Fashions change: when I visited the huge Berri co-operative in the Riverland in 1990 a ton of Pinot Noir was fetching up to $1,000; Grenache yielded only a quarter of that price. The latest news is that the bottom has fallen out of the Pinot Noir market because the public didn't take to the taste of the new grape. At least Shiraz has the advantage of familiarity.

*

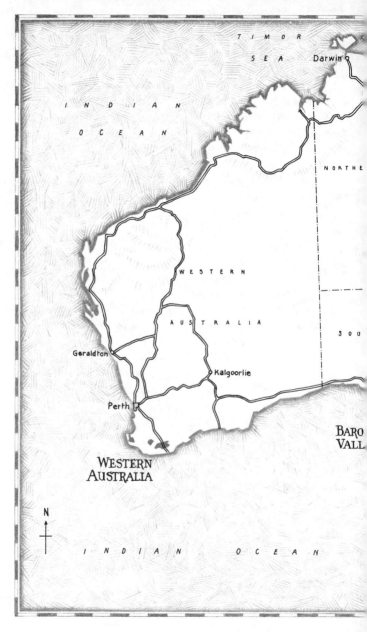

TIMOR

SEA Darwin

INDIAN

OCEAN

SOU

NORTHE

WESTERN

AUSTRALIA

SOU

Geraldton

Kalgoorlie

Perth

BARO
VALL

WESTERN
AUSTRALIA

N

INDIAN   OCEAN

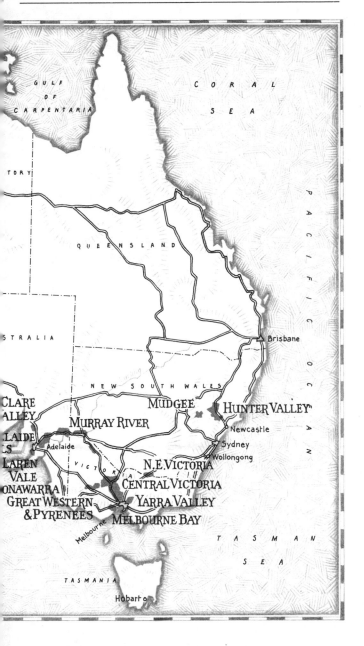

GULF
OF
CARPENTARIA

CORAL

SEA

TORY

QUEENSLAND

STRALIA

Brisbane

NEW SOUTH WALES

CLARE
ALLEY

MUDGEE

HUNTER VALLEY

MURRAY RIVER

Newcastle

LAIDE
S

Adelaide

Sydney

LAREN
VALE

VICTORIA

Wollongong

N.E.VICTORIA

ONAWARRA

CENTRAL VICTORIA

GREAT WESTERN
& PYRENEES

YARRA VALLEY

MELBOURNE BAY

Melbourne

TASMAN

SEA

TASMANIA

Hobart

PACIFIC   OCEAN

Grenache and Mataró

The extensive planting of Grenache and Mataró in Australia dates back to the last century. Like Shiraz their vocation was to make fortified wines, but generally the cheaper, tawny styles. When they are not used for port, Grenache and Mataró are generally blended to make cheap bag-in-box 'claret' or 'Burgundy'.

So far there has been no real rediscovery of the potential of these two grapes. Australian wine snobs have yet to catch on to Bandol or Châteauneuf-du-Pape. On the other hand, with so much of the impetus for change in Australia coming from California, it seems strange that the 'Rhône Ranger' enthusiasm for wines of this style has not taken hold of a few more Australian wine-makers. For the time being we have only Charles Melton and Rocky O'Callaghan in the Barossa who are prepared to show us what they can do with Grenache. Someone should now make a few experiments with some low-yielding Mataró. It could come as a big surprise.

New South Wales

The first plantations in Australia were made only a generation after the first convict ships sailed into Botany Bay. In the course of the nineteenth century, growers moved steadily north until they had settled on the Hunter Valley as the best site for their vines. The ultimate suitability of their choice is still questioned by many authorities in Australia: the Hunter is subtropical, being by turns excessively hot and excessively wet. In recent years, torrential rains have affected red wines in particular.

The climate of the Hunter and the coal-rich subsoil of the region are both possible explanations for the curious 'Hunter character' which develops in old Shiraz wines from the valley (but not exclusively in Shiraz). Certainly this character seems to be absent from the state's other Shiraz-producing region, Mudgee.

Both the Hunter Valley and Mudgee are sustained by their fairly easy proximity to Australia's largest city, Sydney. The Hunter in particular is a favourite target for a day trip, and tourism is well developed.

The Hunter Style

To many people now, the Hunter seems an unlikely place to make wine; in the past, however, this was not the case. The Hunter was planted very soon after the first transports began depositing their human cargo in Botany Bay. Gradually those people looking for a good stretch of land pushed their way up the coast near Newcastle and settled down to raise cattle on the sleek hills around Cessnock and Pokolbin. Soon after that some of them tried their hands at grape-farming and wine-making.

From the very beginning it was clear which grapes gave reasonable results in that temperamental climate: Hunter Valley Riesling (Sémillon) for the whites and Hermitage (Shiraz) for the reds. In the old days the Shiraz lay around in big tuns for years; the grapes picked at a prodigious degree, it was touch and go whether they would be transformed into port or table wine. The size of these wines obviously created something of the famed Hunter style, with all that leathery fruit which every now and then turns into Stilton rinds or horse manure. The Australians generally refer to this as 'sweaty saddles'.

For some people the 'sweaty saddle' is nothing more than a mercaptan: a hydrogen-sulphide compound which is normally created in the course of disinfecting wine by burning sulphur in barrels. If they are caught soon enough, mercaptans may be cured by passing the wine over copper. It has always struck me as unlikely that so many Hunter wines should have been faultily made in this way for so long a period without anyone taking the trouble to do something about it. More probable, it seems to me, is that the 'sweaty saddle' is a product of hot vintages in the Hunter combined with some natural results of the coal-rich *terroir*; or possibly it results from the need to use sulphur-based sprays to combat rot in wet years. The 'sweaty saddle' is not confined to Shiraz, and I have met with this character in both Cabernet and Pinot Noir wines made in the area.

Good or bad, there is still an enthusiastic public for these old Hunter wines. Even so, there are few wineries which adhere to the traditions of the Hunter today. The chief propagators would be McWilliam's and Tyrrell's, although the style is apparent in old vintages of Lindemans and The Rothbury Estate's wines.

The Hunter Valley

The Hunter is an odd place. Unlike most of Australia, where people think nothing of driving for three hours to dine with their nearest neighbour, everything is close by in the Hunter. Among this jumble of wineries you find the traditionalists and a few small wineries who get it right most years, as well as the big boys who seem to use the Hunter more as a base than anything else and make wines in an abstracted style which owes nothing to *terroir* and everything to commercial and marketing considerations.

The Calais Vineyard has been recently acquired by the chemist Ian Peterson. Peterson's emergence in the Hunter had everything to do with the valley's proximity to his chain of shops on the New South Wales coast. Personally he hates the 'Hunter style' and says he'll shoot himself if he ever makes a wine with a 'sweaty saddle' character. Unfortunately for Peterson he actually inherited one or two wines with Calais which were distinctly moulded in that style, like the 1979 Wollundry Shiraz, although later vintages of Calais Shiraz seem to have been made with delicacy.

In his own estate Peterson makes Shiraz in an eviscerated style which impresses show judges but which tends to be too fragile to survive even the half an hour the bottle is open during dinner. It seems to me that Peterson might benefit from feeding back a little press wine into vintages like 1984, 1985 and 1987 to give the wines a bit more tannic backbone.

Hungerford Hill's wines have been changing over the years, moving towards a bland, commercial style. From the 1987 vintage the wine-maker went over to small oak and the change is noticeable in recent vintages. In the new idiom is the 1988, which is a nice big wine ever so slightly reminiscent of rice pudding on the nose with plenty of blackcurrant and blackberry fruit. The 1987 too was good, an even bigger wine reflecting the last good summer in the Hunter before the 1991 vintage. The 1987 has some hints of a wilder style (damp leaves) which has now been phased out. Some older wines are rereleased as 'Collection' Shiraz, which has to be bought from the cellar door. The 1983 'Collection', from a drought year, has a tarry, charred nose with a slight hint of violet. The 1982 Show Reserve Shiraz was made in very small quantities; the wine-maker seemed almost embarrassed how 'Hunterish' this had become.

Hungerford Hill makes some wine from the Abbey Vineyard in Coonawarra. The 1987 is rather jammy with a peppery finish.

Murray Robson is looking for elegance in his wines. The result is that his Shiraz wines tend to look a little eviscerated. I suspect that Shiraz is not really Robson's favourite grape and that he handles it rather more on sufferance than anything else. He likes to pick a little underripe to make wines which are light and drinkable at three years. His 1987 Shiraz had good colour and some blackberry fruit and the desired peppery finish.

Much of the Wyndham Estate's fruit does not come from the Hunter at all, but is brought in from Mudgee. Brian McGuigan and his team are looking for a big, pure-fruit style which typifies much of modern Australian Shiraz-making. Their benchmark wine is the 1988 Bin 555, with its oaky plum and raspberry fruit. The fruit from Mudgee also helps them conquer the occasionally disastrous weather conditions in the Hunter, allowing them to make wines in the same mould, year in, year out.

Of the estates I have not visited, I have only three times come across the wines of Brokenwood. The Shiraz/Cabernet 1989 had a strange chestnut nose; it may have been going through an odd stage when I tasted it in 1991. On the other hand, both the 1990 and the 1989 vintages from the Graveyard Vineyard impressed me deeply, though both need time: the 1990 is full and raisiny; the 1989 is marked by some creamy, oaky notes. The Show Reserve Shiraz 1981 from Saxonvale had become Hunterish over the years, with plenty of leather and game. The 1987 Tulloch Shiraz was also slightly farmyardy, a fairly classic Hunter Hermitage.

See separate entries for Lindemans, McWilliam's, Rosemount, The Rothbury Estate and Tyrrell's Wines.

LINDEMANS

Lower Hunter Valley

McDonalds Road, Pokolbin, NSW 2321

Production of Shiraz: 462,800 litres premium wine (includes Leo Baring, Matthew Lang and Tulloch)

Quality: 🍇🍇🍇–🍇🍇🍇🍇   Price: ★★★★–★★★★★

Best vintages: 1965, 1970, 1973, 1978, 1983, 1986

Lindemans' high-quality operation is in the Hunter, and it is here that the Lindemans story began in 1842. The bulk of Lindemans' wine now comes from its Karadoc winery in Mildura on the Murray, but Lindemans also has interests in Coonawarra and it is there that it makes its superb Limestone Ridge Shiraz–Cabernet.

Lindemans' old wines have a special status for Australian wine-lovers: the old vintages (occasionally rereleased) have become collectors' items, especially old bottles of Sémillon and Hermitage. The wines are released under a confusing coding system, which has been rendered all the more baffling by the fact that it has recently been changed! Essentially it is the last two figures of the four-figure code which count: 03 means a commercial style made from bought-in grapes; 10 means a slow-maturing, exceptional wine; 25 means 'Steven', which is generally the top wine (except when a 10 is issued!). A 00 code *used* to exist, but they tell me this is now extinct.

Lindemans' top wines are now made by Gerry Sissingh, who made the early stars from The Rothbury Estate – although Sissingh is quick to point out that he is not responsible for the 1982, 1984 or 1985 vintages. Sissingh is a highly respected wine-maker who plays an important role in the Australian 'show circuit'; he shares the views of many of the circuit's leading lights, feeling that the 'Old Adam' in Shiraz needs taming. Like many leading wine personalities in Australia, Sissingh denies the existence of *terroir*.

In his pursuit of 'elegance', Sissingh appears to have stripped considerable weight from the wines in recent years and it is now difficult to imagine that these wines will age in the old Lindemans way. Wines like the 1965 Bin 3110 or the 1970 4110 were really built to last; while the 1973 Bin 4810 even shows some strong Hunter 'sweaty saddle' character. Sissingh's benchmark wine is the Bin 6600 of the drought year, 1983: it is certainly an impressively complex wine with masses of fruit. The Bin 7210 (Steven) of 1986 is similar in style, but lighter and more 'elegant'. Both the Steven (Bin 7410) 1987 and the Bin 7625 of 1988 seemed to me sadly dilute.

McWILLIAM'S

Lower Hunter Valley

Mount Pleasant Winery, Marrowbone Road, Pokolbin, NSW 2321

Production of Shiraz: not released

Quality: 🍇🍇🍇-🍇🍇🍇🍇   Price: ★★★–★★★★

Best vintages: 1983, 1984, 1985, 1986, 1987

McWilliam's produces Shiraz wines here in the heart of the Hunter as well as a lighter, more commercial, range at Murrumbidgee on the Murray River. Sadly, McWilliam's concentrates on the irrigated Riverland wines for the export market; outside Australia it is virtually impossible to get hold of the benchmark Hunter Valley Shirazes from Mount Pleasant.

The McWilliam's Mount Pleasant style is controversial in Australia. For the older generation it represents the essence of Hunter Shiraz, with its aromas of 'sweaty saddles'; for the uninitiated, a wine like the 1983 Philip can come as a shock with its horse-manure pungency, and quite a lot of modern Australian wine writers would condemn it as 'sulphidic'. To condemn such wines as faulty, however, would be to dismiss out of hand more than half the old Syrahs of the Rhône Valley (including the entirety of Cornas – currently just about the most fashionable wine in France), and quite a few old red Burgundies too. In reality the style expressed by McWilliam's is little more than the old school which was superseded by the 'squeaky-clean' technique which began to make its mark in Australia in the mid 1970s. As far as Shiraz is concerned, the most notable achievement of the new technique was to make the vast majority of the wine taste of little more than raspberry cordial.

Mount Pleasant's basic 'Hermitage' wine is Philip. More prestigious is the Rosehill wine, of which the 1986 was a rich, gamy wine. The best McWilliam's Shiraz is OP & OH (Old Paddock and Old Homestead) from the 1880 vines on the slope beside the winery. The OP & OH from the cool 1987 vintage is a delicious wine with a toasty, violet character. The same toasti-ness is apparent on the 1986. The 1985, from an extremely hot vintage, has a rather more farmyard nature.

MONTROSE

Mudgee

Henry Lawson Drive, Mudgee, NSW 2850

Production of Shiraz: not released

Quality: 🍇🍇🍇   Price: ★★–★★★

Best vintages: 1982, 1987, 1989, 1990

Not for nothing is Mudgee now boasting Australia's first AOC: the place is all of a piece, 'nestling in the hills' as the name means in Aborigine. There is none of the subtropical climate here; while it pours with rain in the Hunter, it is quite dry here on the other side of the mountains. Mudgee wines don't have problems reaching the right degree of alcohol – indeed they have to take care to make sure they don't go up to 14.

Montrose is now part of the Wyndham group and, with its sister wineries Craigmoor and Amberton, it dispatches large amounts of fruit to the Hunter to buoy up the Wyndham blends. The current wine-maker for all three Mudgee estates is Robert Paul, formerly of Chapel Hill in McLaren Vale, South Australia. He is a quiet, efficient man and very dedicated to his wine-making.

Amberton and Craigmoor make light, commercial-style Shirazes which are not really classic Mudgee stuff, as Paul admits. The most successful Shiraz here to date was the 1982 Special Reserve, a wine which drew high praise from Robert Parker. In 1990 some gamy notes were detectable on the nose, but the wine was still packed with raspberry and blackcurrant fruit with a long coffee-like finish. The 1987 Special Reserve was also good, with a peppery character coming from the cooler year. The 1990 had just been made when I visited the winery; it was a huge wine which will one day be the equal of the 1987 if not the 1982.

ROSEMOUNT

Upper Hunter Valley

Rosemount Estate, Rosemount Road, Denman, NSW 2328

Production of Shiraz: not released

Quality: 🍇🍇🍇   Price: ★★

Best vintages: 1986, 1987, 1988, 1989, 1990

'The future is in Shiraz,' says Bob Oatley, 'because it is a big strong wine which makes you stick your chest out.' Bob Oatley, a former New Guinea coffee-planter with a talent for *non sequiturs*, is the owner of Rosemount. His wine-maker, Philip Shaw, disagrees with him anyhow: Philip thinks the future is in Chardonnay, and he is almost certainly right.

Rosemount tends to turn its back on the Hunter: fruit comes in from elsewhere, including some very good Cabernet and Merlot from Coonawarra. Some of Shaw's Shiraz is also imported, including valuable 'backbone' material from Château Tahbilk in Victoria. The resulting Shiraz is only slightly 'Hunterish' (the slight cabbagy nose on the 1987 is to some extent a certificate of origin), being generally full of raspberry fruit with a good overlay of pepper and spice. Some of the spice character comes from new American oak, of which Shaw uses about 20 per cent for the straight Shiraz and a little more for the reserve wines.

THE ROTHBURY ESTATE

Lower Hunter Valley

Broke Road, Pokolbin, NSW 2321

Production of Shiraz: *c.* 300 tonnes

Quality: 🍇🍇🍇–🍇🍇🍇🍇   Price: ★★★★

Best vintages: 1976, 1979, 1982, 1983, 1987, 1989

The Rothbury was started in 1968 as a result of Murray Tyrrell deciding to let go of some of his Hunter Valley land. A syndicate was formed under Len Evans, and the shareholders hit on the idea of producing just two wines: a Sémillon and a Shiraz. From 1972–9 the wines were made by Gerry Sissingh, who now makes the wines in nearby Lindemans. More recently David Lowe was in charge. Shortly before my visit to the estate in the spring of 1990, Lowe decided to leave The Rothbury; the wines are now made by two young New Zealanders: Peter Hall and Greg Traught.

It is interesting to see how much Sissingh's style has changed over the years. As a result of Len Evans's generosity I was able to taste some of the oldest vintages of Rothbury 'Hermitage'. The 1972 had sadly had it; but the 1976 from the Herlstone Vineyard was still a big wine with a rather Burgundian farmyard character. Sissingh's last wine was the 1979 – a big, buttery wine very different from the sort of thing he is making today.

In the 1980s The Rothbury continued making whole-heartedly Hunter-style Shirazes, like the 1982 with its but-tered-cabbage aromas and the characteristically robust 1983 from the drought year. Good wines followed in both the 1986 and the cooler 1987 vintage. More recently there has been a change of style for Rothbury Shiraz, with the wine-makers trying to avoid the leathery Hunter character and to pursue the pepper-spice low-Baumé style. As an example of this the 1989 seemed to me highly successful.

TYRRELL'S WINES

Lower Hunter Valley

> Broke Road, Pokolbin, NSW 2321
>
> Production of Shiraz: c. 350 tonnes
>
> Quality: ♛♛♛–♛♛♛♛♛   Price: ★–★★★★★
>
> Best vintages: 1966, 1967, 1975, 1981, 1983, 1984, 1985, 1986, 1988, 1989, 1990

Tyrrell's must be just about the most traditional wine-making estate in Australia after Château Tahbilk. The core of the winery is still the old barge-boarded homesteader's shack; the big wooden tuns sit on an earth floor; vineyard yeasts are used for the red wines; and new-oak barrels are few and far between. As far as Shiraz is concerned, this works: Shiraz is a robust grape variety and requires less mollycoddling than most.

Tyrrell's basic Long Flat Red is essentially a Shiraz wine with additions of Cabernet Sauvignon and Malbec. The fruit is bought in from tried and tested suppliers and the wine tends to be reliable, if not particularly exciting – which is exactly what it is meant to be.

Tyrrell's top Shiraz bins are numbered 5 and 9. Vat 5 is the fruitier, 'elegant' style; while Vat 9 is designed to be robust and peppery. When I visited the estate in the spring of 1990 I was offered a range of Vat 9 to taste, running from 1966 to samples of the wines which were to make up the 1990 blend. In the previous eighteen months Tyrrell's had come under heavy attack for having used sorbitol to 'soften' some of its wines, and the Australian wine press was being particularly sniffy about the quality of the estate. Looking at the range I had to admit that these Shiraz wines had few equals either in the Hunter or in the rest of Australia: the 1966 was still holding on pretty well undiminished by time, a wonderful 1967 was without a hint of sulphide character, and the same could be said for the 1975. Of the wines of the 1980s, the 1981 was huge and packed with fruit, and the 1983 from the drought year had a predictably leathery character which was present also on the 1985. Only the 1987 was disappointing.

South Australia

South Australia is the home of the richer, riper styles of Shiraz: not for nothing does Australia's most famous Shiraz – Grange – emanate from this state. Grange is in itself a tribute to South Australian fruit: formerly the product of the Magill Estate in the suburbs of Adelaide, the wine now combines fruit from the Clare Valley with that from the Barossa. Eden Valley and the Southern Vales have all achieved recognition for their full-flavoured Shiraz wines, and the hot McLaren Vale not only makes a useful blending Shiraz but is also the region best known for Grenache and Mataró grapes destined for use in quality tawny ports. Another leading Grenache producer is the Murray River to the east.

In the south of the state are the regions of Padthaway and Coonawarra. Coonawarra is Australia's coolest growing region, and in recent years it has been increasingly turned over to Cabernet and Merlot. There are, however, still significant plantations of Shiraz in Coonawarra, and grapes from the region are particularly valued in blends.

The Adelaide Hills

The Adelaide Hills are the high ground which separates the urban sprawl of Adelaide from the Barossa Valley. The higher altitude naturally makes the region more suitable for delicate wines made from Atlantic or Burgundian grape varieties. Some Shiraz is also grown here, however, and some of it is very good indeed. See the entries for Henschke and Mountadam.

The Barossa Valley

The Barossa Valley owes its existence as a wine-producing area to a typically Victorian blend of altruism and business acumen. George Fife Angas (who was later to lend his name to a sparkling wine called Angas Brut, known affectionately in Britain as 'The Brute') settled in the Valley in 1841 and founded the small town of Angaston. Angas was something of a religious zealot, but for all that he was not unaware of the need for cheap labour. Hearing of the plight of some villages of Silesian Lutheran weavers who had run into trouble with their squires and employers, he had them shipped out to South Australia and settled them in the Barossa. Twenty years later these Protestant Prussians had got the hang of wine-making and the Valley had found its vocation.

Some of the smaller estates are still owned by descendants of these original Lutheran families (see the separate entries for Henschke and Peter Lehmann); other such families are commemorated in companies like Krondorf and Seppelt. At Bethany Wines, the Schrapnel family has pinned up a family tree composed of nothing but Barossa-*Deutscher* names. Their Shiraz is called Schlenke's Gully to commemorate yet another.

The Barossa Valley floor is hot, and the Shiraz grape was early seen to be the solution to this problem, along with Grenache and Mataró. The idea was, of course, to make port, and the Valley continued to lead on fortified wines until the 1960s and 1970s.

There is still quite a bit of Grenache around, although the quantity of Mataró is fast diminishing. It should be possible to make a Châteauneuf look-alike, and one or two experiments of this sort have already been made. Charlie Melton makes a Shiraz/Grenache blend called 'Nine Popes', which is said to be an allusion to Châteauneuf (see separate entry). Next door, Rocky O'Callaghan of Rockford Wines makes a full-coloured Grenache from ancient vines, with proper plums-and-chocolate character, as well as his Basket Press Shiraz. Possibly O'Callaghan's best wine of all is Black Shiraz, a version of the famous Seppelt Sparkling Red Burgundy (see the entry for Seppelt). He uses a blend of old wines, injecting new life into the wine by the sparkling wine yeasts.

Basedow occasionally makes an uncharacteristically light Shiraz, for the Barossa is a rather old-fashioned 'claret' style, but the 1986 was good stuff, with lots of raspberry/violet fruit.

The Kies Estate makes a Shiraz/Grenache blend called Classic Dry Red, of which the 1987 had a curious apricot-crumble bouquet. Kies's best wine is the Old Vineyard Shiraz, made from 100-year-old vines. The 1987 has huge raspberry fruit with a touch of singed spinach on the nose: a classic Barossa Shiraz.

One of the best Barossa Shirazes is the St Hallet's Old Block. With its great creamy, blackberry aromas, the 1988 has some stylistic affinities to Henschke's wines, although the American oak is slightly less well integrated.

The Clare Valley

The Clare Valley was named after County Clare in Ireland, but there is little resemblance: County Clare is drizzly and cold, while the Clare Valley is arid and hot. Indeed, Clare is even hotter than the Barossa and Rutherglen. Shiraz is still the main grape in Clare, and there is also a good deal of Grenache. As in the Barossa, most of the Mataró is being phased out.

The potential for good hot-country Shiraz fruit has lured

many of Australia's top wine companies into the Clare Valley in the past, and Stanley Leasingham is now part of the huge Hardy group; its Domaine Shiraz is a big 'claret-style' wine built to last with plenty of oak. The 1988 Mitchell's Peppertree Shiraz had an enchanting plums-and-violets bouquet, but the 1989 (tasted in 1991) seemed to be going through an odd stage when I last tried it. Another good Clare Valley Shiraz is Taylor's 'Hermitage'; sadly I have only tasted the 1988 'Château Clare', but I was impressed by its full raspberry/violet fruit. The best Shiraz I have had from the Clare Valley was Tim Adams' 1989: again a marked bouquet of violets and a palate which seemed to combine raspberries with incense.

Coonawarra

Coonawarra means 'honeysuckle' in Aborigine, but land has become so highly prized in this *terra rosa* limestone belt that there would be little room for any such frivolous shrub now; vines are now pretty well the only form of vegetation. The first experiments with growing grapes in Coonawarra date back to the last years of the nineteenth century, but fifty years passed before the first Redman Rouge Homme wine drew attention to the qualities of the soil. In the meantime a vast tract of land had been acquired by Wynns (see separate entry), whose wines began to appear in the early 1950s. In 1955 Mildara (separate entry, under Victoria) began investing in the region. Penfolds (separate entry) followed in 1960, and Lindemans (separate entry, under New South Wales) five years later.

Back in the 1950s the big companies were less clear about the uses of Coonawarra's cool climate than they are today. At first Wynns planted Mediterranean as opposed to Atlantic grape varieties, including nearly 1,000 acres of Shiraz and 85 acres of Grenache. Although its Michael Hermitage was a considerable success, it became increasingly clear that Coonawarra was better suited to Cabernet (although this view is disputed by Penfolds' former wine-maker Max Schubert). Coonawarra's climate means that Shiraz grapes tend not to ripen fully, giving the wine a particular minty aroma which sets it aside from other

South Australian Shirazes. To some extent this is also true of Padthaway to the north, where Lindemans has an estate planted with 250 acres of Shiraz and Grenache.

Of the small estates using Coonawarra fruit, I found Rouge Homme slightly disappointing. The 1986 seemed a bit hot and clumsy. The most interesting new venture is Kim Tolley's Penley. Penley combines Coonawarra and McLaren Vale fruit to make a Prestige Blend Shiraz/Cabernet. The 1989 is superb, with its huge, slightly gamy/toasty raspberry aromas and its pure raspberry-pastille fruit on the palate. The Bowen Estate uses pure Coonawarra fruit. The 1988 is elegant, with a bouquet of fresh raspberries. The Zema Estate's wines have less charm perhaps but none the less exude that minty character of Coonawarra and are technically extremely proficient. Ian Hollick's Wilgha Shiraz is classic stuff with plenty of minty, raspberry fruit and just a hint of varietal smokiness in the 1989.

McLaren Vale

McLaren Vale is a sultry region just beyond the southern suburbs of Adelaide. Not surprisingly the area was famed for port until recently, and Shiraz and Grenache were naturally the most popular of the black grapes. The wines of Chapel Hill used to be made by Robert Paul (see the separate entry for Montrose, under New South Wales), but they are now the work of Bevan Wilson. I found the 1989 rather raw and tough, but it might pull through this stage. Another highly regarded estate is Coriole; again I found the 1989 rather unyielding in 1991, although it seemed to have more potential than the Chapel Hill.

McLaren Vale's great personality is the ebullient, moustached Geoff Merrill, of Mount Hurtle. Merrill is rare among Australians in seeing some good in *rosé* wines. For his Mount Hurtle *rosé*, Merrill uses 90 per cent Grenache and 10 per cent Shiraz, making a 'blush' syle with 9° residual sugar. The result is very well made, but rather too sweet for my personal taste. The Mount Hurtle *rosé* appears to have replaced a Grenache red wine which elicited high praise in the past.

BERRI-RENMANO

Murray River
> Sturt Highway, Glossop, SA 5344
>
> Production of Shiraz: 3,100 tonnes from Riverland, 200 tonnes from Lauriston
>
> Quality: 🍇–🍇🍇   Price: ★–★★
>
> Best vintages: 1986, 1987, 1988, 1989, 1990, 1991

Bulk is the essence of this huge co-operative on the Murray River, and much of the output is issued as 'cask wine', as the Australians cutely call bag-in-box. Here the top grapes are Grenache for red wines and Doradillo for white. From the Grenache, Berri makes a rare *rosé* which smells of fresh apricots. Blended with Mataró, the Grenache makes a 'Beaujolais'.

Berri owns the Barossa Valley Estates in the Barossa, which produces a Shiraz which I personally have never found impressive. Its best Shiraz wines come out under the Arnold or Chairman's Selection label, of which the 1990 was very promising with its peppery, plum-and-blackberry fruit. Both the 1988 and 1989 were big, unabashedly fruity wines which spent twelve months in German-oak hogsheads.

Berri makes several different ports: Cromwell, which is the cheapie, made from Grenache, Shiraz, Tokay (Muscadelle) and Muscat; Rumpole tawny, made from Shiraz, Grenache and a little Muscat; and a nutty Lauriston Show Port, made from Grenache, Tokay and a little Shiraz.

WOLF BLASS

Barossa Valley
> Bilyara Vineyards, Sturt Highway, Nuriootpa, SA 5355
>
> Production of Shiraz: 1,200 tonnes

Quality: 🍷🍷-🍷🍷🍷   Price: ★★—★★★

Best vintages: 1976, 1977, 1979, 1981, 1982, 1983, 1986, 1987, 1990

Wolf Blass is a small, beady-eyed German from Thuringia who wears ready-made bow-ties and drives bottle-green Rolls-Royces (sometimes he drives them into electricity pylons and plunges the whole of Adelaide into deepest night). His style of life is flashy, and this vulgarity extends to his wine-making. Blass was the first man to go positively overboard with oak (generally American, but recently he has experimented with Russian oak too: clearly hedging his bets), giving the public a taste for oak-induced vanilla and spice flavours. The Cassandras said it wouldn't work and the wines wouldn't age; but it did, and they did. Blass simply proved them wrong.

Blass makes no bones about being commercial, and to some extent it comes as a surprise to learn that he sets some store by the not so fashionable Shiraz grape. In Australia the Yellow Label Cabernet is 40 per cent Shiraz (in export markets it is 100 per cent Cabernet), and both the Grey and Black Label wines contain 20 per cent. The Brown Label 'Hermitage' is his pure Shiraz wine; it is made from Barossa, Langthorne Creek and Eden Valley fruit.

In the spring of 1990 I drank a range of Brown Label going from cask samples of the 1990 all the way back to 1971. It was a remarkably consistent series of wines: only the 1971 seemed to have gone off, with some hydrogen-sulphide character; the 1976 was a lovely old wine with some autumn-leaf aromas; the 1979 too had classic Shiraz gamy notes. In the 1980s a slightly different style emerged with a big fruity 1982 and a slightly more complex medlar-scented 1983 and 1986. The best vintage before 1990 was the 1987, which was still in cask in May 1990: a big luscious wine full of creamy black fruits.

Wolf Blass also makes a port, but this was made from 80 per cent Cabernet until 1978. The 1980 still has 30 per cent Cabernet; it is a big, dense, peppery wine.

*

THOMAS HARDY & SONS

McLaren Vale
> Reynell Road, Reynella, SA 5161
>
> Production: figures not released
>
> Quality: 🍇🍇–🍇🍇🍇   Price: ★★–★★★
>
> Best vintages: 1986, 1987, 1988, 1989, 1990

Thomas Hardy is a huge, unashamedly commercial operation with outposts in Coonawarra (Redman), Clare (Stanley Leasingham – see entry under Clare Valley), Southern Vales (Château Reynella), Barossa (Siegersdorf) and Western Australia (Houghton). The Bird series provides a decent introduction to Australian Shiraz at an attractive price – honestly fruity with no frills. The Redman Shiraz appears to have adopted a light, Beaujolais-style persona which used to characterize the now discontinued Nottage Hill Shiraz. The best is clearly the Eileen Hardy Shiraz, which is billed as Hardy's answer to Grange Hermitage. The 1987 has dense – rather lifted – blackberry fruit.

An occasional old vintage is released as Museum Stock; the 1975 Shiraz made from virtually shrivelled McLaren Vale fruit was a big wine reminiscent of blackberries, raspberries and pepper. Needless to say, it is a considerable rarity.

HENSCHKE

Adelaide Hills
> Moculta Road, Keyneton, SA 5353
>
> Production of Shiraz: c. 198,000 bottles
>
> Quality: 🍇🍇🍇–🍇🍇🍇🍇🍇   Price: ★★★–★★★★
>
> Best vintages: 1986, 1987, 1988, 1989, 1990

Stephen Henschke is a descendant of one of the original Silesian Germans who colonized the Barossa Valley in the

1840s. He is a quiet, studious man who learned his wine-making at the top German school of Geisenheim after a basic scientific education at the University of Adelaide. Henschke successfully blends modern and traditional methods, and his wines are an unashamed mix of old and new.

Part of the secret of Henschke's success with the Shiraz grape lies in the good schisty soil of that part of the Barossa combined with the great age of his vines – some are over 100 years old.

Henschke's basic Shiraz wine is Keyneton, which is made from 70 per cent Shiraz blended with Cabernet Sauvignon and Malbec. The 1987 has a characteristically gamy, peppery palate from the high proportion of Shiraz.

Mount Edelstone is 100 per cent old Shiraz. Again the 1987 is a triumph, with dense cherry flavours. The 1988 has delightful incense/raspberry/violet fruit. His top wine is the Hill of Grace, from a vineyard by Keyneton's Lutheran church which was called the Gnadenberg until 1914: both the 1987 and the 1984 were wonderful in 1991; the 1986 should open out soon.

HILL-SMITH/YALUMBA

Barossa Valley

Eden Valley Road, Angaston, SA 5353

Production: 2,020 tonnes Shiraz and 540 tonnes Grenache crushed

Quality: 🍇–🍇🍇🍇🍇   Price: ★★–★★★★

Best vintages: 1987, 1988, 1989, 1990

Best years for port: 1967, 1971, 1979, 1981, 1987

Hill-Smith is a family-owned firm which has played an important role in the development of the Barossa Valley and South Australia. Until he earned enough money to set up his winery at Yalumba, Samuel Smith worked for a while as a gardener for George Fife Angas, the founder of Angaston, who first saw the potential of settling the valley with the Silesian Protestants who later turned their hands to viticulture with such success. The famous Yalumba building with its blue marble tower was built by Samuel's son Sydney.

Through Hill-Smith, Yalumba, Heggies and Angas, the firm tries its hand at an enormous range of wine styles: Shiraz is just a small part of its range. A lot of the fruit is bought in and, like Penfolds, the firm works on a system of sweeteners – paying up to 400 per cent more in order to get the best fruit from the northern side of the Barossa.

One of the most interesting uses to which Shiraz is put at Yalumba is in Angas Brut *rosé*. The popular sparkling wine is more than 50 per cent Shiraz, topped up with Cabernet Sauvignon, Grenache, Carignan and Cinsault, all vinified *en rosé*! The resulting brew has taken Britain by storm with its lively apple, lemon and pineapple character.

Brian Walsh and his Yalumba wine-makers tend to hedge their bets when it comes to making straight Shiraz: they make two styles – a low-Baumé pepper-spice style using Barossa and Coonawarra fruit, and a full-bodied plums-and-mace style from fully ripened Barossa fruit. The bigger wines go into American oak; the peppery, lighter wines into two-year-old French oak casks. Of the two I have a preference for the smokier Barossa style.

A small amount of Shiraz is released under the Family Reserve label, but theoretically this is available only from the cellar door. The best widely distributed range is the Signature series: it is into the Signature wine that most of the Barossa fruit goes, mixed with some grapes from Coonawarra to give it an elegant finish. Wines thought capable of longer ageing are bottled or reissued under the Galway label: the 1987 is classic plums-and-mace ripe Shiraz.

The 1988 Signature is from Coonawarra and therefore picked at a lower Baumé. It is a pleasant chocolate-and-cherry-style wine. The 1988 Family Reserve combines Coonawarra with Barossa fruit to produce a real blockbuster. The 1987 is the best Family Reserve I have tasted: packed with dark fruits – morello cherries, plums and blackberries. An idea of how long these wines can last can be gauged from the 1973 Wyndham

Blend, Galway Vintner Reserve Claret: the wine, aged in Yugoslavian oak, was still full of cherry, pineapple and blackberry fruit in 1990.

Until 1960 or so, Yalumba was a port house, and its ports are still among Australia's best. The top range is called Yalumba V.P., although some decent ports come out under the Dulcify label. The 1987 V.P. is typical of the style: plenty of mulberry and blackberry flavours. The 1981 had a more caramel/chocolate character. The Dulcify 1979 was closer to a tawny in style, more orangey; the V.P. 1971 was all raspberries and liquorice; the 1967 more like coffee and cream. The oldest port I tried at Yalumba was the 1923: still on excellent form with its fleshy-plum fruit.

PETER LEHMANN

Barossa Valley

> Samuel Road, Tanunda, SA 5352
>
> Production of Shiraz: 1,400 tonnes
>
> Quality: 🍷🍷🍷–🍷🍷🍷🍷🍷   Price: ★★–★★★
>
> Best vintages: 1981, 1983, 1986, 1987, 1988, 1989, 1990

The baron of the Barossa, Peter Lehmann, holds sway over the rump of the otherwise unenfeoffed Barossa-*Deutschen*. The son of a local Lutheran pastor, he understands their needs and, as a result, they loyally deliver up their grapes to his weigh-house. Few people know as much about the *terroir* of the Barossa as Peter Lehmann; every year it becomes a battle of the cheque-books between Lehmann, Hill-Smith and Penfolds to see who gets the best Shiraz fruit from the northern side of the Valley. Anthropologists wishing to study the genus Barossa-*Deutschen* would find the Lehmann weigh-house a source of endless fascination. Here these Rip-van-Winkle look-alikes gather at harvest time, after offloading their grapes, to enjoy a few Metwurst sandwiches and a pickled gherkin or three. The grapes they deliver – Shiraz, Grenache and Mataró – go to make the wines made under the Peter Lehmann label.

Lehmann is an open-minded wine-maker: 'Château Yquem? Let's make some!' When I suggested a Châteauneuf-style wine, he seemed all ears; he had the Shiraz, Grenache and Mataró, 'And I could get hold of some Carignan,' he added. The Barossa, thinks Lehmann, is a 'wine-makers' playground'.

Lehmann makes a good, straight Shiraz wine. The earliest I was able to taste was the 'Futures' from the 1980 vintage. Like the rest of his best Shiraz, Lehmann makes this wine from a plot of vines planted in 1890. As its name implies, there was plenty of life in the 1980; a wine with enough fruit to last another decade. The Shiraz Dry Red tends to be a lighter wine made in a more commercial style. The best is issued as Show Reserve wines. The 1987 wears more medals than Marshal Göring, but it deserves them; it is quite delicious, young yet with all its raspberry, chocolate and pepper fruit; it will be ready to drink from 1992.

For me the highlight of the tasting at Lehmann's was his 100 per cent Shiraz vintage ports. These are probably the best that Australia has to offer, and it is a great pity that the pedantic EC legislation makes it so difficult for them to reach a wider public in Europe. The 1981 suffers a bit from being too thick and liqueurish, while the 1983 seemed to have overdone the spirit. The flight tasted began in earnest with the 1986 from the Eden Valley; then came the stunning 1987 (release 1993), with its nose of incense, and the 1988, which suffered just a mite from being too fiery. Time will mellow it. The best of the lot is the 1989 – a port with decades ahead of it.

Lehmann also makes a tawny port with the suspiciously Catholic name of Old Redemption. It contains some Grenache as well as a touch of Sémillon and Muscadelle. It is between fifteen and twenty years old, with a nutty, custardy palate.

CHARLES MELTON

Barossa Valley

Krondorf Road, Tanunda, SA 5352

Production: 12,000 bottles

Quality: 🍇🍇🍇   Price: ★★★

Best vintages: 1990, 1991 (no earlier vintages tasted)

If for no other reason, Charlie Melton would deserve a place in this guide for being the only man in Australia to follow the lead of the Rhône Rangers in the United States and begin cultivating a Barossa garden of Rhône varieties. Until 1990 'Nine Popes' was a blend of 60 per cent Grenache from very old vines with 40 per cent Shiraz. With the 1991 vintage Melton finally went the whole hog and began adding Mataró (Mourvèdre).

Some explanation should be given for the name of the blend. In the Barossa they will tell you that Charlie calls it 'Nine Popes' because he thinks that is the translation for Châteauneuf-du-Pape. On the telephone Melton promised to send me an explanation, but this never arrived. I am now obliged to accept the story current in South Australia.

The wines too proved elusive. Finally Craig Smith of London's excellent Australian Wine Centre put on a tasting for me. The range began with a Rose of Alexandria made from pure Grenache. The 1991 was fresh, with a toffeeish nose: given the absence of competition, I think I can easily dub this Australia's best *rosé*. Melton's 1990 Shiraz was deep-coloured, brooding wine which will repay long keeping with its damson, spice and leather aromas. The 'Nine Popes' was also marked by a damson character, but the vines gave off none of that Virginia-tobacco aroma of Grenache in Châteauneuf. I liked the wine, but look forward to the 1991 vintage to see the extra complexity which should be supplied by the Mataró.

MOUNTADAM

Adelaide Hills

High Eden Road, High Eden Ridge, SA 5235

Production of Shiraz: all grapes bought from
contract growers

Quality: 🍇🍇🍇–🍇🍇🍇🍇   Price: ★★–★★★

Best vintages: 1987, 1988, 1989, 1990

The Wynns' estate is 2,500 feet up on the High Eden Ridge
between Adelaide and the Barossa. David Wynn bought the
land with the specific intention of making cool-climate wines,
and it is exactly in those that Mountadam excels.

The present wine-maker is David Wynn's son Adam. Adam
studied at Bordeaux University under Professors Peynaud and
Ribereau-Gayon and graduated top of his class. He retains a
rather more authentically French view of wine-making than
most growers in Australia, which he puts to good use on his
Chardonnays and Pinot Noirs.

Adam Wynn's Shiraz is made from bought-in fruit and is
issued under the secondary, David Wynn label. The 1987 was
the first vintage, and this was unoaked and bottled straight from
the vat as no wood was available. It is a delicious wine, with
plenty of body and frank, nutmeggy spice. The 1988 I found
over-oaked, and this was also my view of the 1989 until I
retasted it in London in 1991. I pleaded with Adam not to put
the excellent 1990 into oak and am much gratified to learn that
he did not do so.

ORLANDO

Barossa Valley

Sturt Highway, Rowland Flat, SA 5350

Production of Shiraz: 75,000 tonnes

Quality: 🍇–🍇🍇   Price: ★–★★★

Best vintages: 1986, 1987, 1988, 1989, 1990

Jacob's Creek 'claret' is Australia's biggest-selling red wine by a long chalk; it trounces its nearest rival (Seaview Cabernet Sauvignon) by three bottles to one. Jacob's Creek is predominantly Shiraz ullaged with quantities of Cabernet and Malbec. It is certainly not bad wine and begins to look positively superior when put next to the Englishman's favourite red: Piat d'Or. It has good, rather honeyed, blackcurrant fruit with an ever so slightly stewed finish; but at this price who's complaining?

Next up the scale is the RF Shiraz: a good, uncomplicated wine with masses of raspberry and blackberry fruit and also excellent value at the price.

Orlando's best widely distributed Shiraz is Lawson's. The 1985 is rather good: plenty of tarry raspberries and blackberries. It proves that the quality is there when the company wants to splash out.

In Australia a small amount of Show Shiraz is also sold. This is naturally the top of the range.

PENFOLDS

Barossa Valley

Tanunda Road, Nuriootpa, SA 5355

Production of Shiraz: 778,000 litres premium wine (including Kaiserstuhl and Tollana)

Quality: 🍇–🍇🍇🍇🍇🍇   Price: ★–★★★★★

Best vintages: 1980, 1981, 1982, 1983, 1984, 1985, 1986, 1987, 1988, 1989, 1990, 1991

Best vintages for Grange: 1966, 1970, 1971, 1975, 1976, 1977, 1980, 1982, 1983, 1987

Penfolds is Australia's leading producer of Shiraz wines. Even when you leave aside the Penfolds-owned South Australian companies where the wines are vinified by the same team, the range of Shiraz is quite astonishing. It runs from the commercial Dalwood or Glenloth wines (🍇) to Australia's great Shiraz wine: Grange (🍇🍇🍇🍇🍇).

Both Glenloth and Dalwood can be pleasant enough, they are made deliberately light in order to appeal to a wide market; but the real quality begins with the Bin 2 Shiraz/Mataró (🍇🍇/★★), a chunky deep wine with plenty of tannin. Shiraz predominates in the blend, and there is a rumour that Penfolds intend scrapping the Mataró altogether to make it a 100 per cent Shiraz wine. Although I have reservations about blending two varieties with such similar aromatic and tannic structures, I should be sorry to see the Mataró go; it is, after all, one of the very rare instances when Mataró appears on the label in Australia, and the wine has been a considerable success (notably in Britain). Perhaps Penfolds should try its hand at bottling a 100 per cent Mataró from low-yielding vines. The result could be an eye-opener.

Next up the scale for price and quality is the Koonunga Hill Shiraz/Cabernet blend. Koonunga Hill is one of the main sources for Grange, and it should come as no surprise that the wines are deep and slow-maturing. Doubtless the Cabernet is there to soften it, but I none the less believe that Koonunga Hill is put on the market absurdly young given its ageing potential. Both the 1987 and the 1988 were successful (🍇🍇–🍇🍇🍇/★★).

Bin 28 Kalimna Shiraz (🍇🍇🍇/★★) comes in part from another vineyard now associated with Grange, although the Kalimna fruit is topped up with Shiraz from Langthorne Creek, McLaren Vale and the Clare Valley. In years like 1985, the

Kalimna fruit gives the wine a gamy character. In others (such as 1986) this is more muted, tending to a more typical high-Baumé Penfolds style: plenty of plum and chocolate.

Bin 128 (☆☆☆/★★) is made from 100 per cent Coonawarra Shiraz. The cooler climate and limestone subsoil are apparent in the rather different flavour of the fruit. Bin 128 is marginally more expensive than Bin 28, and gets some 20 per cent new Nevers oak to round off the raspberry/minty Coonawarra style. In cooler years there is a pronounced pepperiness to the wine which comes from using slightly underripe fruit. In general, however, Penfolds is not looking for the hallowed 'pepper-spice' character in its Shiraz wines.

St Henri (☆☆☆–☆☆☆☆/★★★) is billed as a 'claret', which often leads otherwise trustworthy wine writers to put it down as a Cabernet/Shiraz blend. Actually St Henri is almost pure Shiraz, aged in big tuns as opposed to small oak. Here John Duval and his team are trying to preserve fruit aromas while softening the tannins and prolonging the structure of the wine. The fruit is mostly from Kalimna, although some Coonawarra wines are blended in to give the wine 'elegance'. Successful St Henri was made in 1985, 1986 and 1987. The 1986 had opened out the last time I tasted it, becoming a pleasant toasty wine with plenty of soft red-fruit character. The 1987 was superb, with more characteristic Kalimna fruit: buttery blackberries, leather, raspberry and cloves. In Stephanie's restaurant in Melbourne I was also able to try the 1965, an intensely toasty, caramelly old wine with a long after-taste of raspberries.

Magill (☆☆☆☆/★★★★) is Penfolds' second-best Shiraz and possibly also its second-best red. The wine comes from the Magill Estate in the suburbs of Adelaide, and it was Magill fruit which was the original mainstay of Grange before Grange started moving up the north side of the Barossa. Magill is a rarity among Penfolds wines in its adherence to the 'estate' idea. The 100 per cent Shiraz fruit is aged in a mixture of French and American oak. No efforts are made to allay the slight gamy nature of Shiraz fruit, but there are also masses of ripe red fruits and sufficient depth and colour to keep the wine fit for decades.

Grange Hermitage (or just Grange, as it has been called since the Australians began to run into trouble with the EC) is a masterpiece (👑👑👑👑👑/★★★★★) created by misunderstanding and making do with the materials to hand. In 1950 Penfolds' winemaker Max Schubert paid his first visit to Bordeaux, where he was a guest of Christian Cruse. He returned with an ambition: to make a world-class red made according to Bordeaux principles. The problem was that Australia did not at that time possess sufficient stocks of Cabernet, Merlot and Cabernet Franc to make such a wine feasible; moreover, French oak was unobtainable. Schubert proceeded to use Shiraz fruit from Magill and another private vineyard near Adelaide for his experimental wine. He housed it in 100 per cent new American oak, although it was unlikely that even the First Growth Bordeaux wines were using 100 per cent new oak in the early 1950s.

Schubert's tannic bruiser was slow to find admirers. When a selection of vintages was aired for the first time in the late 1950s, one critic found the wine tasted of 'crushed ants', another wrote it off as 'very good dry port'; others saw aphrodisiac uses for his wine. In 1957 Schubert received instructions to stop production. Fortunately for the Australian wine business, he carried on making it on the sly until 1960, when he was again given permission to produce Grange openly. 'Since that time,' writes Schubert, 'Grange Hermitage has never looked back.'

It is touching, perhaps, that Australian wine commentators have continued to see Grange as a 'claret', even despite its 100 per cent Shiraz nature; it was, after all, yet another attempt to come up with a claret-style wine. Grange, however, is far from claret-like in style: with age, it develops all that leathery, gamy, almost cheesy character of hot-country Shiraz, but combined with luscious raspberry, blackcurrant and blackberry fruit, damp leaves, black olives, herbs, tobacco and, in the best vintages, a waft of violets.

Grange has remained consistent in its quality despite the glaring truth that the wine is no longer made from the original fruit; Grange is a brand, not a wine made from a defined *terroir*. The wine had outgrown the stocks from Magill and Morphett

Vale by the early 1960s. Kalimna Shiraz made its first appearance in 1961, and by 1970 it had become the majority ingredient of the blend. That same year the team began to use some Shiraz from the Clare Valley. The final vital ingredient – Koonunga Hill pressings – was introduced in 1975. Every now and then a little Cabernet was used, but the last time this was done was in 1976.

Grange is virtually unique among Australian wines in being undrinkable before it is ten years old or more. In 1990 the 1971 was still massive, and most British commentators who tasted the 1976 a year later found that it needed a few years yet. For the time being only the 1980 and possibly the 1982 seem ready to give their best.

Penfolds makes a couple of decent ports from a blend of Shiraz, Grenache and Mataró: Club and Penfolds 10 Year Old. The latter has a pleasant nutty, *rancio* character.

The same team, headed by John Duval, is responsible for making the rather commercial Shiraz wines of Seaview (🍇/★). A far better bet is Tollana, of which the 1987 was made in a herbaceous, peppery smoky style (🍇🍇🍇/★★). Another wine made by Duval is Kaiserstuhl (literally 'imperial seat'). The 1986 won a great many medals in Australian shows, but I found it undistinguished and marked by raw, American oak.

For Penfolds' 'Wynns' brands, see the separate entry; for its 'Tulloch' brand, see under Hunter Valley, New South Wales.

SEPPELT

Barossa Valley

Seppelt, Seppeltsfield via Tanunda, SA 5352

Seppelt Great Western, Moyston Road, Great Western, VIC 3377

Production in Great Western: not released

Production in Barossa: not released

Quality: 🍇🍇🍇–🍇🍇🍇🍇   Price: ★★★–★★★★★

Best vintages: 1985, 1986, 1987, 1988, 1989, 1990

The Seppelt family were originally Barossa-*Deutschen*, settling at the place now known as Seppeltsfield. The Seppelts bought into the Great Western vineyard in 1918. The Seppeltsfield complex is still much as it was: a picturesque group of wine buildings around the old homestead which justifiably attracts numerous tourists during the summer months.

Strangely enough, the best fruit seems to come from Victoria where the flagship Great Western Hermitage is made. It is a big, dense wine packed with raspberry, cherry and plum fruit. The best recent vintage is the 1985, a wine which apparently sells at high prices in Australia, but one which proved elusive during the time I spent there. I finally tracked it down in Paris!

Also made in Great Western is Seppelt's Sparkling Red Burgundy, another 100 per cent Shiraz wine which is some-thing of a cult wine in Australia. One can see why: wines like the 1972 or the 1967 were simply packed with virtually black Shiraz fruit rejuvenated by the action of the yeasts used in the champagne method. Production was discontinued for a while during the 'puritan' years of the 1970s, but I'm pleased to say that Seppelt is making it again and is even exporting a small amount to Britain.

The Seppeltsfield complex is famous for Para Port, Australia's best-known and most expensive liqueur Shiraz. Para Port is made by the solera system, using wines dating back to the 1878 vintage. The current release comes mainly from the 1952 harvest, but obviously contains both older and younger wines; some Mataró is used. The current release is a rich, dark wine redolent of nuts and cloves.

WYNNS

Coonawarra

Memorial Drive, Coonawarra, SA 5263

Production of Shiraz: 761,500 litres

Quality: 🍇   Price: ★★

Best vintages: 1986, 1987, 1988, 1989, 1990

The Wynns are one of the great families of Australian wine. Originally called Weintraub (a name which must have encouraged Samuel Wynn to enter the business), they changed their name to the more prosaic Wynn during the anti-German days of the First World War. It was Samuel's son David who had the foresight to buy a big chunk of Coonawarra in 1951. For this alone he will be long remembered as one of the pioneers of modern Australian wine-making, and Australian wine writers still get dewy-eyed at the mere mention of some of the famous vintages of Coonawarra Hermitage released during the 1950s and 1960s.

Wynns was first taken over by Tuohy's, the brewers, and then swallowed again by Penfolds in the 1980s. The Wynn family ceased all connection with the company in 1981 and withdrew to High Eden Ridge to launch another pioneering wine estate (see the entry for Mountadam).

Wynns still leads on the Coonawarra estate wines. The Hermitage (or Shiraz, as it is labelled for export) is a good introduction to a now rapidly vanishing Coonawarra Shiraz style, the wines all having that slight minty nuance from the effects of soil and cool climate. Personally I find the Wynns' Hermitage goes overboard on the American oak, but it is a style which is immensely popular in Australia.

Wynns makes another Shiraz from fruit grown in the Ovens Valley in North East Victoria. In contrast to the Coonawarra style, the Victorian wine has all the hot-country characteristics – the bouquet of roasting coffee and dried figs – and is something of a winter warmer. There is some talk of phasing it out of the Penfolds range, but this, I think, would be a pity.

Victoria

Stylistically, Victoria produces the most interesting variety of Shiraz wines of any state in Australia. A relatively cool climate in all but the Murray River and Rutherglen areas of Victoria has allowed for the development of the 'pepper-spice' character of Shiraz which is so beloved of Australian wine writers.

Central Victoria

Central Victoria is the birthplace of the modern 'pepper-spice' school of Shiraz beloved of those writers and wine-makers who wanted to castigate the old style of Shiraz-making as represented by the Hunter Valley. The wine which initiated this trend back in Shiraz's darkest days was Knight's Granite Hills from Macedon. The Knights' estate is at 1,800 feet and the fruit ripens only with difficulty. The idea of cool-country, underripe grapes created a fashion for Shiraz-makers which may have saved many estates from being pulled up in favour of Cabernet and Merlot. There is not a lot of Knight's Granite Hills about, but I tasted the 1981 vintage at Stephanie's restaurant in Melbourne. It was like a classic Rhône wine, very smoky with an autumn-leaf character plus a sprinkling of white pepper. Craiglee from Macedon is also star-rated. The 1985 was well structured with plenty of blackberry fruit.

In the Bendigo region is the Balgownie Estate (see Mildara) making anything but light, peppery wines. Château Le Amon, owned by Philip Leamon (geddit?), makes another big, solid Shiraz. The 1985 was an excellent rich, tarry, raspberry-and-violet-scented wine.

In the central Goulburn district are both Château Tahbilk and Mitchelton (see separate entries). Alister Purbrick, the wine-maker at Tahbilk, is also responsible for Longleat in Murchison. Its 1987 was classic Shiraz, with plenty of tar and wood smoke and a rather lemony palate.

*

Great Western and the Pyrenees

It was gold which brought settlers to Great Western, not wine. The gold-diggers planted vines however, and when the gold ran out they consoled themselves with wine.

Seppelt's is just about the biggest thing in the area (see separate entry, under South Australia). Neighbouring Best's produces big strapping Shirazes for its Bin No. 0. The 1987 in particular seemed built to last for decades: in 1991 it was showing a raspberry/violet bouquet; emerging from its compact body, it was immensely long. I was impressed by a 1985 Shiraz from Cathcart Ridge which was also made in a very rich style a bit like Black Label Seppelt.

Mount Langi Ghiran enjoys an excellent reputation in Australia: the 1987 had a good blackberry nose and a very dense palate marred only by a slightly dry finish; the 1986 I found very austere and unapproachable in the spring of 1989; the 1985 (tasted in 1990) had a slight redolence of pickling spice with plenty of raspberry and blackcurrant. The palate revealed very fine tannins. I was impressed by both the 1984 and 1986 Montara wines, with their cinnamon and leather character, and especially by the 1984, with its huge blackcurrant fruit.

In the Pyrenees, Dalwhinnie lies somewhat in the shadow of Taltarni (for which, see the separate entry); the 1988 was rather closed when I tasted in 1991, its style rather lighter than its neighbour with a slightly clumsy, spirity finish.

Redbank is largely a Cabernet house, although some Shiraz goes into its Sally's Paddock wine, along with Cabernet Sauvignon and Malbec. Its 1986 straight Shiraz was a bit pongy, but the owners denied that this was the result of a mercaptan.

Melbourne Bay

The last twenty years in Australian viticultural history have been marked by, among other things, a perpetual quest for a cooler climate in order to be able to reproduce European wine styles. Sometimes there is something rather comic about this desire to climb mountains and plant wind-swept coasts in the hope of getting away from the obtrusive Australian sun. The rise of Geelong and the Mornington Peninsula has much to do with these trends, and the grapes planted (Cabernet, Pinot Noir and Chardonnay) reflect the novelty of these wine-producing districts.

There is not much Shiraz on the Mornington Peninsula to the east of Melbourne Bay (though there are good reports of Paringa): Merricks made a good 1988 which I met once in a restaurant in Gloucestershire; it was full of pepper and black fruits and marked by a long finish. Another Mornington Shiraz I found on a restaurant list was the Dromana Estate Schinus Molle, which Gary Crittenden makes from Great Western fruit. The 1988, drunk in the Bayswater Brasserie in King's Cross, Sydney, was in the plums-and-mace style, with a slightly flashy use of oak.

See the separate entry for Bannockburn Vineyard.

North East Victoria

The North East Victoria region centres on the area of Rutherglen, one of the hottest growing regions in Australia. The speciality here is fortified wines – ports and liqueur muscats – but there are exceptions like the Browns at Brown Brothers (see separate entry), Campbells (see separate entry), St Leonards and Baileys of Glenrowan.

St Leonards is now part of Brown Brothers, but Browns leave Roland Kaval very much to his own devices. Kaval is a fan of the Knight's Granite Hills style, and from 1984 to 1986 he made his Shiraz from underripe grapes to get that 'pepper-spice' character. Since 1986 he has returned to the fuller style. The 1988 had me thinking of smoky bacon – a spicy wine with a strong element of plums or prunes. The 1987 seemed closed up in 1990, but the 1986 was at its peak, with plenty of ripe cherry and chocolate fruit. The 1982, made before the 'pepper-spice' influence, was a lighter wine with an orangey, mushroomy character – a distinguished but definitely *old* wine.

Baileys of Glenrowan used to make the sort of Shiraz you frightened adults with, but over the years its style has been tamed, though not necessarily to its advantage. The 1986, for example, was a great monster of a wine with huge tannins and great burnt, leathery aromas. The 1988, on the other hand, seems to have shed an element: the fruit is more classic black-berry, although the Baileys style is recognizable by the tannins. The 1989 was closed up in 1991, recognizable only by its tan-nins. Baileys comes fairly close to the traditional style of Château Tahbilk.

The enormous castellated winery of All Saints is best known for its wonderful fortified wines; but the Sutherland-Smiths do make unfortified wines too, such as their rather porty 1987 Hermitage. I visited All Saints with the infectiously enthusiastic Andrew Sutherland-Smith, the young wine-maker. He moved from cask to cask like the proverbial blue-arsed fly, uncovering delights like a 100 per cent Shiraz tawny still in cask with a delicious nuts and raisin fruit, an Old Shiraz port that was all chocolate and figs, and an unmarked pre-1900 cask containing a marvellous concentrated treacle which was presumably old Muscat. I also tried a couple of vintage ports: a 1979 100 per cent Shiraz with plenty of blackberry and mango, raspberry and violet and a 1970 with smokier raspberry and blackcurrant fruit. All Saints should be remembered for its ports.

The same applies to Stanton & Killeen down the road. Nor-man Killeen and his son Chris make a small amount of Shiraz as an unfortified Moodamere Red, which did not impress me. Like many Rutherglen growers, they seemed to be getting better results from the Durif vines. On the other hand they made some delicious ports: the vintages 1988 and 1985 were excellent, with their strong redolence of cloves; of the older vintages, look out for the 1972. A liqueur port is made slightly sweeter. The tawny contains Muscat, Touriga, Tokay (Muscadelle), Shiraz and Grenache.

The Yarra Valley

Despite the relative antiquity of wine-making in the Yarra, its rediscovery was part of the quest for cool climates in order to perfect European wine styles in sunny Australia. Once again the most important thing was to perfect the Chardonnays and the

Pinot Noirs – Shiraz was not considered to be of much importance compared to these vineyard aristocrats.

Shiraz was made none the less – and some of the best Shiraz
in Australia if Yarra Yering is taken into account (see the separate entries for Yarra Yering and for Yarrinya). When I visited
the Yarra in 1990, James and Suzanne Halliday very kindly put
on a tasting of Yarra Shirazes for me which showed how in
certain cases the Yarra may have been unwise not to concentrate more on the old Australian stand-by.

The tasting kicked off with an excellent Warramate 1988
with plenty of spice and body. The Shirazes which Halliday
himself makes from bought-in fruit at his Coldstream Hills
estate included a spice-and-cherry-scented 1985. I was not
impressed by the Shirazes of either Kellybrook or Bianchet. I
was also once again disappointed by the St Huberts 1987, which
reminded me of the rather dilute 1984.

Later that morning I had the chance to visit Dr Peter McMa-
hon of the Seville Estate. Seville's wines enjoy a certain reputation in Melbourne, where they appear on the wine lists of top
restaurants like Mietta's. The Shiraz is made in a modern style.
Both the 1989 and the 1988 had a lentil character. The 1986
had a little tinned asparagus on the nose, which may not bode
well for the future. The 1980 seemed to me too cooked and
jammy; but the 1987 was a return to form: it had aged gracefully, giving off plenty of toast and caramel but retaining its
raspberry fruit.

BANNOCKBURN VINEYARD

Melbourne Bay

Midland Highway, Bannockburn, VIC 3331

Production: between 4,800 and 9,600 bottles – should double
in the next few years

Quality: 🍇🍇🍇🍇   Price: ★★★

Best vintages: 1984, 1985, 1986, 1988, 1989

The main thrust at Bannockburn is towards Burgundian varieties, and the quantities of Shiraz produced have always been small. Recently a further two and a half acres have been planted and there will now be a little more to go round. All the wine is aged in (second-hand) French oak, there is no filtering and the wine spends two years in cask.

I have never visited Bannockburn and have tasted the wines only by chance. The excellent 1985 I found in the Bayswater Brasserie in Sydney: a wine distinguished by the subtlety of its use of oak and a fine wood-smoke, plum and violet nose. Both the slightly light 1982 and the much better 1984 I tasted at trade tastings in London. The 1984 was marked by a delicious smell of nutmeg. The 1986 I brought back from Australia in my suitcase. It also has a spicy character and a pleasant overlay of violets and raspberries.

More recently I have lunched with Bannockburn's talented wine-maker, Gary Farr, in the Australian Sydney Street restaurant in London. Here we tasted the 1987, 1988 and 1989 vintages. The best of these were the powerful 1988, with its tight structure, and the more opulent 1989.

These are wines to watch: buy them if you can.

BROWN BROTHERS

North East Victoria

Milawa, VIC 3678

Production: figures not available

Quality: ♛♛-♛♛♛   Price: ★★-★★★

Best vintages: 1981, 1985, 1987, 1988, 1989, 1990

John G. Brown is in charge of wine-making at this old-fashioned winery in the north of the state, although his two brothers and more especially his father – Old John – put all their experience to good effect. Milawa itself is all 'Brown' as far as wine is concerned; but there is an excellent cheese dairy, a mustard-maker and a good little restaurant for anyone looking for something else after a call at the cellar door.

Brown's wine-making style is marked by caution; he rarely produces remarkable wines, but then again he is almost incapable of fault. When it comes to Shiraz, he wants to tame its more earthy, animal nature by ensuring that the pH of his wines never rises above 3.4. The basic Shiraz is a ripe Victorian Shiraz made from bought-in grapes, of which the 1985 was a notable success with its wood-smoke, autumnal character. Single-vineyard wines come from the Buffalo Vineyard, with its lentilly, low-Baumé character, and from the 1,000 feet Koombala Vineyard, where the Browns are looking for a style reminiscent of Knight's Granite Hills: plenty of black pepper, lentils, mint and strawberry. Brown Brothers release an occasional Estate Selection; look out for the 1981, a particularly luscious wine.

Brown Brothers market a couple of ports made from a blend of Shiraz and Grenache: the Old Reserve (in fact only three to four years old) has a pleasant, nutty, figgy character; while the Very Old Port, made from 50 per cent Shiraz and 50 per cent Grenache, is a darker wine with a concentrated palate of blackberries and chocolate.

CAMPBELLS

North East Victoria

Murray Valley Highway, Rutherglen, VIC 3685

Production of Shiraz: 95 tonnes

Quality: 🍇🍇🍇   Price: ★★

Best vintages: 1972, 1981, 1985, 1986, 1987, 1988, 1990

In 1985 Colin Campbell had a change of heart. For ten years he had been making wines to please the 'show circuit' judges, in the new approved Shiraz style, but at the same time he had never fully come to terms with this. Between 1975 and 1985 so many techniques had been applied to the business of cleaning up Shiraz that it had begun to lose its character: all Australian Shiraz tasted the same.

Campbell thinks he refound his way with the 1986 vintage of his top Shiraz wine: Bobbie Burns. It is certainly a high-class wine, with an attractive burnt-sugar character overlaying a complex tannic structure and good raspberry fruit. The 1981, though coming from the Dark Ages at Campbells, I found equally good – full of luscious raspberry fruit. Both the 1985 and the 1988 are also recommended.

His second wine is Campbells' straight Shiraz, of which a 1972 was still showing considerable style after eighteen years. I actually preferred the violet-scented 1987 to the cedary Bobbie Burns of that year, but time may reverse that judgement. The 1990s I tasted straight from the press house showed great promise.

In the middle of Rutherglen, it comes as no surprise that Campbells should make fine ports. These are made from 100 per cent Shiraz. The best of all I tasted was a magnificent 1972. The 1983 was also stylish; the 1986 a little too jammy.

MILDARA

Murray River

> Wentworth Road, Merbein, Mildura, VIC 3505
>
> Production of Shiraz: 1,500 tonnes
>
> Quality: 🍇🍇–🍇🍇🍇🍇   Price: ★–★★★
>
> Best vintages: 1986, 1987, 1988, 1989, 1990

'In my house there are many mansions' might sum up Mildara's ownership of so many prestige vineyards and wineries. From the outside of the winery, situated on a particularly arid stretch of land on the banks of the Murray River, it would be hard to credit that Mildara controls Balgownie in Victoria and Krondorf in the Barossa as well as a good stretch of land in Coonawarra which is used to make (among other things) the prize-winning wines of Jamieson's Run.

Mildara's own wines, made from fruit grown along that irrigated stretch of the Murray, are not to be despised either, although they are made in an unabashedly commercial style. One of their more popular lines is a rather raspberry-yoghurt-like Mildara Nouveau wine made to resemble Beaujolais *primeur*. Not all their wines are made in this style, however, and I was able to taste a 1964 Cabernet/Shiraz Bin 33 which was still on excellent form. A 1973 Bin 42 Shiraz/Cabernet combined fruit from Coonawarra, McLaren Vale and the Hunter; it was a very toasty old wine, the colour having turned almost orange over the years. Mildara is also responsible for two 'liqueur' wines: Stratford Old Tawny, made from Shiraz with a little Grenache, and the rather more Grenache-dominated nutty Cavendish.

Some of the Coonawarra fruit is shipped up to Mildura where it is bottled as Mildara Coonawarra Hermitage (or Shiraz for export); look out for the 1987. The fruit is best put to use in Jamieson's Run, a blend of 80 per cent Shiraz combined with Cabernet Sauvignon, Cabernet Franc and Merlot aged in heavily toasted French and American oak. The 1986 had a little more Shiraz and a drop of Malbec, giving it a slightly farmyardy, mulberry-and-blackcurrant character. The 1987 appeared to have rather riper blackcurrant fruit. The 1988, which won the prestigious Jimmy Watson Trophy for the year's best young red, had a highly attractive wood-smoke and autumn-leaves bouquet allied to chunky raspberry fruit and great length.

The former Barossa-*Deutscher* estate of Krondorf was made famous in the days when it was owned by the dynamic Burge and Wilson partnership. Under Mildara's ownership, Krondorf makes a Shiraz/Cabernet wine using Barossa, McLaren Vale and Coonawarra fruit which starts in European oak and finishes its maturation in American barrels. The wine is rather dominated by the minty flavours of Barossa Cabernet. A preview of the 1990 Shiraz augured well for the 1990 vintage.

Also made at Krondorf is Premier Cuvée, a blend of 50 per cent Shiraz from Balgownie with Coonawarra Cabernet. I found the 1988 overpoweringly oaky, but time should mellow it. As ever, the Balgownie fruit seemed tough and unapproach-able.

Anyone calling at the Krondorf cellar door is well advised to invest in the superb Show Liqueur Port, made from 45 per cent Shiraz, 45 per cent Grenache and 10 per cent Mataró. The port is fifteen years old and has a marvellous, rich complexity of coffee, liquorice, butter and *rancio* flavours.

Lastly there is Mildara's 'boutique' division in Balgownie, Victoria. Stuart Anderson is left alone to get on with making the wines which made the estate famous before Mildara acquired it. The Shiraz wines are among the biggest in Australia. The 1986 seemed to me to be excessively closed and meaty in 1988, though by mid 1990 it was showing some rather more attractive raspberry fruit. The 1988 tasted in 1990 was black and tarry, although some pleasant violet character was showing through. There are excellent reports of the 1990.

MITCHELTON

Central Victoria

Mitchellstown via Nagambie, VIC 3608

Production of Shiraz: not released

Quality: 🍇🍇🍇   Price: ★★

Best vintages: 1986, 1987, 1988, 1989, 1990

Just up the river from Château Tahbilk, the modern Mitchelton seems deliberately to want to upstage its venerable neighbour. In the place of the old vineyard tower of Tahbilk, Mitchelton's creators built a huge, space-age 'feature tower', equipping it with a (sadly lacklustre) restaurant with views over the whole Goulburn Valley.

Wine-maker Don Lewis shares a trait with the *régisseur* of Château d'Issan in the Médoc: he is an expert pickler. He is also a pretty good wine-maker; but he has elected to go for a no-nonsense, modern approach, like the architecture. One of Lewis's specialities is his 'Cab Mac' – as the name implies, a wine made by carbonic maceration in a Beaujolais style, but from Shiraz, Grenache and Cabernet Sauvignon rather than the usual Gamay. It is a good, light summer wine.

Lewis also makes a Goulburn Valley Shiraz and, in most years, a Reserve Shiraz. The vines are grown on red, sandy loam, and some of them are almost eighty years old. The wines are aged for a couple of years in American oak casks, Lewis believing that the spicy character of the oak complements the Shiraz fruit. Potentially the best year for some time is the 1990, which will be bottled in the spring of 1992; it is a huge deep wine in a hefty plums-and-mace style, and was the winner of the prestigious Jimmy Watson Trophy for the best young red in 1991. Both the straight 1989 and 1988 are lighter: correct without being remarkable. The 1987 Mitchelton Reserve seemed to smell of paprika while the palate was marked by a distinct pepperiness. The 1986 Reserve was more smoky, more classic old Australian Shiraz.

CHÂTEAU TAHBILK

Central Victoria

Tahbilk, VIC 3607

Production of Shiraz: *c.* 200 tonnes

Quality: 🍇🍇🍇-🍇🍇🍇🍇   Price: ★★-★★★

Best vintages: 1968, 1971, 1980, 1981, 1982, 1984, 1985, 1987, 1990

Best vintages of Special Claret: 1981, 1982, 1985

Château Tahbilk is a historic monument in more senses than one. Here is Australia's oldest functioning wine estate in its original buildings on the Goulburn River, and over in a corner of the 355 acre estate are almost certainly Australia's oldest Shiraz vines, 1.7 acres which date back to 1860. They are still in production for a few cases of Special Claret made only in exceptional years.

Old Eric Purbrick's father bought the property in 1925, and

in that year the Cambridge graduate made his first visit to the estate. Eric Purbrick still lives in the vineyard house, while his son John handles marketing. John's son Alister is now the wine-maker both here and at Longleat in Murchison.

Appropriately enough for Australia's oldest estate, the wine-making has an old-fashioned air: there is no new wood used for the reds, and the wines mature in big tuns. A huge tannic backbone coupled with a powerful acidity contrives to make Tahbilk one of the longest-living wines in the country. The 1961, made in a generally light year, is evidence of this. Tasted in London in the winter of 1991, it was full and toffeed with plenty of butter and caramel tastes. There was no sign of fad-ing. Of the more recent vintages, the 1982 was the best vintage for a while, though there is every sign that wines like the 1984, 1985 and 1987 will prove able replacements. There are high hopes for the 1990 too. The estate went through a bad patch at the end of the 1970s, when Alister Purbrick had yet to find his way. Both the 1988 and the 1989 vintages were also disappoint-ing, made in a light, commercial style which is definitely *not* typical Tahbilk.

TALTARNI

Great Western and the Pyrenees

Taltarni Road, Moonambel, VIC 3478

Production of Shiraz: *c.* 40 tonnes

Quality: ♛♛♛–♛♛♛♛   Price: ★★

Best vintages: 1981, 1983, 1984, 1986, 1988, 1990

Taltarni was created by American businessman John Goelet in 1972, as a sister operation to his Californian winery Clos du Val. The wine-maker at Clos du Val was Frenchman Bernard Portet; in this Victorian vineyard Goelet installed Portet's brother Dominique, who is assisted by Greg Gallagher.

Between 1977 and 1981, Taltarni's Shiraz style was slightly

hesitant, more claret-like than anything from the Rhône Valley, say. A change occurred in 1981, when Portet decided to change the name of the wine to 'French Syrah' (this name can't be used in Europe) to herald a new, more Gallic, style of wine-making. Since then, Taltarni's track record has been excellent. The 1984 is possibly its best wine to date, with a wild, peppery character, although this may have had something to do with the failure of a cooling jacket on a fermenting vat. The 1985 returned to a fruity style; the 1986 had an aristocratic violet bouquet. The 1987, on the other hand, was less successful: rather flabby and short. The 1988 was the recipient of a Gold Medal in the 1991 International Wine Challenge.

YARRA YERING

Yarra Valley

Briarty Road, Coldstream, VIC 3770

Production of Shiraz: 400–500 cases in the past; less now

Quality: 🍇🍇🍇🍇–🍇🍇🍇🍇🍇   Price: ★★★★★

Best vintages: 1982, 1984, 1987, 1989, 1990

Bailey Carrodus bought Yarra Yering in the Yarra Valley in 1969. An Oxford-trained botanist, he already had a far more international conception of Shiraz when he started making his superb Dry Red No. 2. Carrodus had no desire to blend Shiraz with Cabernet (Cabernet Sauvignon is the mainstay of Dry Red No. 1), not holding this typical Australian combination in high regard: 'They both need friends,' he says of Shiraz and Cabernet, 'but not one another.' Instead, Carrodus looked to the Rhône Valley. He planted Mataró, but found that the Yarra Valley was not hot enough for either Mataró or Grenache. He looked further up the Rhône, to Côte Rôtie and Hermitage, and planted Viognier and Marsanne. Now his Dry Red No. 2 is made from some 85 per cent Shiraz with additions of the two white grapes.

Another way in which Carrodus defied the normal Australian

conception of Shiraz was to house the wine in between a third and a half new *French* oak. Carrodus told me that he was 'utterly unconvinced' by American oak and doesn't use it for any of his wines.

Dry Red No. 2 has always been made in small quantities. In 1975 and 1978 none was made at all, the weather being too cold. The best recent vintages have been the 1982 and the 1984. The former is slightly gamy, pointing to a hot year in the Valley, but with a splendid redolence of violets. The 1984 is *my* favourite: lovely smoky, violet-scented wine. The 1989 should be as good: when I tasted it in 1990 it reminded me of a young Côte Rôtie; it was made with 6 per cent Viognier and 10 per cent Marsanne.

The latest craze to grip Australia is Pinot Noir, and Carrodus is once again among the front-runners. The only problem is that, with his Pinot Noir fetching $50 a bottle at the cellar door, he has lost interest in Shiraz and has T-grafted many of his vines over to Pinot. This would be a catastrophe if it weren't for the fact that he was able to purchase the neighbouring Underhill estate, where he continues to make reasonable quantities of Shiraz under the Underhill label. The 1989 Underhill is made in typical Carrodus Rhône style, though the last time I tasted it (1991) it seemed strangely forward.

YARRINYA ESTATE

Yarra Valley

Pinnacle Lane, Dixon's Creek, VIC 3775

Production of Shiraz: not released

Quality: ♦♦♦   Price: ★★

Best vintages: 1983, 1985, 1988, 1990

Yarrinya is the Yarra Valley branch of the big De Bortoli firm. (The name used to be Château Yarrinya, and the De Bortolis are threatening to change it again, to De Bortoli.) Most of De Bortoli's wines are made at Griffith in the Irrigated Region, where their most successful wines are the pudding wines they make from nobly rotten fruit. They make some Shiraz in New South Wales, but it doesn't measure up to the quality they can obtain here in cool, maritime Victoria.

The 'château' (in fact more of a crenellated shack) was owned by Graeme Miller until 1985, and the De Bortolis still retain some of the wines made under the old ownership. For me, the best was the 1983, from a drought year, with its toasty nose and blackberry/violet palate. The 1985 was good too, made in a Hunterish style, with plenty of game and leather.

The new owners dismiss wines like the 1985: they want more fruit, and they are rare in advocating French oak for Shiraz. The 1988 shows something of the buttery, raspberry new style at its most successful. I was less happy with the 1989 in cask, but early indications for the 1990 looked good.

The estate has an Italian restaurant for visitors looking for lunch in the Valley.

Western Australia

Although vineyard planting in Western Australia dates from the time of the colony's foundation in 1829, most of today's top estates were created during the rediscovery of the region's potential which has taken place in the last twenty years. The timing is significant: Western Australia received this huge fillip at precisely the moment when Shiraz was going through the nadir of its popularity in Australia. Most of Western Australia's top estates prefer to concentrate on Cabernet and Chardonnay wines.

There remain a few well-known Shiraz wines from Western Australia which deserve mention here, however – not least as a result of their unusually wide distribution. The 1987 Plantagenet wine from the Lower Great Southern Area seems to take the pie-and-peas style to extremes, reminding me of nothing more than fresh pork sausages. The 1988 was much better in a chocolate-and-raisin style. In the Margaret River, Cape Mentelle makes a highly acclaimed Shiraz; the 1987 is a nicely structured wine with a pronounced spice and violet character, while the 1989 is more tarry and leathery. One of Western Australia's biggest producers (and exporters) of Shiraz is Houghton Wines, now part of the Hardy group.

AUSTRIA

| Production: experimental only

With the red-wine revolution currently taking place in Austria, a wide variety of new grapes has been planted in the hope of finding a big red wine which can be made in Austria's warmer, drier regions like Burgenland and the north-western Weinviertel. Only one or two growers have latched on to Syrah, but their number could increase over the next few years. Paul Triebaumer in Rust on the Neusiedlersee has planted an acre of vines which his son brought back from South Africa, but he has yet to vinify the grapes for Austria's first Syrah. On the Czechoslovak border near the town of Retz, Gerhard Redl of the Landwirtschaftliche Fachschule told me that he was planting his first Syrah vines in the spring of 1992.

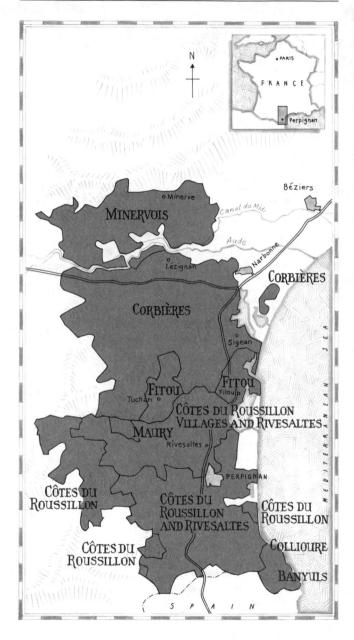

FRANCE

Languedoc-Roussillon

Not so long ago Languedoc-Roussillon was the source for little more than oceans of cheap plonk. Départements like the Aude and Hérault were deemed 'a problem' to be faced by successive French agriculture ministers. The progress this large region has made in less than two decades has been phenomenal, and we may yet live to see the Languedoc become the byword for decent-quality wines at modest prices.

Syrah, Grenache and Mourvèdre have played a leading role in reforming the viti/viniculture of the region. After the war, the flat lands and even some of the slopes were planted with big-yielding grape varieties like the Aramon and the Alicante Bouschet. The first task was to remove these vines; the next was to find flavours and structures to make up for some of the drawbacks of the Carignan grape which remained. Syrah, Grenache and Mourvèdre were called for as *cépages amélio-rateurs*. A little Syrah or Mourvèdre provided not only aromas and tannins but also an anti-oxidant which allowed the wines to age with dignity. Grenache provided the texture for the new wines, and, where possible, Grenache Noir has actually replaced Carignan as the mainstay of these Mediterranean vine-yards. The resulting wines have a complexity which cannot be found at this price among the cheaper 'varietal' wines of the New World.

While the basic red wines of Languedoc-Roussillon cried out for reform, there was a range of neglected liqueur wines in the region which has only recently been rediscovered by wine-lovers (chiefly in Paris): the great Grenache-based *vins doux naturels* (VDNs) of the Pyrénées Orientales. These superbly complex dessert wines have a long history in French and Spanish Catalonia and deserve a wider audience.

Banyuls AOC and Banyuls Grand Cru

Production: 2.8 million litres of Banyuls and 1.5 million litres of Banyuls Grand Cru from the communes of Collioure, Banyuls, Port Vendres and Cerbère

Great claims are made for the antiquity of Banyuls as a wine. One I've heard (and not believed) is that Hannibal planted the vines on his way to the Alps, Italy and an appointment with Fabius Cunctator (which the latter wouldn't keep). Clearly the style of wine has centuries of tradition on this coastline, as wines of the type can be found all over Catalonia, both French and Spanish. The early wine authority Jullien certainly attests to their existence in 1816, and after phylloxera decimated the port vineyards there must have been a renewed enthusiasm for passing them off as port on the British market.

Banyuls is on a great series of schist outcrops marking the foothills of the Pyrenees to the extreme east. Within the area there are considerable variations of soil which also affect the unfortified wines of Collioure. Basically the wines are lightest to the north, in the area around Collioure, and heaviest to the south as you move up through Port Vendres towards the communes of Banyuls and Cerbère. Yields are poor: officially growers may make up to 30 hl/ha (1,210 litres per acre) but in reality they are happy with half of that.

Banyuls is essentially Grenache. At least 50 per cent of Banyuls must be Grenache Noir (the majority of the rest should be Grenaches Gris and Blanc), and Grand Cru must be 75 per cent Grenache Noir. With both wines there is an allowance for 10 per cent *cépages accessoires*. This generally means Carignan, but some growers use Syrah or even Mourvèdre.

Banyuls may be made in a variety of styles, which can resemble vintage port (here called 'rimatge', which is the Catalan word), tawny port or Madeira. Whatever form the wine takes, there is a difference between Banyuls and port in that the

French wine uses rectified spirit as opposed to brandy. Alcohol can be added at different stages of the fermentation, but the favoured process for the better wines is *mutage sur marc* or *macération sous alcool*, where the grapes ferment with the alcohol. The resulting wine is lower in strength than port, at around 16.5° alcohol.

Originally Banyuls must have tended towards the 'Madeira' style. The idea was to bake the wine in the sun in big glass jars. Only one of the co-operatives now does this regularly and that is the Cave de l'Étoile. The G.I.V.B. still rolls barrels out into the sunlight during the hot summer months, but does not actually expose the wine to the sun's rays. Treated in this way, the wine takes on a strong roasted character which is called *rancio* in Spain and Catalonia as it exudes smells of leather, coffee and dried figs. More recently, Banyuls producers have favoured the vintage or 'rimatge' style which produces wines of dense colour and a good, fresh fruit character which take on further characteristics when they get a chance to grow old.

Two names to watch in Banyuls are the Mas Casa Blanca (see also under Collioure) and the Domaine de la Tour Vieille (see also under Collioure). At Casa Blanca the former lawyer Alain Soufflet makes wines of immense character. The 'dry' 1986 Banyuls was rich in fig and nut characters, while the vintage wine was spicy behind a weight of red-fruit tastes.

See separate entries for S.C.V. l'Étoile, G.I.V.B., Château de Jau, Domaine du Mas Blanc, Domaine de la Rectorie.

Collioure

Production: *c.* 800,000 litres from the communes of Collioure, Banyuls, Port Vendres and Cerbère.

Much like modern Bandol, in Provence, Collioure's AOC is the creation of one man; and it is no accident, perhaps, that Lucien Peyraud of Bandol and Dr André Parcé of Collioure should be good friends.

For years the Parcés had been making a dry, unfortified wine within the boundaries of AOC Banyuls. With Parcé's many contacts in the gastronomic world of France, this wine enjoyed a certain reputation. In the 1960s the wine managed to achieve a sort of temporary AOC (which was then possible); a full AOC followed in 1971.

At that time, however, Parcé was pretty well the only man about who had made a dry wine of this type. There were dry *rancio* wines to be sure – made not unlike the wines of Priorato, in Spain – but they were rarely bottled, lying in big tuns and gradually oxidizing. Much of their charm for the locals lay in their prodigious degree of alcohol. At first there weren't many takers for Collioure. In 1972 only four domaines vinified an unfortified wine in the region. The figure of 100,000 litres was passed for the first time in 1977, but it was not really until 1982 that the AOC began to gain ground.

The first Collioures had relied chiefly on the Carignan grape, but over the twenty years of the AOC this position has changed considerably. Grenache Noir is now the mainstay of the wine, along with Syrah, Counoise and increasing quantities of Mourvèdre. Mourvèdre is actually proving better adapted to the schisty soils than is Syrah, and the best recent experiments have almost all been made with a high proportion of Mourvèdre.

In the summer of 1989 I conducted a tasting in Collioure of as many wines as could be found at the time. Top marks went to a 1982 from the G.I.V.B., with wines from both the Parcé brothers at Domaine de la Rectorie and Dr Parcé at Domaine du Mas Blanc coming near the top (see the separate entries for all three). Other leading lights were Jules and Petra Campadieu's Domaine de la Villa Rosa, Alain Soufflet and Laurent Escarpa's Mas Casa Blanca (for which I noted 'well-hung game, cats on heat, leather and spices'), Rémi Herre's Cave Tambour, and Vincent Cantié and Christine Campadieu's Domaine de la Tour Vieille in Collioure itself.

See also the description of Clos des Paulilles under the entry for Château de Jau.

*

Corbières

| Production: 53.7 million litres

The rapid progress made by Corbières in the past two decades is a classic instance of the effect of the *cépages améliorateurs*. In the past, the best that Corbières had was low-yielding Carignan; the worst (and that was bad) was Aramon and Alicante Bouschet. Even before Corbières became an AOC in 1985, growers had realized that the only grape worth saving was the Carignan, and then only the hillside old vines. Grenache proved a popular replacement throughout the region; over towards the coast, experiments were made with Mourvèdre, and Syrah was the favourite among the newcomers up in the schisty soils of the Massif.

More recently, the authorities in Corbières have isolated individual areas of Corbières in which the wines have a family resemblance; these are Sigean, Durban, Queribus, Termenès, Fontfroide, St-Victor, Lagrasse, Servies, Montagne d'Alaric, Lézignan and Boutenac. Naturally there has been more Mourvèdre planted in the maritime region and more Syrah planted in inland areas.

See separate entries for Château Hélène, Château du Parc and U.C.C.M. Portel.

Côtes du Roussillon and Côtes du Roussillon Villages

| Production: 202 million litres of Côtes du Roussillon; 9.7 million litres of Côtes du Roussillon Villages

Twenty years ago the Roussillon could boast few if any unfortified wines which would have lured the wine-conscious traveller off the main road to Spain and Spanish Catalonia. In this arid, rugged region the wines were made according to virtually prehistoric practices under the blazing sun of the hottest corner of France. The only people who stopped for wine were canny *négociants* from Bordeaux, who had prized these wines as *vins médecins* for nearly two centuries: strong, black wines capable of shoring up the claret in an ill-favoured year.

It was the oenologists who changed all that: first André Brugirard and later Jean Rière and Pierre Torrès. Brugirard still
jokes that his labours turned him prematurely grey, but no one
would now question that all his work has paid off.

The reforms started in the vineyards, with the grapes themselves. For most growers the best grape they had was the
Carignan; but since 1977, however, the Carignan has been
limited to a maximum of 70 per cent, and in 1993 this will be
reduced to 60 per cent. The intention is to give more and more
attention to the *cépages améliorateurs*: essentially Grenache
Noir, Syrah and Mourvèdre.

The only differences between the Côtes du Roussillon AOC
and that of Côtes du Roussillon Villages are that the latter
comes from a more privileged *terroir* on either side of the River
Agly, is half a degree stronger and has yields of 40 hl/ha (1,620
litres per acre) as opposed to 45 hl/ha (1,820 litres per acre).

The Roussillon is still dominated by co-operatives which,
with the guidance they receive from Jean Rière and others,
often produce wines of real class. The better co-operatives in
the Fenouillèdes, such as La Tour de France and Caramany, are
marketed by Les Vignerons Catalans. La Tour de France and
Caramany are the two Roussillon Villages allowed to put their
names in bold on the labels; Caramany is the better of the two,
notably for its Cuvée Presbytère, which has more Syrah.

Jean Rière also vinifies the wines of René-Jean Camo at Mas
Camo in Força Réal. This vineyard was planted in 1976 with a
majority of Grenache Noir. A small amount of Syrah is added
to the wine, which is aged for a few months in new oak.

Over towards the coast, beyond the sprawl of Perpignan,
Raymond Laporte farms the 99 acre Château de Roussillon
estate. Laporte makes an excellent pure-Syrah *rosé* by *saignée*,
then uses the hulls from the grapes to beef up his Côtes du
Roussillon made from 60 per cent Syrah and 40 per cent
Grenache.

Laporte is one of the more enterprising growers of the
younger generation who is using Syrah and Grenache to good
effect. In general, the Roussillonais have had difficulty with
Mourvèdre, which fails to ripen except on the coast by Col-

effect. In general, the Roussillonnais have had difficulty with Mourvèdre, which fails to ripen except on the coast by Collioure. One grower who has had some success with the grape, however, is Jean Gauby in Calce. Gauby farms 148 acres of vineyard on different sites in the Agly Valley. His *rosé* is made from 70 per cent Mourvèdre and 30 per cent Grenache Noir. Gauby is also steadily increasing the amount of Mourvèdre he puts into his Côtes du Roussillon Villages: the 1988 had 10 per cent, with 40 per cent Grenache and the rest old Carignan; with the 1989, however, he was up to 30 per cent Mourvèdre, making the wine deep and tannic. The 1990 was 25 per cent each of Mourvèdre, Syrah, Grenache and old Carignan, producing a wine most uncharacteristic for the region with its dense tannins. It will not be ready to drink for several years yet.

See also Cazes Frères, Château de Jau, Domaine Sarda-Mallet.

Fitou

| Production: 9.9 million litres of red Fitou

Fitou has long been recognized for the quality of its Carignan wines: it was for this reason that this small coastal pocket was created the first of Languedoc-Roussillon's unfortified-wine AOCs, in 1948. To a great degree Fitou remains what it was, although the Carignan has been brought down to a maximum of 75 per cent, allowing Grenache, Syrah or Mourvèdre to be used should the grower wish. This has liberated some of the domaines which were interested in broadening the range of their wines. On the coast, Mourvèdre has been favoured as it has always given better results there. In the more mountainous regions of Paziols, Tuchan, Cascastel and Villeneuve, Syrah has been the favoured *cépage améliorateur*.

See separate entries for Caves de Mont-Tauch and Cave Pilote de Villeneuve.

Maury

| Production: 4 million litres of VDN

Maury is a nineteen-mile-long valley some seven miles due west of Perpignan. The soil is shaly and hard, and the heat of the valley produces Grenache-based wines of great concentration and colour, most of which are used for the VDN AOC Maury.

There are 4,200 acres of Maury, but very few of the growers vinify their own wines. The two best-known names are the co-operative Les Vignerons de Maury and Mas Amiel. In addition to these two there are the estates of Jean-Louis Lafage, René Martinez (owned by Mme Lydie Baissas) and Marc Majoral.

The wines are made in much the same way as Banyuls, but on most occasions they lack Banyuls' finesse. At the co-operative they make a fine Six Ans d'Âge, and a Vieille Réserve. There is also a vintage wine.

Minervois

| Production: 188 million litres of red wine

Another area of the vast Midi which has been revived by the use of Syrah, Grenache Noir and Mourvèdre grapes, Minervois was granted full AOC status only in 1985. Since then, growers have been making a determined effort to use the new grapes in preference to the old.

Under the current rules, Carignan may enter the vats at a maximum of 60 per cent, while Syrah, Grenache or Mourvèdre (or, indeed, all three) must represent a minimum of 30 per cent.

See separate entries for Château du Donjon, Château de Gourgazaud and Château Villerambert-Julien.

Rivesaltes

| Production: 4 million litres of VDN

Eighty-six communes in the Pyrénées Orientales (some 45,000 acres) have the right to make a Grenache VDN as Rivesaltes. As the soils vary enormously from one commune to another, it is hard to give an overall picture of the styles involved. Some estates now make a 'vintage' style by bottling the wine early, to keep its fruit character; two of the best of these are Cazes Frères and Domaine Sarda-Mallet (see separate entries). Les Vignerons Catalans markets a good vintage wine under the Cap de Fouste label; otherwise I've tasted fine young Grenache VDNs from Mas Rous, the Coopérative de Planèze, the Domaine de Rombeau, Les Vignerons de St-Vincent and Les Maîtres Vignerons de Tautavel.

Older wines tend to have a higher proportion of Grenaches Gris and Blanc than Noir.

CAZES FRÈRES

4 avenue Ferrer, 66600 Rivesaltes

Production: 370 acres of vines, about 110 acres of which are used for Côtes du Roussillon and Côtes du Roussillon Villages; 37 acres of Syrah planted in 1991

Quality: 🍇🍇🍇   Price: ★★

Best vintages: 1984, 1985, 1986, 1987, 1989, 1990

Possibly the most enterprising wine-makers in the Languedoc-Roussillon region, the Cazes brothers make seventeen different wines. The elder of the two brothers, André, started out modestly with the former estate of the Maréchal Joffre in 1956, at the end of his military service. By the time his younger brother, Bernard, had joined him, he had managed to make inroads into the Parisian market. Since then there has been no looking back.

With their constant experimentation, however, the brothers are increasingly unhappy with the wines they make as Côtes du Roussillon and Côtes du Roussillon Villages. The AOC imposes too much of a strait-jacket on them with its insistence on the grapes associated with the region. They despise Carignan: when you bring up the subject of good, low-yielding old Carignan, André dismisses it as 'a five-footed sheep' (i.e. a fabulous beast). Mourvèdre doesn't ripen on their soils, and the *fond de sauce* is Grenache Noir. Syrah is the best grape they have, but so far the legislation will not allow them to go beyond 30 per cent; nevertheless, they say, 'It's the Syrah which makes the difference between a good and a bad wine.'

To some extent they protest too much: their 1986 Villages was superb, and year in year out even their second-string Côtes du Roussillon wine is one of the best in the appellation. Also from Grenache Noir is the wonderful VDN Rivesaltes Vintage. Only 20 per cent Grenache Noir goes into the Rivesaltes 'Vieux', which is largely made from Grenache Blanc. The magnificent Très Vieux is 100 per cent Grenache Blanc.

CHÂTEAU DU DONJON

Bagnoles, 11600 Conques-sur-Orbiel

Production: 57 acres in Minervois AOC; 111 acres altogether

Quality: 🍇🍇🍇   Price: ★★

Best vintages: 1985, 1986, 1989, 1990

The sister château of Château du Parc in Corbières (see separate entry), the Château du Donjon is housed in a proper old keep, with the vats in the dungeons! The wine is made from 30 per cent Syrah, 30 per cent Grenache Noir and 40 per cent Carignan. The 1988 struck me as being a trifle short, though with a promising amount of fruit. The 1986, labelled Panis-Miailhe (the name of the owners), was giving off some old, leathery notes. The best wine by far was the 1985, with its intense blackcurrant/blackberry fruit.

S.C.V. L'ÉTOILE

26 avenue du Puig-del-Mas, 66650 Banyuls-sur-Mer

Production: 420 acres of vines producing Banyuls and Collioure

Quality: 🍇🍇🍇🍇🍇 for Sélect Vieux, 🍇🍇🍇🍇 for Grande
Réserve, 🍇🍇🍇 for Rimage, 🍇🍇 for
Collioure   Price: ★★–★★★
Best vintages: 1967, 1972, 1977

L'Étoile is above all the Banyuls house which continues to produce sensational old Banyuls wines which conform to the *rancio* style once prevalent in the area. If you wish to experience Banyuls as it was historically, then L'Étoile is the place to go; here you will find with the Sélect Vieux, for example, all those coffee, leather and fig aromas which typify classic Banyuls. The modern-style wines are less successful, and this is true also for the Collioure, which is not one of the front-runners.

The Rimage 1989 is an illustration of this. The Étoile Rimage seems to have missed the point; with its coffee, malt and tobacco characters it is already halfway to traditional Banyuls and not the vintage-port-inspired 'rimage' or 'rimatge'. The Grande Réserve is more in the line which distinguishes this house: all walnuts, figs and coffee, with a spice-and-tobacco finish. The Sélect Vieux 1974 is very pale, with a creamy coffee-and-fig aroma and a touch of leather. This is Banyuls as it ought to be.

G.I.V.B.

S.I.V.I.R.

S.I.C.A. DES VINS DU ROUSSILLON

CELLIER DES TEMPLIERS

Route des Crêtes, 66650 Banyuls-sur-Mer
Production: no figures released
Quality: 🍇🍇–🍇🍇🍇🍇   Price: ★★–★★★
Best vintages: 1970, 1975, 1978, 1982, 1985, 1989, 1990

This is the largest of the three big co-operatives in Banyuls and the best for across-the-board quality. Here the wines are vinified by Jean-Pierre Campadieu, a professional oenologist who was not slow to see the potential in Collioure and whose 1982 proved the best wine in a tasting of twenty or so wines assembled in the Parcé bunker in 1989.

The G.I.V.B. now produces a wide range of Collioures under a confusing variety of labels. The 1982 which proved such a winner is now sold both as 'Collioure' and as 'Guy de Barlande'; both the 1986 and the 1988s are classic Collioures, as is the Domaine de Baillaury 1988, which is made from a domaine vinified separately. Château Les Abelles contains a certain amount of Syrah, while the Abbaye de Valbonne relies more on Mourvèdre, some of it aged in new oak. In 1988 Campadieu made an experimental cuvée containing as much as 40 per cent Mourvèdre, some of it aged in new oak. Once again Mourvèdre appears to be proving the clue to improving the infant AOC of Collioure.

The G.I.V.B. also makes some of the greatest of all Banyuls, yet in a style quite distinct from those made by the Caves de l'Étoile. There is a 'rimatge', of course – here vinified *sur marc*. The Grand Cru Amiral François de Vilarem is aged for fourteen years in oak, producing an elegant, tawny wine with a redolence of strawberries, figs and cooked peaches.

CHÂTEAU DE GOURGAZAUD

34210 La Livinière

Production: 173 acres, of which 86 acres in red Minervois AOC

Quality: 🍇   Price: ★–★★

Best vintages: 1979, 1986, 1989, 1990

This up-market Minervois estate is well known abroad for its presence in big retail outlets such as Sainsbury in the UK.

Gourgazaud uses a high proportion of Syrah in its red wines and has on a number of occasions made a 100 per cent Syrah wine. The oldest of these that I was able to taste at the property was a 1979 with a big, old toasty nose but good raspberry fruit after the wine had been aired for a while. The 1986 Étiquette Dorée was also pure Syrah, the last experiment of its type; it is toasty again, with a weight of tannin which has yet to be subdued by age.

The normal cuvée at Gourgazaud is 50 per cent Syrah, 10 per cent Mourvèdre, 5 per cent Grenache Noir and 35 per cent Carignan. The Carignan is vinified by carbonic maceration. The 1989 has good Syrah violet character with plenty of raspberry fruit. The tannins are quite aggressive (or at least they *were* in 1990). 250,000 litres of the Cuvée Normale were made in 1988; here again were the violets and raspberries, but the wine lacked the weight of tannin of the 1989 and fell a mite short.

CHÂTEAU HÉLÈNE

Montagne d'Alaric region

11800 Barbaira

Production: 74 acres, of which two-thirds in *vin de pays*; 11,000 bottles of *primeur* made annually; 200,000 bottles of Syrah *vin de garde*

Quality: 🍇🍇–🍇🍇🍇   Price: ★★

Best vintages: 1987, 1988, 1989, 1990

Marie-Hélène Gau is a rather forceful little woman who inflicts her personality on to her wines: none is typical of the region, something borne out by the very high proportion of Syrah she pours into her fermenting vats. Only one of her reds is made within the framework of old-fashioned Corbières and that is labelled 'Corbières Tradition' lest you make a mistake. The wine is, however, only 55 per cent Carignan, with the rest made up of Syrah and Grenache, giving it good plum and tobacco notes.

Marie-Hélène's *primeur* wine is 80 per cent Syrah (the remainder being Cinsault). Tasted soon after it was made in 1990, it had all the *primeur* aldehyde aromas of pears and bananas.

Her main Syrah wine (up to 90 per cent, with a little Carignan and Grenache to top up the vats) is housed in new-oak casks for two years. The best is released with a gold label to distinguish it from less favoured wines. A brand-new must in 1990 was immensely deep, with good dense chocolatey flavours covering plenty of cherry and raspberry fruit. The 1987 Gold Label (only 60 per cent Syrah, with 10 per cent Grenache and 30 per cent Carignan) was also aged in new oak and has plenty of good plums-and-mace character from the Syrah with touches of vanilla from the oak.

A new, experimental 80–90 per cent Syrah wine is called Hélène de Troie! It is aged in new oak for eight months. The 1988, tasted in 1990, was still very closed, exuding little more than tomato and some chocolatey tannins on the palate.

CHÂTEAU DE JAU

Cases-de-Pène, 66600 Rivesaltes

Production: 294 acres, producing 180,000 bottles Château de Jau and 200,000 bottles Château de Jau Second Label in Côtes du Roussillon, 35,000 bottles red and 25,000 bottles *rosé* in Collioure and 8,000–19,000 bottles in Banyuls

Quality: 🍇🍇–🍇🍇🍇   Price: ★★

Best vintages for Côtes du Roussillon: 1986, 1988, 1990

Best vintages for Collioure: 1989, 1990

The Daurés of Château de Jau are rather rare birds for the rustic Pyrénées Orientales. The 'château' (rather more a villa) houses a collection of avant-garde art which seems to have been assembled more for its modernity than for its artistic quality.

Madame Dauré reads Hegel to cure insomnia, and daughter Estelle travels the world to promote the wines, breaking hearts with every step.

Their Côtes du Roussillon wines have always been reliable, and in the past they have supplied the British high-street chain Oddbins with a good-value red wine which beat all comers in its price range. The wines labelled Château de Jau, however, have, with the exception of the 1986, left me cold: technically they are fine, but they lack a spark of imagination somewhere.

Far more exciting has been the development of their vineyard in Collioure. The Clos des Paulilles made its first wines in 1989 with a 50/50 Syrah/Mourvèdre *rosé*. By 1990 Collioure *rosé* was officially recognized by the INAO. In only two years the Paulilles *rosé* has taken the local market by storm with its fresh strawberry fruit.

The red Collioure from the Clos des Paulilles is made from 80 per cent Mourvèdre, 10 per cent Syrah and 10 per cent Grenache Noir. It is housed for a year in one- and two-year-old barrels. I was sceptical about this wine at first – it appeared to me that they had overworked the tannins – but after a year in tank and a year in cask it was beginning to evolve into something really good. This first wine and its successor from 1990 are wines to watch out for.

The Daurés also produce a Banyuls under the Robert Doutres label. The classic 1986 has a good, typical figs-and-chocolate character. The wine to look out for is the Rimatge (vintage) 1988, which is exceptionally good and made from 100 per cent Grenache Noir with a huge redolence of blackberries and a long raisiny finish.

DOMAINE DU MAS BLANC

9 avenue du Général-de-Gaulle, 66650 Banyuls-sur-Mer

Production: 35 acres in Banyuls, 20 acres in Collioure

Quality: 🍇🍇🍇   Price: ★★★

Best vintages: 1977, 1985, 1987, 1989, 1990

Dr Parcé's pioneering Banyuls and Collioures are now made by his son Jean-Michel. The doctor himself now lives in Perpignan and makes only occasional visits to the town where he was once mayor and president of the largest co-operative. One sometimes feels that he regrets the passing of the days when he was the only independent fish in the Banyuls pond; he dislikes competition, especially from his cousins the Parcé brothers at the Domaine de la Rectorie.

The Domaine du Mas Blanc still makes exciting, innovative wines. Carignan, the staple grape of the earlier Collioures, has been grubbed up, and the Grenache is not long for this world: from 1989 the domaine's top Cosprons label was made from 30 per cent Syrah, 60 per cent Mourvèdre and 10 per cent Counoise. Les Piloums is 30 per cent Grenache, 40 per cent Syrah and 30 per cent Mourvèdre. The new Clos du Moulin is a blend of 60 per cent Mourvèdre with 40 per cent Counoise.

Cosprons is a big wine, built like a Führerbunker to last a thousand years. When I tasted it in 1991, the 1990 was still full of CO_2, though it looked set to become something good. The 1989 was big and peppery, the 1988 a disappointment on the middle palate. Neither the 1987 nor the 1985 was ready to drink, though both will become splendid wines.

Parcé made his reputation for his VDNs, which include a delicious 'Solera' wine, inspired by sherry-making techniques, which tastes of honey and coffee with a long, figgy finish. The best of his Banyuls is possibly La Coume, which is made from 80 per cent Grenache Noir topped up with Syrah and Mourvèdre. The 1989 still seemed ungainly and hot in 1991, but it was young yet; the 1985 is already magnificent; and the 1977, with its mature aromas of coffee and figs and its rich, chocolatey finish, is perfect mature Banyuls. Look out also for his 'rimatge' or vintage Banyuls.

CAVES DE MONT-TAUCH

11350 Tuchan

Production: 2,470 acres in Fitou

Quality: 🍇 Price: ★–★★
Best vintages: 1985, 1988, 1989, 1990

This efficient co-operative produces good quantities of well-made wine. It sees its ideal Fitou as being a blend of 60 per cent Carignan, about 25–30 per cent Grenache Noir and the rest Syrah. On the other hand, it has made Fitous where the Grenache has predominated, as in 1985. Its Château de Ségure is 30 per cent Syrah, 28 per cent Grenache Noir and 42 per cent Carignan, with some pretty cigar-box/cigarette-packet notes. Mont-Tauch makes a classic *rancio* VDN (AOC Rivesaltes) by putting jars of Grenache wine out into the sun for the summer months.

CHÂTEAU DU PARC

Lézignan region

Avenue des Vignerons, 11200 Conilhac-Corbières

Production: 124 acres in Corbières

Quality: 🍇–🍇🍇 Price: ★–★★

Best vintages: 1988, 1989, 1990

The sister château of Château Donjon in Minervois, Château du Parc produces an up-market Corbières, making its reds from 50 per cent Grenache Noir, 20 per cent Mourvèdre and 30 per cent Carignan. I tasted two 1988s at the property: one aged without small oak, the other with. The unoaked wine had a pleasantly creamy strawberry palate with some typical Grenache tobacco character. The oaked wine was made in roughly the same proportions but was a selection of the better vats. It seemed to have more raspberry aromas than the non-oaked cuvée, with some big, ripe fig fruit from the Grenache. The oak was wisely subdued.

*

CAVE PILOTE DE VILLENEUVE

11360 Villeneuve-les-Corbières

Production: 1,110 acres in Fitou

Quality: 🍇   Price: ★–★★

Best vintages: 1988, 1989, 1990

This is another Fitou co-operative which is making good use of Syrah, Grenache and Mourvèdre as *cépages améliorateurs*. Carignan still accounts for some 70 per cent of the vines planted here, but the tally of *améliorateurs* is mounting steadily. As in many cases in the region of the Corbières and the Fenouillèdes, the co-operative puts much (too much?) faith in the use of carbonic maceration.

In 1988 Cave Pilote made a pleasant 50/50 Grenache/ Carignan blend with some pleasant raisiny Grenache character. The top wine is the Château de Montmal, which is 45 per cent Carignan, 45 per cent Grenache and 10 per cent Syrah, the 1988 having slightly meaty flavours with a hint of tobacco. Its Domaine de Courtal is another straight split between Carignan and Grenache Noir.

The co-operative makes a proper *rancio* VDN (AOC Rivesaltes) with an enchanting character: lavender and cherries; incense, coffee and figs.

DOMAINE DE LA RECTORIE

28 et 54 avenue du Puig-del-Mas, 66650 Banyuls-sur-Mer

Production: 49 acres in Banyuls and Collioure

Quality: 🍇🍇   Price: ★★–★★★

Best vintages: 1986, 1987, 1988, 1989, 1990

Marc and Thierry Parcé started vinifying their own grapes in 1984. They are third cousins of Dr André Parcé, but there is no love lost between the inventor of Collioure and his *petits cousins*.

Marc is entirely self-taught, but Thierry took a few courses after they arrived in the area – not least with the oenologist André Brugirard.

Originally the brothers were associated with Jules and Petra Campadieu, who have now gone off to make excellent wines of their own at the Domaine de la Villa Rosa. They had a few teething troubles with their earliest wines, including a 1985 Collioure marred by too short a maceration which ended up disappointingly brief on the palate. Since then they have gone from strength to strength. More recently they have acquired an old Wehrmacht bunker built into the cliffs, which provides them with some of the best cellaring in steamy Banyuls.

Unlike the Doctor, the Parcé brothers have experimented with using reasonable amounts of new oak on their wines. The earlier Collioures contained large amounts of Carignan, but over the years the total has diminished in favour of Syrah, Mourvèdre and Counoise.

The brothers have now abandoned filtration for their wines, allowing them to retain all the goodness from the must. The best of their Collioures to date were probably the two 1988s, especially that made exclusively from Mourvèdre, Counoise and Carignan.

The Parcé brothers also make superb Banyuls from their Grenache vines, called Cuvée Léon Parcé, and this is aged in new oak. Wines like the 1985 and 1986 were superbly concentrated Banyuls of the new school. The 1986 in particular was very rich in blackberry/violet aromas. A dense 1988 was spiced up with some Mourvèdre.

More recently their straight Banyuls (at 16° here and not the usual 16.5°) showed good depth of colour, with a big nose of blackberries and chocolate and a very long, tobacco-dominated finish. The Léon Parcé 1989 is very young, yet with a whacking great 'Ovaltine' malty nose and lashings of chocolate and figs.

DOMAINES VITICOLES DES SALINS DU MIDI
LISTEL

68 cours Gambetta, 34063 Montpellier

Production: 4,450 acres of vineyards in total, of which 3,400 acres in Languedoc and the rest in Provence and the Côtes du Rhône

Quality: 🍇   Price: ★★

Best vintages: 1988, 1989, 1990

This salt-producer is also the biggest vineyard-owner in France. The salt flats of Aigues-Mortes were owned by the church until the Revolution, when they were sold off to various *bourgeois* in Montpellier. In 1856 a company was formed to process the salt. The potential of the sandy beaches around the salt flats was not realized until 1863, however, when the phylloxera which devastated the vineyards of France failed to touch all those vines grown on sand. From that moment on, the salt flats began their double vocation.

Listel is now a semi-organic company using a number of clever schemes to maximize on recycling in its vineyards. Its best-known wine is the Gris de Gris *rosé*, which is Grenache Noir with some Carignan and Cinsault. The colour is natural, as grapes grown in sand cannot achieve any depth of pigment. Its best Languedocian *rosé* is the Gris from the Domaine de Jarras: a pure Grenache Noir with a fine peach, honey and raspberry character (🍇🍇🍇). In Provence, Listel makes another *rosé* at the Château de Gourdonne, with pleasant toffee-apple and strawberry flavours. A red wine from the Château de Gourdonne is 70 per cent Grenache and Carignan, with 10 per cent each of Syrah, Mourvèdre and Cabernet Sauvignon, making for a chunky, plummy brew.

DOMAINE SARDA-MALLET

12 chemin de Sainte-Barbe, 66000 Perpignan

Production: 128 acres of vines, 44 acres reserved for the top Étiquette Noire

Quality: 🍇🍇🍇   Price: ★★

Best vintages: 1986, 1987, 1989, 1990

Having long admired the wines of Gérard Chave in Hermitage, Jacques Reynaud of Château Rayas in Châteauneuf and Éloi Durrbach at the Domaine de Trévallon, Max Mallet had a fair idea about the sort of wine he wanted to make when his wife, Suzie, inherited the family domaine. Cuttings for his planting of Syrah came from Chave, and Mallet began to house the resulting wine in Tronçais oak for his special, Black Label, cuvée. The results were quickly recognized, and in 1988 the French magazine *Gault-Millau* named him the Roussillon's wine-maker of the year. His best vintages to date have been the 1985 and the 1986 Étiquette Noire.

The Mallets also make a small quantity of excellent Rivesaltes: a young 'ruby' made entirely from Grenache Noir and a *vingt ans d'âge* made from a blend of Grenaches Blanc, Gris and Noir.

ROBERT SKALLI
FORTANT DE FRANCE

278 avenue du Maréchal Juin, B.P. 53, 34210 Sète Cedex

Production: Syrah 1.5 million litres, Grenache *rosé* 1 million litres, red 3 million litres

Quality: 🍇🍇🍇   Price: ★★

Best vintage: 1990

The varietal king of the Midi, Robert Skalli has also turned his hand to Syrah and Grenache. The wines are made from reasonable yields in the Aude, Gard and Hérault départements. With the whole of the Midi's cultivars to play with and a commercially on-the-ball policy as far as fruit flavours are concerned, Skalli seems to be on to a winner. Naturally the thrust has been towards Cabernet and Chardonnay (the latter being the most successful wines Skalli makes), but the Syrah is interesting too.

In the autumn of 1991 I tasted a range of Syrahs from Skalli's 1990 vintage. The basic fruit was authentic Syrah, with a pretty violet/raspberry aroma. The wine had been oaked in three different ways: 30 per cent, 70 per cent and 100 per cent, using a mixture of 50 per cent new oak and 30 per cent one-year-old barrels. Of these I thought that, given the comparative lightness and readiness of the fruit in the unoaked sample, going beyond 30 per cent was a mistake. The 30-per-cent-oaked Syrah was a very pleasant wine. At 100 per cent there was nothing there but oak: wine for Mr Chip.

Also available were three Grenache samples blended with a little Syrah. With 10 per cent Syrah the Grenache didn't appear to have benefited much from the experiment, possibly because once again the base wine lacked a little concentration. Some tobacco scents emerged with the 20 per cent Syrah, while the 30 per cent seemed to have overdone the Syrah as its violet character dominated.

The samples proved an interesting toy: I found myself making some new blends from what I had, and was particularly excited by my Syrah + 30 per cent oak with Grenache + 10 per cent Syrah; but perhaps this is not the varietal game which Skalli wants to play.

When are we going to get some 100 per cent Mourvèdre?

U.C.C.M. PORTEL
ROCBÈRE

Sigean region

11490 Portel

Production: 10 per cent of the AOC Corbières (5–6 million litres)

Quality: 🍇 Price: ★–★★

Best vintages: 1988, 1989, 1990

A large co-operative which has seen the need to plant more and more *cépages améliorateurs*, the U.C.C.M. now has 300 acres of Mourvèdre, 740 acres of Grenache Noir and 120 acres of Syrah. Mourvèdre is valued for its resistance to oxidization, which makes it a perfect partner for the Grenache here. Many of the wines are released under the curious Vent Maritime label, which depicts two Greek sailors holding hands; but if you can get over that then you will find the wines reliable.

The Vent Maritime *rosé* is a pure Syrah made by *saignée*, with good plummy length. The Vent Maritime red 1989, made from 80 per cent Grenache Noir and 20 per cent Syrah, has an enchanting nuts-and-raspberries nose. The 1988 Château de Mattes is 20 per cent Mourvèdre with 40 per cent Grenache Noir topped up with 40 per cent Carignan, made by carbonic maceration. Naturally it is a more tannic wine than most Corbières, with a pleasant bouquet of apricots.

CHÂTEAU VILLERAMBERT-JULIEN

11160 Caunes-Minervois

Production: 148 acres in Minervois

Quality: 🍇🍇 Price: ★★

Best vintages: 1988, 1989, 1990

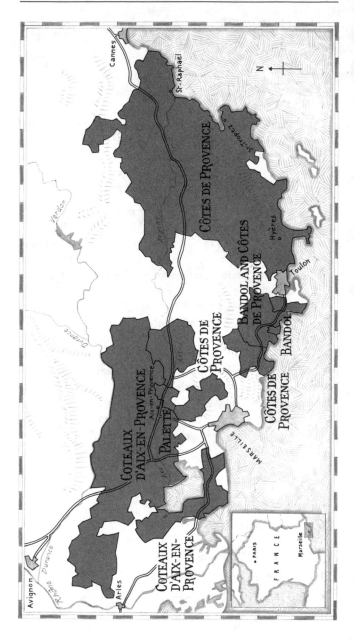

This progressive estate lives in the same château as Château Villerambert-Moureau. The basic wines here are dominated by old Carignan, but the top cuvées – Trianon and Prestige – are made to a formula of 50 per cent Syrah, 10 per cent Syrah pressings, 20 per cent Mourvèdre and 10 per cent old Carignan. The Grenache which makes up the other 10 per cent is actually grown on pink marble! Given the presence of the press wine, the 1989 Trianon is remarkably accessible, with plenty of pastille-like fruit. The Prestige 1988 spent six months in new oak, and oak dominates the wine for the present, although the blackberry fruit will break through before long. A pure-Syrah 1990, tasted straight from the fermenting vat, had a good len-tilly character betraying its relatively low Baumé: 11.95°.

Provence

Bandol

| Production: 2,350 acres (4 million litres)

Pace Randall Grahm of California's Bonny Doon, Bandol is the world showplace for the Mourvèdre grape. California and Collioure may have made impressive experiments, but nowhere but Bandol can boast such a concentration of growers who understand how to get the best out of it.

That Bandol should have emerged as the torchbearer for quality Mourvèdre wine is very largely due to one man: Lucien Peyraud. Peyraud arrived in the region in 1940 when he married a *demoiselle* Tempier whose father owned a small vineyard which still forms the core of the estate in Le-Plan-du-Castillet. Soon after his arrival, he made the acquaintance of a Swiss who was farming a few acres in retirement. Together they worked out plans for improving the overall quality of the wines.

In those days Mourvèdre had dwindled to just over 10 per

cent of the vineyard area. The wines of Bandol owed their character to the heavy-yielding Aramon and Alicante Bouschet grapes: they were strapping red plonk and no more. Peyraud and one or two other growers decided to form a *syndicat* to protect the region's wines; in 1941, Bandol was granted an AOC.

Peyraud became president of the growers' union in 1944 and remained in office for nearly forty years. Everything positive which has happened in the recent history of Bandol occurred during that time. Peyraud looked into the wine history of the region and learned that the Mourvèdre grape had formerly dominated the mix in Bandol at a time when the wines had enjoyed a far higher reputation than they did then. From his position in the *syndicat*, Peyraud encouraged members to up the percentage of Mourvèdre, first to 20 and later to 30 per cent. By 1980 the figure had risen to 50 per cent, and a survey carried out today would reveal a figure of around 60 per cent.

In the meantime, the enthusiasm of certain growers had created in Bandol one of the best-policed AOCs in France. The members of both *syndicats* (personality problems led to the cre-ation of a second union) agreed not only to limit yields to 35 hl/ha (1,416 litres per acre) but also to waive the PLC automati-cally granted in most parts of France which allows growers to harvest around 15 per cent more than the permitted yield. Since then the growers have agreed that no red Bandol will be made from vines under eight years old. Mourvèdre juice from vines aged between four and eight years is run off as *rosé*.

Most of the Alicante Bouschet and Aramon vines of Bandol have now been eliminated. The secondary *cépages* which work best with the Mourvèdre are the Carignan (old vines) and the Cinsault. Grenache Noir tended to get too alcoholic to make it popular for the best wines, although most growers still have a little in their vineyards. To my knowledge, the only estate to possess Syrah is the Domaines Ott at Château Romassan. Increasing numbers of growers are now bottling 100 per cent Mourvèdre wines; in the majority of cases these are stunningly good and repay all of Lucien Peyraud's labours with interest.

Bandol currently possesses some four dozen growers who

bottle their own wines, while the others take their wines to one of two co-operatives. The best of the co-ops is the Moulin de la Roque, which now employs Roger Pouteau (a one-time *meilleur sommelier du monde*) to act as a consultant. Its straight red Bandol is 65 per cent Mourvèdre, and the 1988 is a fine example with its strong 'winegum' character. With the 1990 vintage it experimented with a pure Mourvèdre cuvée and I was able to taste a highly promising unfiltered wine with a powerful violet aroma.

M. Boyer at the Domaine des Salettes is famed for his fresh, lively *rosés*, but he also produces some decent red Bandols, of which the 1989 was the best I tasted.

At the Domaine de la Noblesse, young Agnès Gaussen has taken over the wine-making from her father; there have been one or two problems with recent vintages, but it is a domaine to watch.

La Laidière has a good local reputation, above all for its whites and *rosés*. The red from the 1985 vintage seemed to me a rather old-fashioned Bandol which was dominated by Grenache rather than Mourvèdre.

More promising is the Domaine de la Vivonne, where the Scottish-sounding Walter Gilpin makes the wines. (His family does appear to have hailed from Scotland, but he is himself unaware of how long ago that was.) Since 1985 the Vivonne wines have been pure Mourvèdre. I have only tasted the 1987, but that seemed to place Gilpin's Vivonne among the leaders of the AOC.

See separate entries for Domaine de Cagueloup, Domaine Le Galantin, Château de Pibarnon, Château Romassan, Domaine Ray Jane, Château de la Rouvière, Château Ste-Anne and Domaine Tempier.

Coteaux d'Aix-en-Provence and Coteaux d'Aix-en-Provence-les-Baux

| Production: 14.2 million litres of red and *rosé*

Coteaux d'Aix-en-Provence is an AOC on the move. The decree was passed in 1985, when both Georges Brunet and Éloi

Durrbach had set the trend of using a majority of Cabernet Sauvignon in their wines. As a result, an upper limit of 60 per cent was established for the Bordeaux variety. Both Brunet and Durrbach reserved Syrah for the remainder of their wines (Brunet had a little Grenache), thereby becoming the only growers in France to produce wines with what has over the years become a classically Australian mixture. Durrbach, however, could claim support from Dr Guyot's *Étude du vignoble de France*, which had first advocated the blend in 1868.

Not everyone within the region has been happy to get into bed with the interloper from Bordeaux. In Les Baux itself, Mas de la Dame makes classy Provençal reds with Grenache, Cinsault and Syrah (and very good olive oil too!): see the separate entry. At the Château de Fonscolombe (which also goes under the names of Domaine de Boullery, Domaine du Paradis, Domaine de la Crémade and Domaine du Temps Perdu) they use a little Cabernet but otherwise content themselves with Grenache, Carignan and Cinsault. The organically grown Terres Blanches wines are made from Grenache, Cabernet Sauvignon, Syrah, Mourvèdre and Cinsault; the 1985 was a superb wine, but quality has been a little shaky since then.

The Mas Ste-Berthe also produces traditional Les Baux wines of quality. The basic wine is a blend of 52 per cent Grenache with 20 per cent Cabernet Sauvignon, 12 per cent Carignan and 8 per cent Cinsault, making for a deep, herby wine with a flavour of liquorice. The Cuvée Louis David has 36 per cent Grenache Noir, 33 per cent Syrah and 31 per cent Cabernet; the 1988 is a particular success, with its intense *garrigue* aromas and liquoricy palate.

Côtes de Provence, Cassis and Palette

| Production: 79.3 million litres of red and *rosé*

In what now seems like another lifetime, I used to stay frequently with friends in Provence. It was an area far from the touristy coastline, up in the hills between Draguignan and Grasse. Those were pleasant unspoiled days before Wicked

Willie was even a leer in his inventor's eye and long, long before the latter had had the idea of traipsing off to Provence to find that simple life which would earn him a second and a third fortune.

In the mid 1970s the neighbouring farm was owned by a rugged individual with the Pagnolesque name of Marius. Marius and his wife and family lived a life which seemed for the most part unaffected by the twentieth century: he had his vines, goats, some vegetables and corn. The wine was nothing to write home about: we rarely talked grape varieties, but I assume from hindsight that it was largely Cinsault if not Aramon. Marius sold it direct from the vat to anyone with a few francs in his pocket and a plastic cubitainer to take it home in; bottles were not his thing.

Then Marius hurt himself badly in a fight with a tractor. For several days he was obliged to take to his bed. When he was on his feet again, it appeared that the uneven combat had affected his mind to some degree. When I next sat down at his table, he went into his cellar and came back with a dusty bottle: it was his 1974, the best wine he had ever made, he said. Could he, he asked, aspire to the AOC with wines like that? 'Well, Marius,' I replied, somewhat taken aback, 'if you were to plant some other grape varieties . . . Syrah, perhaps? Possibly some Grenache?'

I doubt whether Marius ever took my advice, but other Provençal growers read the writing on the wall in the 1970s and 1980s and began to set aside a portion of the traditional grapes in favour of the *améliorateurs*. Apart from getting the grape mix right, another practical necessity seems to me that the wines (the reds at least) should be put into sensible bottles and not that overelaborate, baroque-onion-dome of a thing which is impossible to stack. In the past I have enjoyed the wines of Château Barbeyrolles, Castel Roubine, the Commanderie de Peyrassol, Château de Selle and of course the Domaines Ott (despite the frightful skittle-bottle – see my comments under the separate entry for Château Romassan). More recently I have tasted Château Ste-Roseline (60 per cent Mourvèdre, 30 per cent Cabernet Sauvignon, 10 per cent Grenache) with its real Mourvèdre character of Russian leather. The Domaine du

Jas d'Esclans, just below Le Muy, is made up of half Grenache/Syrah/Mourvèdre with the other half Cinsault; it has always been a favourite when I've been in that part of the world. The Domaine Gavoty makes a 60/40 per cent Grenache/Syrah wine with concentrated raspberry/strawberry fruit flavours, as well as a light, fruity *rosé* which is 50 per cent Grenache.

The Domaine St-Baillon is something of a Provençal star. The *rosé* is made from 45 per cent Grenache, 45 per cent Cinsault and 10 per cent Syrah while the élite cuvée Opale is 80 per cent Syrah with 20 per cent Grenache. Of its reds, the green label 1986, with 30 per cent Syrah, 30 per cent Grenache, 30 per cent Cabernet and 10 per cent Cinsault, was a big, mulberry-scented wine. The red label is two-thirds Cabernet to one-third Syrah.

In St-Tropez, the Château de Pamplonne shares the name of the resort's most famous nudist-infested beach. The wine contains Syrah, Grenache and Mourvèdre as well as Tibouren and Cinsault. The 1988 was big and plummy. The Château de Pamplonne is the flagship wine of the Maîtres Vignerons de St-Tropez; their Côtes de Provence also contains all three varieties and is generally tightly made to last longer than the usual Provençal wines.

The small Cassis AOC is better known for whites than for reds, although one or two domaines make a red wine on Bandol lines. The Domaine de la Ferme Blanche makes a slightly jammy wine from Grenache, Mourvèdre and Carignan.

The recent success of the Château de Simone has introduced the small AOC of Palette to a wider range of wine-drinkers. The red wines are increasingly based on Mourvèdre, a little Grenache Noir, Cinsault and Plant d'Arles.

DOMAINE DE CAGUELOUP

83270 St-Cyr-sur-Mer

Production: 44 acres, producing 30,000 bottles of red Bandol annually

Quality: 🍇🍇🍇   Price: ★★

Best vintages: 1971, 1978, 1987, 1988, 1989, 1990

Down in the old *village perché* of La Cadière d'Azur, Mme Bérard, the charming proprietor of the Hostellerie Bérard, will tell you that the word 'Cagueloup' means something scatological in Provençal. Fortunately for her cousin, M. Prébost, none of this manages to seep into the estate's wines.

Prébost is an eccentric bachelor with, by his own admission, 'many mistresses' and a collection of lame dogs. His red Bandol is 60 per cent Mourvèdre with 40 per cent Grenache Noir. In the 1989, 1990 and 1991 vintages, however, Prébost has set aside some wine with the idea of making a pure Mourvèdre cuvée.

The soil of Cagueloup is poorer than in many parts of Bandol and gives the wines a more leathery character when young. Added to this, even the non-Grenache wines seem to give off some of that Woodbine character which is normally associated with Grenache Noir. Both the 1990 and the 1988 are good commercial wines with some of the winegum aroma of young Mourvèdre. Prébost prefers his 1987 to the 1988, which he finds more quintessentially 'Bandol' with its leathery character. The estate made superb wines in 1978 and 1971, with plenty of gingerbread aromas.

DOMAINE LE GALANTIN

Le Plan-du-Castillet, 83330 Le Beausset

Production: 47 acres – 43,000 litres red Bandol, 18,000 litres *rosé*

Quality: 🍇🍇🍇🍇   Price: ★★

Best vintages: 1979, 1982, 1985, 1987, 1988, 1989, 1990

From the outside, Le Galantin looks like any other small Provençal wine estate; nor does the steady trickle of German tourists traipsing in for half a dozen bottles of *rosé* inspire confidence in Achille Pascal's wines – just another grower living on the holiday trade is what you might think. You'd be wrong: Pascal is one of the best wine-makers in Bandol.

Pascal began to get it right when he decided to make his red from 100 per cent Mourvèdre. Earlier vintages had about 30 per cent Grenache, which made the wines more approachable but far less memorable. The 1987 is nice now; the 1985 is prematurely old, with a slight gingerbread character. Both the 1979 and the 1982 on the other hand, were rather dense, muted and impenetrable in 1991.

Most Bandol wine-makers put their wines into big oak tuns, but Pascal has experimented with small new-oak *barriques* for the 1988, 1989, 1990 and 1991 vintages. The casks are not 100 per cent new, and I think that too much new oak might well detract from the delightful aromas of the wines. The 1990 has a wonderful scent of violets; the 1989 is if anything even better, with its blackberry/bilberry fruit. The 1988 has a hint of game, deeply concentrated with a pronounced bouquet of cinnamon.

MAS DE LA DAME

Les Baux-de-Provence, 13520 Maussane

Production: 86 acres (200,000 bottles) in Coteaux-d'Aix-en-Provence-les-Baux

Quality: 🍇🍇🍇   Price: ★★–★★★

Best vintages: 1984, 1985, 1986, 1988, 1989, 1990

This is one of the better growths in Coteaux-d'Aix-en-Provence-les-Baux which is not yet using a majority of Cabernet Sauvignon. The basic wine here is 62 per cent Grenache Noir, with the rest being Carignan and Cinsault. The estate also makes a Cuvée Gourmande and a Réserve du Mas. The latter is 36 per cent Cabernet Sauvignon, 17 per cent Syrah and 47 per cent Grenache Noir. The 1985 had developed all sorts of gamy notes when I last tasted it, in 1990. A 1984

Réserve du Mas containing a slightly higher percentage of Grenache and a smidgen of Carignan was also marked by some animal notes.

CHÂTEAU DE PIBARNON

83740 La Cadière-d'Azur

Production: 119 acres planted in Bandol; not all in production

Quality: 🍇🍇🍇🍇🍇   Price: ★★★

Best vintages: 1982, 1985, 1987, 1988, 1989, 1990

The Château de Pibarnon must come as close to paradise as any estate on the Côte d'Azur. From the comparatively simple Provençal manor house, you look right out over the wide blue sweep of the Bay of Bandol. In the foreground are the vines, arranged in an amphitheatre facing on to the ocean and covering a richly varied soil which lends its character to the wines.

The Comte de St-Victor bought Pibarnon in 1978. Until that time he had been in the property business and had only the barest notion about how to make wine. In those days there were only 30 acres planted on the estate, but St-Victor has set about shaving the hills of their scrub and every year more and more land comes into production.

St-Victor's Bandol is virtually pure Mourvèdre. In years when the Grenache gets through bud-burst there is about 5 per cent of Grenache in the wine. He gets added concentration from feeding back the grape hulls from his *rosé* into the *grand vin*, making wines with a good weight alongside considerable elegance.

The 1990 for me had some affinities with the top Peyraud wines, with its classic blackberry/bilberry character; the 1989 was suppler, though still superbly concentrated. The 1988 was 100 per cent Mourvèdre, with its appealing winegum bouquet; the 1987 all violets. The best of all for the time being is the 1985, with its wonderful redolence of blackberries.

CHÂTEAU ROMASSAN

83330 Le Castellet

Production: 57 acres in Bandol, plus 42 acres farmed for other growers and 62 acres on short-term contracts

Quality: 🍇   Price: ★★★

Best vintages: 1985, 1987, 1988

Château Romassan is the Domaines Ott's outpost in Bandol. Ott wines are part of the folklore of the South of France and anyone who has spent any time in the region has encountered them, high up on the wine lists of the best restaurants. To some extent, however, the Otts are prisoners of their own image: the peculiar skittle-shaped bottles which cannot be induced to stack properly; the high prices; the renunciation of the arid southern *terroir* from which they come.

To some degree the prices are justified by the incredible work that went into the creating of the vineyard at Romassan. Jean-Daniel Ott showed me photographs of before and after the bulldozers went in: the entire topsoil and subsoil have been changed. In the wines themselves, the blend is noticeably less 'Mourvèdre' than any other leading grower in Bandol: 50 per cent, with the rest made up of Cinsault, Grenache and 5 per cent Syrah. Jean-Daniel says he is not against increasing the proportions of Mourvèdre, but it would take time.

The wines are Ott rather than Bandol: remarkably consistent in style, but lacking in that exciting, slightly wild, character found elsewhere – too well mannered by half. The best for the time being are the 1985 and the 1987. The 1988 will follow in the same style, but it was still tough when I last tasted it in 1991.

DOMAINE RAY JANE

83330 Le Castellet

Production of Bandol: 32 acres in red and *rosé*

Quality: 🍇🍇🍇🍇   Price: ★★
Best vintages: 1985, 1986, 1987, 1988

M. Constant, the owner of Domaine Ray Jane, is an eccentric who collects antique wine-making tools. He has strong opinions about wine: he doesn't like *rosé*, for example – 'It's like water!' he says. Yet he adds that his *rosé* is probably the best in Bandol. Hydrophobia characterizes his reds too: 'the most tannic wines in Bandol' he calls them. They are certainly concentrated, and almost need to be pummelled out of the bottle like tomato ketchup. Constant believes that their high tannin levels are actually good for one's health: 'They chase away cholesterol,' he says.

I liked Ray Jane's massive wines, which are made without filtering or fining. The 1988 is a classic: a huge great brute reeking of leather, tar and blackberries. The 1987 is slightly suppler (all is relative, you understand), with a redolence of tar and cherries: only 80 per cent Mourvèdre was used, along with 10 per cent each of Cinsault and Grenache. Constant showed me a 60 per cent Mourvèdre from this wet year which he treated with some scorn: true, it had a rather prematurely aged, gingerbread character. Then he brought out the pure Mourvèdre which he had put into small oak for *four* years! It was no surprise that this was another bruiser, with plenty of leather and well-hung game on the nose. Constant also contrasted an 80 per cent Mourvèdre 1985 with its pure-Mourvèdre cousin of the same vintage. The former was approachable with its ripe, leathery character; the pure Mourvèdre was incredibly gamy after four years in oak – a wine to drink with a pungent cheese.

CHÂTEAU DE LA ROUVIÈRE
MAS DE LA ROUVIÈRE
MOULIN DES COSTES

Mas de la Rouvière, Le Castellet, 83330 Le Beausset

Production: 198 acres – *c.* 300,000 bottles of red, *rosé* and white Bandol

Quality: 🍇🍇–🍇🍇🍇   Price: ★★

Best vintages: 1985, 1989

This large estate is run by the Bunan brothers – Paul and Pierre – and Paul's son Laurent. The Bunans were originally wine-makers in Algeria, but they had to leave with the rest of the *pieds noirs* and with the money they were able to take with them to France they purchased their land in Bandol.

It's an impressive place: the Bunans have literally moved mountains to give their vines the best possible exposition – here the Mourvèdre really can see the sea – and the winery is lined with the latest technology. The Bunans make a wide variety of wines on their land, but not just wines: they also distil a *marc* and make honey from their bees and olive oil from their olive trees.

As far as Bandol is concerned, Moulin des Costes and Mas de la Rouvière are basically the same wine under two different labels. The Bunans' top wine is the Château de la Rouvière, made from 100 per cent Mourvèdre.

Château de la Rouvière has less charm than some of the new-wave Bandols made from pure Mourvèdre. The 1990 seemed to be going through an odd stage when I tasted it from cask. The 1989 was the best, with its big, blackberry aromas. The best of the rest was the 1985, with its herby *garrigue* character.

CHÂTEAU STE-ANNE

Ste-Anne-d'Évenos, 83330 Le Beausset

Production: 62 acres, producing 25,000 bottles of red Bandol

Quality: 🍇🍇–🍇🍇🍇   Price: ★★

Best vintages: 1982, 1985, 1987, 1989, 1990

The Marquis Dutheil de la Rochère lives in a refreshingly informal style in this simple eighteenth-century château and makes Bandols of an old-fashioned sort. He is not keen on the idea of making 100 per cent Mourvèdre wines, finding them 'unbalanced' without the element of Cinsault or Grenache. In 1990 and 1989 he none the less put some wine aside to see how a pure Mourvèdre wine would look. I liked both: the spice-and-violet-scented 1990 and the violet-and-winegum-like 1989. With the *accessoires*, Dutheil's wines have a pleasant herb and tobacco character. His most successful wine to date seems to have been the 1982, with its big, full, strawberry fruit.

DOMAINE TEMPIER

Le Plan-du-Castillet, 83330 Le Beausset

Production: 40 acres of land producing red and *rosé* AOC Bandol; 60,000 bottles of Bandol produced annually

Quality: 🍇🍇🍇🍇🍇   Price: ★★★–★★★★

Best vintages: 1971, 1975, 1978, 1982, 1983, 1985, 1987, 1988, 1989, 1990

The man who led the revival of Bandol is now about to enter his ninth decade. He is a short, lively man with a military moustache and hair cut *à la brosse*. Lucien Peyraud no longer makes the wine at Domaine Tempier, but he takes an active interest in the work of his two sons who are now in charge. Naturally he is an extremely able ambassador both for his wines and for those of Bandol in general.

Tempier produces no white wine, but it does make an exceptionally fresh, clean *rosé* which is 30 per cent Mourvèdre. One of Mourvèdre's chief advantages is its anti-oxidizing nature; this allows the Peyrauds to bottle their *rosé* without using any SO_2.

In recent years the Peyrauds have begun bottling a confusing array of cuvées based on the wines of different sites and soils. The Cuvée Spéciale 1990 with its classic blackberry and bilberry aromas turned out to be 84 per cent Mourvèdre and 16 per cent Grenache Noir. The 1989 Cuvée Tourtine, on the other hand, was a mere 60 per cent Mourvèdre but, with a pebbly soil and yields of 28 hl/ha (1,130 litres per acre), was a dense, buttery wine tasting of cherries, blackcurrants and coffee. The top wine is the Cuvée Cabassou, which is 100 per cent Mourvèdre. The yields here are even lower than for the Cuvée Tourtine, and the Cuvée Cabassou is a great basket of black fruits and violets.

Bandol ages extremely well, which was borne out by two older wines I tasted with the Peyrauds. These were the 'ordinary' wines of the domaine, but superb wines for all that. Peyraud described the 1982 as being 'like a great aristocrat who keeps you waiting': in 1991 it had only just opened out, giving off those leather and undergrowth aromas which are the hallmark of good old Mourvèdre. The 1971 had gone a stage further, with all the gingerbread character of old Bandol.

The Rhône Valley:
the Northern Rhône

Despite the ever increasing competition from the New World, the Rhône Valley still produces 70 per cent of the best wines made from Syrah, Grenache and Mourvèdre grapes. In the northern Rhône the Syrah reigns supreme, occasionally blended with a little Viognier in Côte Rôtie or a dash of

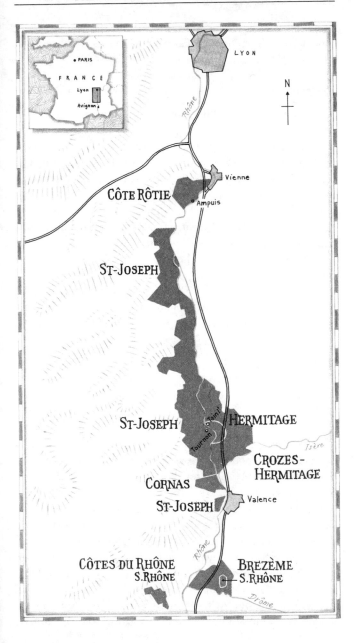

Marsanne in Hermitage. The wines from the top estates of Côte Rôtie, Hermitage and Cornas continue to represent most of the world's finest.

Brezème

| Production: c. 50,000 litres of pure Syrah wine

Brezème is an often forgotten AOC which was first established in 1943 for a mere 25 acres of vines. In the 1970s the AOC was revised. In the intervening period the area designated for planting had been extended to 208 acres.

Brezème is 100 per cent Syrah grown on sandy soils twelve miles south of Valence around the confluence of the Rhône and the Drôme. There are only two estates bottling wine: the co-operative and Jean-Marie Lombard. Neither is easy to find.

Jean-Marie Lombard's wines are imported into Britain by the Rhône specialist Robin Yapp. In my relatively slight experience, I have always found them tough and lacking in fruit.

Cornas

| Production: 173 acres making 250,000 litres (or more) of red
| wine

'Cornas' is an AOC limited to the commune of Cornas itself. A small stretch of land to the east of the Route Nationale 86 has the right to the AOC Côtes du Rhône. The wines are pure Syrah: no white grapes are admitted.

The very recent explosion of interest in the wines of Cornas has created a curious atmosphere in the village itself. In what was by all reports the sleepiest of places, jealousies now run wild and no one speaks to anyone else for fear of giving something away. For the visitor from outside, the place can inspire feelings of paranoia. 'Did that curtain just twitch?' you ask yourself as you walk down one of the four or five streets; 'Am I being watched?' And then there is the interrogation you have to face each time you arrive at a grower: 'When is X going to put his 1989s on the market?' 'Has Y got those new vats working yet?' 'Is Z using new oak on his wines?'

Up in Hermitage, the big *négociants* still write off Cornas as Clochemerle. One told me that he was down in Cornas at dawn on the first day he was allowed to remove his wine, in order to get it safely into his cellars; he didn't trust the villagers not to dip into the barrel and fill it up with water. I'm sure this is unfair: for ten years or more the Cornassiens have been courted by dealers from all over the world; they've had to grow up quickly, but they have grown up.

And yet there are some suspicious dealings none the less. Vines are literally everywhere: sprouting from the back gardens of the villagers in the village down by the muddy stream; right next door to the bleak modern cemetery or on other stretches of bad, flat land which does not produce wine worthy of the name of Cornas. Somebody is bottling this as Cornas; and it doesn't go to the co-operative in Tain.

If all the excitement of being discovered was not enough, Cornas has also been shaken up by the arrival of an oenologist, rumoured to be from Bordeaux (which might as well be Tim-buktu as far as most people in Cornas are concerned), called Jean-Luc Colombo. Colombo has brought with him all the usual Bordeaux baggage: new oak, *pigeage* and hiking up the prices in order to tell the world you have something truly special. Colombo has been making wine of his own since 1987. That vintage I have tasted, but none since; it is called 'Les Ruchets', and it comes in a Bordeaux-bottle(!). It was aged in 100 per cent new oak for sixteen months after a twenty-day *cuvaison*. I liked its spicy, violet aromas and chocolatey finish; it seemed quite able to handle the oak.

Apart from Jean Lionnet (see separate entry), few Cornas-siens seek Colombo's advice. There is still some small-scale wine-making going on here, with growers like Pierre Lionnet selling to faithful private customers (his 1988 is excellent). One or two new boys have started up in the past few years, of whom the most notable is Jacques Lemenicier, who rents about 9 acres of vines. Lemenicier has already attracted considerable notice for his 1988, which was quite beautiful in 1991. Both his 1989 and 1990 vintages should develop into something special.

Sylvain Bernard (see St-Joseph) has taken over the old vines which used to be the mainstay of Guy de Barjac's wines. So far he has only made one Cornas, which I tasted at the property. This 1990 wine seemed to have the necessary concentration, but it remains to be seen what it is like in bottle.

Among the old guard, Marcel Juge makes some of the best wines in Cornas. Juge has adopted the laudable policy of separating his *pieds de coteaux* wines from those grown on the high slopes. The 1990 *cuvée des coteaux* wine was quite delicious, but in 1991 the 1989 was going through a difficult stage. I was most impressed by a barbaric 1988 (a good sign in Cornas), which mingled earthworks with violets; leather with liquorice. Of Juge's *pieds*, both the 1989 and the 1988 are pleasant, lighter, fruity wines. 'I don't make hard wines,' said Juge defiantly.

Alain Voge has 17 acres in Cornas and makes two cuvées: one from his younger vines and another from the old vines. The wines are lighter than some, and this is especially true of the 1988. The 1989 Vieilles Vignes is another good example of his approachable style.

Noël Verset is a little old man in a cloth cap with some ancient vines in his 5 acre hillside plot. Longevity seems to be a thing with these Versets: his father died a few years ago soon after his hundredth birthday. If you visit the cemetery, his moustached image looks at you from a black marble tomb. Verset's wines are in great demand for export and he has little to show callers. The 1990 I tasted there was quite seductive some six months after the vintage, but it is bound to close up. The 1989, like so many from that ferociously hot year, seemed to lack the aromas of the 1990, although that too may have been a stage. A 1988 tasted in London was a splendid wine: all tar and blackberries. I liked the 1986 less.

There are signs that a new star is emerging in Thierry Lallemand.

See separate entries for Cave de Tain-l'Hermitage, Auguste Clape, Maurice Courbis, Guy de Barjac, Jean Lionnet, Robert Michel and Robert Michelas.

Côte Rôtie

'Côte Rôtie' is an AOC for red wine covering 320 acres of the communes of Tupin-Semons, Ampuis and Saint-Cyr-sur-Rhône. The Syrah grapes may be complemented by up to 20 per cent Viognier. Thirty-seven people bottle Côte Rôtie made from their own vines.

The main *lieux-dits* (from north to south) are La Vallière, Montuclos, La Viria, Les Rochains, Rosier, La Landonne, Les Moutonnes, La Côte Boudin, Ravin des Arches, Le Grand Taille, Les Bannevières, La Chevalière, La Brocarde, Le Moulin, Pavillon Rouge, La Pommière, La Turque, Fongent, Le Truchet, Le Grêt, Les Trialles, La Châtillonne, La Mouline, La Grosse Roche, La Garde, La Blanchonne, Le Combart, Le Clos, Le Car, Les Prunelles, Maison Rouge.

If one were obliged to name one place where the Syrah grape was wholly in its element, it would not be the Barossa, Clare or Hunter Valley or the granite outcrops of Cornas or Hermitage, but here just a few miles to the south of Lyon at Côte Rôtie. Côte Rôtie is often cast as a feminine complement to the more robust and indeed occasionally awkward wines of Cornas and Hermitage. The watchword here is that much abused noun 'elegance'. Generally when wine-makers talk about elegance one is tempted to reach for one's gun; but good Côte Rôtie, I feel, fits the word like a glove.

Côte Rôtie is no monolith, however, and there are styles within styles: some caused by differences of opinion on vinification, others the result of the famous variations in the soils which cover the granite slope. Basically there are two styles resulting from geology: Côte Brune and Côte Blonde. The Brune *terroir* is more clayey with a high proportion of ferrous oxide, giving a more masculine, slower-maturing quality to the wines. The Blonde *terroir* has more sand, and here are the aromatic, sensuous wines, which are frequently enhanced by cutting with a little Viognier, the most enchanting of all white grapes.

But not all Côte Rôtie's wines obey the norms: Gilles Barge makes long-ageing, masculine wines on the Blonde with no Viognier, while his father makes Brunes with classic aromatic

flowers-and-apricots aromas. And there is also the factor contributed by the plateau which lies behind the slope; this flat,
undistinguished land is responsible for around a quarter of Côte
Rôtie. New oak too is increasingly becoming an element in the
wines; Guigal uses as much as 100 per cent new oak in his *crus*.
Under the influence of Jean-Luc Colombo in Cornas, a grower
like Bernard Burgaud contents himself with about 20 per cent.

On a 55° slope, wine-making can't be easy in Côte Rôtie, and
one can see why the steeper sites were being abandoned until
the revival of interest in Côte Rôtie in the 1970s. In the spring
of 1991 I went with Gilles Barge to look at the vines trained
high on their bundles of four stakes. I was grateful for those
stakes; had it not been for them, I'm sure I would have tumbled
all the way to Ampuis. Barge smiled sympathetically at my
discomfort: 'Yes,' he said, 'we growers have flat stomachs and
well-rounded calves.' It must also help to have a goat in the
lower branches of your family tree.

Wine-making in Côte Rôtie has often suffered from an
amateurish tendency which was born in the years when the
wines were hard to make and brought in but little return. Down
on the alluvial lands bordering the Rhône there is an extensive
market garden growing fruit and vegetables for the tables of
Lyon and Vienne. Many of the vine-growers doubled up as
vegetable-growers, tending their vines when they had the time.
Then the prices of Côte Rôtie went through the roof after it
was discovered in Paris and New York, and the vegetable men
began to climb up the hill to have a look at a new source of
profit. One or two of them have proved enlightened wine-
makers; others have not. Barge was easily able to identify
one of these by the fact that he had forsaken the traditional
goblet training for wire. Easier to work, yes; but not Côte
Rôtie.

Côte Rôtie is rare. The estates are tiny, and there is very little
land to go round. Something of a price revolution was created
by Marcel Guigal's new *crus* which began selling in New York
at sums exceeding even those of Château Pétrus in Pomerol.
Fortunately, few Côte Rôties match these prices, and some
Côte Rôties (one thinks notably of Delas's Seigneur de Mau-

giron) are particularly reasonable. One must continue to bear in mind that these are handmade wines grown on estates which are a fraction the size of some mechanized, semi-industrial Bordeaux concern, and that you are paying for workmanship which only a man of intense dedication could or would achieve.

One of the best places to discover a wide range of Côte Rôties from small growers is in local restaurants. The most famous of these is La Pyramide in Vienne. This restaurant was once the instigator of everything that was good in French cuisine, when it was in the hands of Fernand Point; recently his widow sold out, and reports vary on the quality of the kitchens these days. Similarly the Beau Rivage in Condrieu has changed hands. There used to be a wonderful list of Côte Rôties at this riverside restaurant, and it was there that the *sommelier* wisely counselled me to take a 1983 Côte Blonde from de Boisseyt – a wonderful mouthful of black fruit. The restaurant Magnard in Vienne has an excellent list of well-priced Côte Rôties, including the superb 1980 from Dervieux with its toast, blackcurrants and game flavours. It is, however, a pity that the food does so little justice to the wines on the list.

See separate entries for Pierre Barge, Gilles Barge, Bernard Burgaud, Émile Champet, Marius Gentaz, Marcel Guigal, Joseph Jamet, Robert Jasmin, René Rostaing, Vidal-Fleury, Chapoutier, Delas Frères and Paul Jaboulet Aîné.

Crozes-Hermitage

Production: 3.7 million litres from 2,200 acres of vines situated in the communes of Érôme, Gervans, Serves, Larnage, Tain-l'Hermitage, Mercurol, Chanos-Curson, Beaumont-Monteux, La Roche-de-Glun and Pont-de-l'Isère

The watchword here is *caveat emptor*: Crozes-Hermitage can be a fairly unreliable wine. Half of the total production is vinified by the co-operative in Tain (see the separate entry) and is released either under its own label or under that of whatever supermarket or high-street chain has bought that particular vat. Then, with the exception of a handful of star growers, the rest of Crozes is ropy stuff, given the right to the AOC by the usual silly tale of compromise and pusillanimity.

The original AOC was established in 1937, to cover the vines to the north of the great hill of Hermitage or on the northern slope which did not benefit from the same exposition as Hermitage. Then, in 1952, the AOC was extended to include not only the good hill villages to the north, like Gervans and Érôme, but also the flat, alluvial lands around La Roche-de-Glun to the south. These days the majority of Crozes comes from these unsuitable southern soils.

Mercifully there are some good people in Crozes, and some of these have made their presence felt in the last few years. The best at the moment are probably Étienne Pochon and Alain Graillot (see separate entries).

Of the rest, Tardy et Ange went through a fine period in the early to mid 1980s but appear to have trailed off a bit since then. I've tasted a very good 1988 from Bernard Chave (apparently no relation of Gérard) with an enchanting bouquet of carnations and violets. Desmeure makes reliable wines in an authentic Syrah style, as does Ferraton. As for the Fayolle brothers, their wines have always seemed to me a little patchy and unreliable, although their top 1989 cuvée, which I tasted from cask, had a pretty peony nose. This cuvée, however, is apparently hard to find.

There are also good reports of the Cave des Clairmonts.

See separate entries for Chapoutier, Alain Graillot, Paul Jaboulet Aîné, Robert Michelas, Étienne Pochon and Cave de Tain-l'Hermitage.

Hermitage

Production: 320 acres producing some 400,000 litres of red wine (as well as around 100,000 litres of white)

For the early history of Hermitage, see the Introduction (pages 2–4). Syrah must account for a minimum of 85 per cent of

Hermitage; some growers continue to add Marsanne and Roussanne grapes as permitted under the 1937 decree.

The main *lieux-dits* in Hermitage are the following vineyards, travelling from west to east: Les Varognes, Les Bessards, Le Gros des Vignes, Les Greffieux, Le Méal, L'Hermite, La Chapelle, Chante-Alouette, Beaumes, Péléat, La Maison Blanche, Les Rocoules, Les Diognières, La Pierreille, Les Murets, La Croix, L'Homme and Les Signaux.

Good Hermitage is the sum of its parts, or, as Philippe Jaboulet told me (but then he would, wouldn't he?), 'The *assemblage* is always preferable to a *lieu-dit*.' Jaboulet's family firm naturally has the wherewithal to make such a blend, and so indeed do the other great merchant houses: Chapoutier and Delas. Only Gérard Chave and the co-operative cellar can compete with them here. The rest of the growers are left with little bits of the vineyard and lack the ability to bring together wines from all over the great granite rock.

The reason for the variety in these wines lies in the topsoils: although the rock itself is mostly granite, the soils which cover it are varied and the wines produced are very different. Les Bessards, which is on granite shale, gives delicate, fine wines which are short on alcohol. Le Méal, in the centre, is on sand and loess, giving strong alcoholic wines helped by its full, south-facing outlook. Les Greffieux is on a clay soil which gives the wines body. The chalky soils are generally reserved for the whites: Rocoules, Maison Blanche, Murets and Diognières. All the wines must be vinified separately; only when the grower is ready to bottle the wines does he blend in the desired proportions.

Hermitage is a steep hill, as I know from experience. Once with a friend and equipped with an impromptu picnic of a bottle of Hermitage and a brace of *caillettes* (faggots) from the best charcuterie in Tournon I climbed that hillside on a parching late-summer day. Snakes slithered out from under rocks as we rose out of a sea of Syrah vines, their trunks attached to long stakes or *échalas*. It was easy to see why the wine was both rare and expensive: those terraces cannot be easy to work, and there is no question of mechanization; only man can handle conditions such as you find in Hermitage, Côte Rôtie or Cornas.

But, though the conditions are superb for the making of great Syrah wines, the experience of tasting Hermitage can often be disappointing. There are not many more than a dozen vineyard-owning 'names' in Hermitage, and half of these are rustic outfits which sell more as a result of the AOC's prestige than because of any inherent quality in their wine-making. Many do not have access to the good sites and use old wood which should have been thrown out years ago. Cellars are not always squeaky clean. Many of the growers are only part-timers when it comes to wine. This is a region famed for its fruit, particularly apricots, and in the summer months, while the grapes are ripening on the hillside, these growers are making a quick killing shipping their fruit crop off to Lyon and Paris. During these times the vines are only of secondary importance.

When good, Hermitage is very good. Starting out with a combination of fruits and flowers – raspberries, blackberries and blackcurrants; carnations, violets and peonies – the wines often develop the flavours of cereals and tobacco in ageing. When mature, Hermitage regains some of that fruit but adds roasted, truffly, wild, liquorice tastes which tend to gaminess and leatheriness with age.

The estates of the smaller producers are often incredibly small. The Fayolle brothers, for example, have only 3.7 acres (see Crozes-Hermitage for their other holdings). Much of this is in Diognières and naturally goes to make white wine. On my visit to the domaine in Gervans I was able to try a rare red. Of the two casks of 1988, one was decidedly musty but the wine from new oak was clean and appealing; we must wait to see how it will turn out in bottle. Also in cask (after four and a half years!) was the 1986. This had already shed its primary fruit and was exuding aromas of cereals, tobacco and game. I couldn't for the life of me see why Fayolle still had this in cask. My note-book contains the cryptic line *'perdrix au chou'* (partridge cooked in cabbage); I wonder now whether this was a judge-ment of the wine or simply a suggestion of what to eat with it. I confess that it is a complete mystery to me.

Caves Desmeure's Domaine des Rémizières has a 3.7 acre plot for its red wines. It makes intensely fruity Syrah wines which tend to be more 'Syrah' than Hermitage. They are generally fairly priced.

Bernard Faurie's chunk of Greffieux and Méal adds up to a scant 4.2 acres, although he has little domaines in St-Joseph and Crozes and a few apricot trees for that vital summer cash injection. His wines are unfiltered, produced traditionally in a cluttered cellar full of old oak tuns. Faurie blends the Méal with Greffieux to achieve fine, balanced wines: the Méal is fleshy and chocolatey, while the attractive Greffieux gives off those carnation/peony aromas which are so enchanting in young Syrah. The 1989 is a good deep wine with silky tannins which should be excellent at the turn of the century. The 1985 was already turning gamy in the spring of 1991.

Michel Ferraton is too busy writing poetry to speak to wine writers.

See separate entries for Chapoutier, Gérard Chave, Delas Frères, Jean-Louis Grippat, Marcel Guigal, Paul Jaboulet Aîné, Robert Michelas, Marc Sorrel and the Caves de Tain-l'Hermitage.

St-Joseph

| Production: in excess of 1.6 million litres

St-Joseph is produced by the communes of Chavanay, Malleval and St-Pierre-de-Bœuf in the Loire département and by Andance, Ardois, Arras, Champagne, Charnas, Félines, Limony, Ozon, Peyraud, St-Désirat, St-Étienne de Valoux, Sarras, Sécheras, Serrières and Talancieux in the Ardèche, as well as by the original six communes of Glun, Mauves, Tournon, St-Jean-de-Muzols, Lemps and Vion.

The story of St-Joseph is another sorry tale. In the beginning there were the wines of Tournon, which were grown on the steep hill to the back of the town, proudly facing the more famous *cru* of Hermitage on the other side of the Rhône. Some of the best of these came from the *lieu-dit* of St-Joseph, which lay on the borders of Tournon and Mauves to the south. At the time of the Revolution, these were some of the most expensive wines in the whole area.

After phylloxera passed through the region at the end of the last century, many of the vines were replanted not on the granite-based rocks but rather on the alluvial plains beside the Rhône. This process of debasement continued during the depression, when more and more of the difficult terraces were forsaken for the valley floor. When the original appellation was drawn up in 1956 there can have been precious little St-Joseph grown where it should have been.

The original decree extended only to the vineyards around Tournon, stretching south to meet the AOC of Cornas. As St-Joseph had been the most famous growth in the area, the authorities baptized the new region with this name. Then, in 1969, the INAO decided to upgrade the Côtes du Rhône vineyards on the left bank of the Rhône, taking in a forty-three-mile stretch all the way to Côte Rôtie. This they included in St-Joseph. The result is a big, characterless AOC, and most of the wine frankly does not deserve the high price demanded of it.

One of the small band of growers who promote quality in St-Joseph is Émile Florentin. On his 10 acre Clos de l'Arbalestrier estate, Florentin produces about 9,000 bottles of red wine from ancient vines using antediluvian methods. The wines are wholly organic: people who don't appreciate earthy, farmyardy smells won't much like the Arbalestrier wines. The 1988 cask sample I tried seemed to have become prematurely feral, indeed to have a sulphide character; I hope Florentin was able to deal with this before bottling. The 1984 was much more the thing: creamy with plenty of blackberry fruit, yet with some of the earthy Florentin style. The 1983 is the best wine I've had from the domaine: a nose reminiscent of fresh butter, with blackberries, blackcurrants and a splendid elegance to it.

Above St-Péray is the Domaine de Fauterie. Its owner, the youthful Sylvain Bernard, is a pupil of Gérard Chave and has 7 acres of Syrah in the AOC. He seemed in some doubt about his 1990s when I visited him, but I liked them a lot. They seemed to me to have noble, carnation/peony aromas. Both the 1989 and the 1988 were successful wines in this style. The 1987 I liked less, and the 1986 seemed to have gone into a sulk, although there is every chance it will get over it.

Alain Paret makes two St-Joseph cuvées: Les Pieds Dendés and Les Larmes du Père. Pieds Dendés is the suppler wine; Les Larmes du Père is made in a chunky tannic style and takes a few years to pull round.

In the past I've much enjoyed the wines of both Bernard Gripa and the large firm of Coursodon. It is, however, too long since I last tasted either to give an honest judgement on how they are today.

See separate entries for Chapoutier, Gérard Chave, Maurice Courbis, Jean-Louis Grippat and Paul Jaboulet Aîné.

PIERRE BARGE

Le Carcan, Ampuis, 69420 Condrieu

Production: 6 acres (10,000 bottles) Côte Rôtie

Quality: 🍇🍇🍇🍇   Price: ★★★★

Best vintages: 1983, 1985, 1988, 1989

The Barge family, father Pierre and son Gilles, share a large house and cellar in Ampuis; but they own separate parcels of vines and their wines are very different. Pierre's wines are on the Côte Brune and he adds about 5 per cent Viognier. There is no small oak to speak of, and the wines are stored in big tuns. They are uncharacteristic Côtes Brunes with all their delicacy. The 1990, from a very tricky year in Côte Rôtie, was a delicate wine with aromas of peony and pepper, violets and carnations. Pierre Barge's 1989 comes from an easier vintage; the nose is beautifully seductive – aromatic and fleshy.

GILLES BARGE

Le Carcan, Ampuis, 69420 Condrieu

Production: about 6 acres (*c.* 10,000 bottles) Côte Rôtie

Quality: 🍇🍇🍇🍇   Price: ★★★★

Best vintages: 1985, 1988, 1989

Gilles Barge is the president of the growers' *syndicat* in Côte Rôtie: an articulate, reasonable man in his thirties who seems to get on well with the other wine-makers in the AOC. Barge's vines are on the Côte Blonde but, unusually, he uses no Viognier. Unlike his father, he tends to put his wines into small oak, about one-tenth of which is new each vintage. He adds that this is not intended to impart a woody taste to the wines; it is merely in the interests of making clean wine.

In the terrible drought year of 1990, Barge's grapes failed to achieve the proper degree of alcohol as the heat was so intense that the sap ceased to rise. Barge chaptalized half a degree up to 12.5. The result is good Côte Rôtie, with lots of pepper and violets on the nose and some black fruits lurking in the background.

In general, the 1989s were more successful in Côte Rôtie. Gilles Barge's put me in mind of raspberry mousse and cherries. It was a nicely structured wine which should age into a classic.

I have tasted the 1985 twice. The first time was in the hotel-restaurant in Ampuis in the summer of 1988, when the wine must have been at 25 °C. Fortunately the second time I tried it was under more favourable conditions; the wine had become slightly gamy, with a full taste of raspberries and blackcurrants.

GUY DE BARJAC

Grand-Rue, Cornas, 07130 St-Péray

Production: formerly 5 acres (12,000 bottles) Cornas; now much less

Quality: 🍇🍇🍇   Price: ★★★

Best vintages: 1978, 1985, 1990 (according to de Barjac);
   1981, 1986, 1988, 1989 also good

Guy de Barjac intentionally makes rather atypical Cornases. He advances the old arguments to justify the easier, suppler style of his wines: people don't have cellars any more, the old wines lacked fruit, etc. De Barjac wants a 'Burgundian elegance' and therefore destems his bunches. His yields are also at the outside limit, which must mean that there is less concentration in his fruit than that of other producers in the AOC.

After twenty years of selling all his wines in bottle, de Barjac retired in 1989. His civil-servant son had no interest in working those gruelling slopes, and de Barjac *père* decided to rent out his vines. The older ones went to Sylvain Bernard (see St-Joseph), and the younger ones to Jean-Luc Colombo (see the Cornas entry). De Barjac takes some of the fruit in lieu of rent and makes small quantities of wine to please certain customers and friends.

Contrary to most informed opinion in Cornas, de Barjac does not rate either the 1989 or the 1988 vintage highly. True to form, the former is a light wine, not one of the brooding giants found elsewhere in the AOC. The 1988, on the other hand, has begun to develop mature Cornas character, with a leathery, gamy nose. The 1987 he brought in just a day before the heavens opened and he thinks it as good as the 1988 and the 1989: it has a full, ripe cherry character. The 1986 was only partly destemmed: it is a well-structured wine tasting of black fruits. The 1981 was not destemmed at all, and this seemed to have something of the leathery character of the 1988.

BERNARD BURGAUD

Le Champin, Ampuis, 69420 Condrieu
Production: 9 acres (*c.* 12,000 bottles) Côte Rôtie

Quality: 🍇🍇🍇🍇   Price: ★★★★
Best vintages: 1985, 1988, 1989, 1990

Bernard Burgaud is a follower of Jean-Luc Colombo, so it will come as no surprise to learn that his cellar comes equipped with plenty of small oak. Burgaud, however, is restrained in his use of the *barrique* and renews only about 20 per cent annually; he is not looking for oaky tastes on his wines.

Burgaud's best vines are on the Côte Blonde, but he has other little plots, including some land on the plateau. The plateau, he says, saved the vintage in the drought year of 1990, as the parched grapes were able to find some nourishment in that relatively lush soil. I tried the wine from a new cask; it had authentic violet-and-raspberry fruit – an attractive wine.

The 1989 was a denser wine, as the alcoholic degree was achieved by a more normal vegetative cycle. The wine was very deep soon after bottling, with lots of leathery, spicy blackcurrant fruit.

The 1984, from a generally decried vintage, was a very pleasant wine with the advantage of having come round fairly quickly.

ÉMILE CHAMPET

Le Port, Ampuis, 69420 Condrieu
Production: 5 acres (8,000 bottles) Côte Rôtie
Quality: 🍇🍇🍇🍇   Price: ★★★
Best vintages: 1978, 1983, 1985, 1988, 1989

This pocket-handkerchief-sized holding is located on the Côte Brune but, with as much as 6 per cent Viognier, the wines are softer and more approachable than some. I have not come across them as often as I should have liked, especially if Champet's 1988 is a measure of his latest vintages: it is a superb wine with an enchanting bouquet of raspberries, pepper, tar and violets. This is a Côte Rôtie at its most seductive and so perhaps a little atypical of the Côte Brune.

Émile Champet is on the point of retirement, but the reins will be taken over by his son Noël, who has been working closely with his father for years now. No cause for alarm.

CHAPOUTIER

M. Chapoutier S.A., 26600 Tain l'Hermitage

Production: Hermitage, 42 acres for the red wines (32 acres for white); Côte Rôtie, 6.7 acres (11,000 bottles); St-Joseph, 5 acres (c. 8,000 bottles); Crozes-Hermitage, 13 acres (20,000 bottles). 79 acres in Châteauneuf. The firm produces 1 million bottles in all.

Quality: 🍾🍾🍾–🍾🍾🍾🍾   Price: ★★–★★★★★

Best vintages of Hermitage: 1967, 1978, 1982, 1983, 1985, 1988, 1989, 1990

Best vintages of Châteauneuf: 1947, 1978, 1985, 1986, 1989, 1990

Best vintages of Côte Rôtie: 1986, 1987, 1988, 1990

In the middle of the 1980s Chapoutier's reputation had plummeted as a producer of high-quality red wines. This was a great pity, as the firm owned some of the best sites in Hermitage, Côte Rôtie and Châteauneuf-du-Pape. Then in 1987 Max Chapoutier renounced the business of wine-making and handed on the reins to his son Michel. Another son, Marc, travels the world export markets.

Michel Chapoutier is a rather doctrinaire wine-maker who draws analogies from other fields (chiefly music) when he wishes to expound on the subject. According to Michel, wine is about harmony: 'You don't want the violins in the orchestra to play too loudly,' he told me, and 'Too much brass makes for a coarse sound.'

Michel is a stickler for doing the best job in the vineyard –

removing the need to add chemicals by assuring the physical well-being of the vine – and since he took over at Chapoutier the firm has begun to get better reviews. I think this is just: the new wine-making is cleaner and the fruit is less obscured by the muddiness of some of the old wines; there has also been far less emphasis on the strange blended cuvées which the Chapoutiers put out, mixtures of different vintages which were one of Max Chapoutier's passions. There is, however, still a little room for improvement: some of the wines have a rather ungainly bitter, extractive fruit which I personally find unattractive.

The Chapoutier Hermitage is called Monier de la Sizeranne. It is made from fruit coming from the *lieux-dits* Bessards, Greffieux, Murets, Hermite, Méal and Chapelle. I tasted the 1989 in cask twice in the autumn of 1990 and found its soft peach and raspberry flavours particularly attractive. The 1988 was going through an odd stage straight after bottling and it was impossible to give a verdict. The 1987 was already at the cereal/tobacco stage when I tasted it in 1988; it is a fast mover!

Something of that cereal/tobacco character was also present on the 1986. The 1985 had become rather like sugared porridge with sweet tomatoes; it was wonderfully long. The 1983's tastes had intensified with wild, leathery, tobacco notes. The 1982 was rather more reminiscent of prunes. Of the older vintages, the 1979 was very luscious and fruity, the 1978 amazingly structured, and the 1967 sweet and rather like very old claret with a faint hint of strawberries and biscuits.

Chapoutier's Côte Rôtie I know less well. The firm has the advantage on Jaboulet in owning some land there which is half on the Côte Brune and half on the Blonde. The wine is 10 per cent Viognier. The 1989 I found marred by a bitter finish which spoiled the otherwise attractive fruit. I was far keener on the 1987 when I tasted it in cask; it had a lovely violet scent and a tarry palate which reminded Michel Chapoutier of black olives. The 1986 was spicy with a whiff of cloves, raspberry and tobacco.

Chapoutier's has always been proud of its Châteauneuf. With holdings of 79 acres, it does not have a *négociant* mentality when it comes to the wine. Michel believes strongly in Grenache when it comes to Châteauneuf, and the cherry-scented Cuvée Jubilée was as much as 97 per cent Grenache. The 1989 was an encouraging sign of the new wine-making, with masses of ripe fruit and this time no hard finish. The 1988 was rather less exciting, and I'm afraid that I found the 1986 poor in comparison with many other Châteauneufs. The 1985, however, was an excellent wine with a strong blackcurrant character. The 1984 seemed a mite unbalanced.

Of the older wines, a 1978 was one of the best wines I've tasted from La Bernardine: lots of cassis and tobacco, with of the wild herby character of the Provençal hillsides. The 1964 was a marvellously structured wine. The oldest I have drunk was the 1947, which was still buoyant with its creamy cereal/tobacco nose and a wave-like structure which kept coming and going on the palate.

Chapoutier makes a decent Crozes, which was successful in 1989 and 1988, as well as a St-Joseph which I found a little bitter in 1989 and a fraction too light in 1988.

GÉRARD CHAVE

> Route Nationale 86, Mauves, 07300 Tournon
>
> Production: 22 acres of red Hermitage (35,000 bottles), plus the production of the 14.5 acres formerly belonging to Terence Gray, plus 2.5 acres of St-Joseph making 4,000–5,000 bottles a year
>
> Quality: ⬦⬦⬦⬦⬦   Price: ★★★★
>
> Best vintages: 1976, 1978, 1982, 1983, 1985, 1986, 1988, 1989, 1990

When most of Hermitage seems to be an anticlimax, Gérard Chave rarely disappoints; not only does he show us how Hermitage can be made, he is also one of the most skilful handlers of the Syrah grape in the world. When Chave vinifies Syrah it can match any other red grape for subtlety and refinement. Chave's wines don't seem to develop those coarse, rude and barbaric elements found in Cornas or the Hunter Valley; they are reserved and well-mannered, a little like the man himself.

The man who enjoys such an enormous reputation throughout the world of wine lives a life of endearing modesty. He makes his wine and relaxes by shooting, fishing and, more recently, cooking. His house and cellars are in the drab main street of Mauves; he doesn't appear to have any lust for flashy artefacts, nor does he have any truck with new oak as used as a flavouring ingredient in the wine: 'A barrel is like a shoe,' he told me: 'when it wears out, you buy a new one.' His cellar would make many a New World wine-maker's hair stand on end: it is coated in a venerable, candy-floss mould which creeps into every corner, coating the racks in which sleep vintages going back to the time of Chave's father and grandfather.

Fame has had its drawbacks: a friend from Paris who has been buying Chave's wines since the 1970s was lunching with Chave one day in the latter's garden. To their horror and dismay, an American wine enthusiast appeared over the garden wall. Undeterred by polite refusals at the door or the fact that Chave had no wine left to sell, the American wanted to meet his hero. Since then, Chave has installed a television camera at his front door.

Chave has a little more to sell now since he acquired Terence Gray's 14.5 acres. Gray was an Irish archaeologist who lived for most of the time in Monte Carlo, where his wines were occasionally to be found in restaurants. By all reports he made some curious brews, only half-corking bottles in order to make the wine age more rapidly. Chave bought the land after Gray's death in 1989, but he has farmed it since 1984. In the past two years some of it has been replanted. The gossip in Tain is that some of the grapes are being sold to Guigal in Ampuis. Everyone in Tain agrees that the cession of Gray's vines to Chave was the best thing that could have happened to them – and that in a climate of considerable jealousy. Land is short on the hill, and there are no remaining good plots left to plant. No doubt the grapes from Hermite will find their way into Chave's meticulously structured cuvée.

Unlike some growers in Hermitage, Chave is not tempted by the idea of dividing his resources. Every parcel of vines he has plays some role in the final blend. In 1988 I was able to taste the different elements of the 1987 vintage before they were assembled: the Diognières with its butter, plum fruit already quite open; Beaumes with its aromas of violets, peaches and tar; Péléat with its fatter, denser fruit; Bessards which provided the tannins to give backbone to the wine; and Hermite with its rich, fat, plum-skin and raspberry fruit. Clearly Chave had no problems with this difficult vintage. Later I tasted it again for *Wine* magazine. The whole panel seemed to agree that the wine had been built to last for decades. Chave himself believes that you should wait twelve years before opening one of his Hermitages.

The most comprehensive tasting I have made of Chave's wines was organized by Robin Yapp in the autumn of 1991. Chave himself was there and seemed to revel in the bottle of Château Tahbilk (old vines) which I brought for him to try. It was there that I was able to taste his 1989 Hermitage – a wonderful wine which in youth appeared to combine a scent of straw, hamster cages, rose petals and plum skin.

I had last seen Chave in September 1988. A month later he had finished his 1988 – a lovely, seductive wine with classic raspberry and plum fruit. The 1986 was more earthy, with a roasted truffly character and a distinctive aroma of cloves. The 1985 was superbly long with a classic bouquet of tar and raspberries. The 1984 was light for Chave but with authentic ripe flavours. With its carnation scent, the 1983 was already beautiful when drunk in 1991. The 1982 had something of a truffly character, but with all the floral Syrah notes: peonies and violets; again it seemed quite ready in 1991. The 1981 was a shade less complex, with some gamy flavours, while the 1980 was quite mature: an earthy combination of violets and raspberries. The 1979 was a classic again: deep and concentrated; *à point* in 1991 but showing no signs of tiring. The 1978 was also in its prime, with a fruit character which seemed to go on developing for ages.

The 1976, which I drank at a solitary birthday celebration at the Clos de la Violette in Aix-en-Provence in 1991, gave a demonstration of the longer-ageing abilities of Chave's wines. Here was a fifteen-year-old Hermitage from a great year. On opening, the aromas of blackcurrants were intense but the body seemed thin. Half an hour later the whole palate had filled out with blackcurrants and raspberries and the wine continued to expand over the next hour. To use a much abused word, the wine was superbly elegant – and as clean as a whistle.

Chave makes a tiny amount of St-Joseph which is rarely seen outside France. The 1988 is predictably dense, adding a whole dimension of quality to the usual decent wine from this AOC. Even in the autumn of 1991 the nose was still slightly closed, but the palate revealed the beautiful plum-skin Syrah fruit that you would expect from this source.

AUGUSTE CLAPE

Route Nationale 86, Cornas, 07130 St-Péray

Production: 12 acres (15,000–20,000 bottles) of Cornas. A little Côtes du Rhône is made from vines on the eastern side of the Route Nationale

Quality: 🍷🍷🍷🍷🍷   Price: ★★★

Best vintages: 1983, 1985, 1988, 1989, 1990

Clape is the man who started the ball rolling in Cornas. He was the first to sell wine in bottle and the first to find buyers in Britain and the United States. Assured markets have spoiled him little: he still makes very traditional Cornas from the same cramped little cellar on the main road from Tournon to Valence.

Clape and his son make the wine from four different cuvées which are made separately and blended before bottling. Some young vines could occasionally find their way into the Côtes du Rhône if they are not up to scratch.

The first vat is made up of fifteen-year-old vines which give a highly aromatic fruit (apricot/raspberry/peony). The second vat comes from the very top of the slopes and sixty-year-old vines;

these give the tannic backbone to the wines. The third site has thirty-five-year-old vines and lies on the terraces; this gives extremely dense, perfumed fruit reminiscent of damsons. The fourth element is a plot of 1890 vines, of which some 60 per cent are original; these yield a quite lovely peony/carnation fruit and give considerable flesh to the wine. In some ways the Clapes' style of assembling their wines resembles that of Gérard Chave.

Assembled, the 1989 seemed even better than its constituent parts: the flesh was there as well as that haunting floral scent. The 1988 is another powerful wine which will need more than ten years to subdue its tannins. In a ripe vintage, such as the 1983, the wine was typically gamy and dense, with fig and blackberry tastes. After half an hour the wine began to remind me of prunes. In the 1980, the tannins were softer and the aromas tended towards leather and game.

The 1973 I drank in the Walnut Tree restaurant near Abergavenny was also gamy, with lots of chocolate and plum tastes – a gracefully mature Cornas.

MAURICE COURBIS

Châteaubourg, 07130 St-Péray

Production: 35 acres of red and white St-Joseph (c. 50,000 bottles); 4 acres of Cornas (c. 6,000 bottles)

Quality: 🍷🍷🍷–🍷🍷🍷🍷   Price: ★★–★★★

Best vintages: 1985, 1988, 1989, 1990

Maurice Courbis is a rugged man with a Gauloise *papier maïs* glued to his lower lip and a deft hand with a pruning-knife, which he uses alternatively to remove faxes and to scratch his head. He and his two sons are part of a heroic band of growers who are currently replanting the high slopes of St-Joseph; in this particular case in an amphitheatre of rock between Châteaubourg and Cornas. Much of the land has yet to come into production, but when these growers start working from mature vines we are going to see an enormous improvement in the quality of the top St-Josephs. These wines are not so contemptible now: 32 acres come from granite or chalk/granite terraces, with the oldest vines going back to 1910.

The initial vats of 1990 looked fine when I was at Châteaubourg in the following spring, especially those from its oldest domaine, Les Roilles. Les Roilles spends rather longer in cask before bottling and comes from the chalky soils which give concentration and good tarry aromas. The best of the *trois glorieuses* hat trick was the 1988, but I should imagine that the 1990 will be super when it comes round.

Courbis also makes minute quantities of Cornas, separating the flat-land vines from those on the hillside. The flat-land vines are old (planted in 1913) and, despite their position, give good rose-petal-scented fruit. The 1990 from the hillside is one to watch: one of the most impressive Cornases of the vintage with its concentration and silky tannins. In the 1989 vintage the *vin de coteaux* seemed readier than that from the *pieds*, but all that would doubtless have changed on bottling. The 1988 had been bottled: here the *pieds* wine was lighter and more floral in style, while the wine from the slopes was rich in chocolate/raisin aromas with nutmeg/cinnamon spice; in a few years this will become a big, leathery Cornas. Before 1988, Courbis did not separate the two Cornas cuvées. The 1987 Cornas was rather closed in 1991, though clearly not the fullest wine. The 1985 had some cereal/tobacco spicy character; it will need another two years before it becomes archetypal mature Cornas.

DELAS FRÈRES

St-Jean-de-Muzols, 07300 Tournon

Production: 26,000 litres of red Hermitage, 20,000 litres of Seigneur de Maugiron Côte Rôtie, 36,000 bottles of Cornas, as well as wines from St-Joseph, Châteauneuf-du-Pape and Crozes-Hermitage

Quality: 🍇🍇🍇–🍇🍇🍇🍇   Price: ★★–★★★

Best vintages: 1982, 1983, 1985, 1988, 1989, 1990

Best vintages for Châteauneuf Haute Pierre: 1983, 1985, 1988, 1989, 1990

Delas is a large merchant house with vines in Hermitage and Côte Rôtie and which buys in grapes to complement its acreage in the main Rhône AOCs. In the 1970s it went through a bad spell, but during the 1980s things changed for the better and the firm is now one of the most reliable *négociant* houses in the Rhône Valley.

The two Delas strong points are Hermitage and Côte Rôtie. In both AOCs it has its own vines (those in Hermitage are rented from the Marquise de la Tourette who is thus commemorated on the label) and supplements its production with grapes bought in from other growers. The vines in Côte Rôtie and Condrieu are the property of M. Michel Delas, who still sells his grapes to the firm even now that it no longer belongs to his family but to the champagne house of Deutz.

Delas's Hermitage is made from vines from its walled vineyard together with fruit from Bessards. Balance is achieved by adding bought-in grapes from Rocoules and Beaumes. The style is attractive and relatively 'easy' for a wine like Hermitage: no great bruising tannins here. I've not tasted the most recent vintages but I remember the 1986 well. It was a difficult year for Delas, which does not rate it a great wine. There is an attractive violet character to the fruit, but it was far from ready when I last tasted it in 1990. The 1985 was altogether different: an enchanting wine with lashings of the tarry, smoky, raspberry-and-plum fruit that one associates with Syrah at its best. The 1984 was a successful wine for an undistinguished year, very easy to enjoy with its peony aromas. The 1983 was more animal, the fruit having developed one stage further with some cereal/tobacco notes. The 1982 was all chestnuts, plums and chocolate.

From the old bad days of Delas I tasted a 1974 which had developed some authentic old-wine flavours: undergrowth, wood smoke, tomatoes and well-hung game.

The Côte Rôtie has been improving since the 1986 vintage.

The 1987 is rather light, but the 1988 Seigneur de Maugiron is good stuff and won a Gold Medal at the 1991 Wine Challenge.

Delas makes about 85,000 litres of Châteauneuf red under two labels: Haute Pierre and Cuvée Prestige. The Haute Pierre is 75 per cent Grenache with additions of both Syrah and Mourvèdre. The Syrah seems to dominate the 1988, which has a strong violet character. This is also true of the 1986, although the Grenache is beginning to reassert itself with attractive honey aromas. The 1985 is already truffly; while the 1983 is a very fine wine with its complex tastes of violets, wood smoke, chocolate, liquorice and tar.

Delas makes very competent wines in both St-Joseph and Crozes-Hermitage. The Val Muzol Crozes in particular used to be one of the most reliable widely distributed Crozes-Hermitages.

MARIUS GENTAZ

Le Vagnot, Ampuis, 69420 Condrieu

Production: 3.5 acres (7,000 bottles) Côte Rôtie

Quality: 🍇🍇🍇   Price: ★★★★

Best vintages: 1987, 1988, 1989, 1990

Marius Gentaz had three blocks of fifty- to seventy-year-old vines in the *lieu-dit* La Landonne in the Côte Brune. Apart from his vines, Gentaz traded in fruit and vegetables. At the time of writing Gentaz has announced his retirement from wine-making and no news has so far reached me as to the succession.

Being in the Côte Brune, there is not much Viognier in Gentaz's wines: not even 1 per cent. Gentaz is not keen on Viognier anyway, and thinks that 5 or 6 per cent is the very maximum: 'Twenty per cent' he says 'would make the wines too dilute.'

It is a pity that Gentaz has decided to hang up his secateurs; he was a careful old man with an ability to make wines work even in ill-starred vintages. The 1990 proved quite a test, but he seems to have been largely saved by his old vines, which, having longer roots, were better equipped than some to find the liquids needed to sustain life. Gentaz's youngest vines were the twenty-year-olds on La Côte Boudin. After the punishment of the drought there were two days of torrential rain. The grapes swelled up to four times their usual size: 'You would have taken them for figs,' says Gentaz. Sadly there was nothing he could do with them, as they had achieved only 8.5–9° Baumé by the time the vintage came round. They were left for the starlings.

Gentaz saved his 1990 Côte Brune vintage; the wine is very good with lots of chunky black fruits and violets. The 1989 is even better, with the same violet character but with a better structure. Gentaz is justly proud of his 1987, which has the animal side which is typical of the denser wines of the Côte Brune allied to a rich raspberry taste.

ALAIN GRAILLOT

> 13 place du Taurobole, 26600 Tain-l'Hermitage
>
> Production: about 37 acres, producing 40,000 bottles of red wine
>
> Quality: 🍇🍇🍇–🍇🍇🍇🍇   Price: ★★–★★★
>
> Best vintages: 1986, 1988, 1989, 1990

Like the other top grower in Crozes-Hermitage, Étienne Pochon, Alain Graillot favours a limited use of new oak for his Syrah-based wines. For a while Graillot seemed to be trailing a little behind Pochon, but then he produced a superb series of vintages in the late 1980s and released his first wines under his top, La Guerande, label. The ordinary 1987 was a fine wine from an otherwise undistinguished year, while the 1988 had wonderfully aristocratic aromas of tar and violets. Both the 1989 and the 1990 have been huge, chunky wines reminiscent of prunes and chocolate. These wines will age beautifully, but I suspect few bottles will survive long enough to test that.

La Guerande is billed as Graillot's star wine. The 1986 was

nice enough, but a little light – as many were in that vintage. The other vintage I have tasted, the 1988, was another kettle of fish entirely: a huge distillation of violets and blackberries.

JEAN-LOUIS GRIPPAT

Chemin de la Sauva, 07300 Tournon

Production: 10–12 acres of St-Joseph producing 12,000–15,000 bottles of red wine, plus 0.75 acre of Hermitage for red wine, producing 1,800 bottles

Quality: 🍇🍇🍇🍇   Price: ★★★

Best vintages: 1988, 1989, 1990

There are three 'Grippats' making wine in the northern Rhône and they are all cousins. In order to confuse you, they all spell their names differently, so that there is a Bernard Gripa in St-Joseph and a Bernard Grippa in St-Péray. Jean-Louis Grippat has a small property on the edge of the town of Tournon which has been swallowed up by urban sprawl in the last twenty years. From his front door, however, he can survey the work he has been doing in re-creating the façade of vines above the town.

I recall travelling through Tournon years ago and noticing a neatly tended vineyard suspended above the centre of the town. I wondered who could possibly work such a site. The answer is Jean-Louis Grippat, who rents the vineyard from the local hospital; hence the name: Vigne de l'Hospice. Just along to the south, that solitary vineyard has been joined by a second, larger site. Jean-Louis has just cleared this with the help of his *vigneronne* daughter. By 1995 it will be in production.

Then a few miles to the south Jean-Louis, along with the Coursodons and his cousin Bernard Gripa, has revived the *lieu-dit* of St-Joseph itself, shaving the great hill of its scrub so that St-Joseph in two senses worthy of its name is now being produced. Jean-Louis took me up that hill above Tournon the last time I was in town; he wanted to show me how to plant Syrah! When we reached the top, he showed me his little part of the

Hermitage AOC, where he makes a tiny amount of red wine which is naturally all sold long before it leaves the cask.

From his St-Joseph vines, Jean-Louis makes a classic, classy St-Joseph: all peonies and cloves. The 1990s in particular are destined for a long life, with all their raisin and chocolate concentration. His Vigne de l'Hospice is especially good. While I was there I even had a chance to try the last two vintages of his Hermitage, Les Murets: the 1990, with its lusciously fruity palate and haunting violet nose, and the 1989, with its rather more dense, chocolatey character. The Hermitages are housed in about 15 per cent new oak.

MARCEL GUIGAL

Route Nationale 86, Ampuis, 69420 Condrieu

Production: 30 acres of Côte Rôtie (50,000 bottles). Guigal also buys in grapes from other growers to make his wines in Hermitage and Côtes du Rhône

Quality: 🍇🍇🍇–🍇🍇🍇🍇🍇   Price: ★★–★★★★★

Best vintages: 1983, 1985, 1988, 1989, 1990

Marcel Guigal is a quiet, efficient, almost Jesuitical man. He is the biggest cheese in Côte Rôtie, owning about 10 per cent of the appellation as well as the old-established house of Vidal-Fleury where, once upon a time, his recently deceased father Étienne used to work as cellar master. He still buys up as many grapes as he can to make his excellent Côtes Brune et Blonde, and his *négociant* business extends also to the banks of the Rhône and Hermitage. The straight Côtes du Rhône from Guigal has always been one of the most reliable generic wines available, often dominated by ripe Syrah fruit; it is seldom the cheapest.

The Guigal *maison* is rather stylish. When I was last there, Marcel was building a 'Roman' cellar and hoping to install some Roman artefacts he had amassed over the years: an amphora here, a vase there and perhaps a mosaic pavement or two. New-oak casks from Burgundy made their appearance here long before Jean-Luc Colombo started whipping up the smaller growers. All the top reds get at least three years in oak (three and a half for the *crus*); 25 per cent of this is new for Brune et Blonde and 100 per cent for the top wines: La Landonne, La Mouline and La Turque. Guigal says that he works his wine the Bordeaux way and bottles it like Burgundy. At around 25 hl/ha (1,000 litres per acre), his yields are modest.

In the late 1970s Guigal launched his first two single-*cru* Côte Rôties: La Mouline in the Côte Blonde and La Landonne in the Côte Brune. In 1985 a third *cru* was created at La Turque, a *lieu-dit* which straddles the two slopes, or, to use Guigal's own phrase, 'a hyphen between Brune and Blonde'. Quantities of these wines are minute: Guigal makes about 5,000 bottles of La Mouline and 8,000 of La Landonne. When Guigal's British agents received their first allocation of La Turque in 1989, it turned out to be just twelve cases. They gave one to each of the top twelve Guigal customers. They in turn held it back for directors' lunches. It is highly doubtful if any of these bottles will ever reach the shops. The popularity of Guigal's top wines in the United States has gone through the roof now, and the older vintages of La Mouline and La Landonne have become collectors' items which change hands at prices well in excess of Château Pétrus. While it was still in barrel, La Turque was being quoted at over £300 a bottle!

Are they worth it? It is hard to imagine any wine being worth sums like that, but there is a market out there which is eager to have them at any price and that is what is causing the inflation; to do Marcel Guigal justice, he himself does not demand much more for his wines than his neighbours on the slope.

Sadly, my experience of the *cru* wines is pretty limited, confined to a tasting in Guigal's cellars in 1988.

La Mouline is the softer, more feminine wine of the two more senior *crus* and, true to form, it is the one which is enhanced by some 13 per cent Viognier; La Landonne has none. The wines have a three-week *cuvaison* before being run off into new Burgundian barrels. The 1984 La Mouline, from a comparatively light year, was a really full wine with lots of ripe blackcurrants, leather and vanilla from the oak. La Landonne was far more closed up. A great tannic bruiser typical of the Côte Brune, it was hard to see this 1984 wine softening out much before 1995.

The La Turque I tasted was the 1987, which had been in new oak for one year. This wine receives about 5–6 per cent Viognier. When I tasted it in autumn 1988, the wine still had an attractive *primeur* fruit with lots of blackberry and violet. The new oak was dominant. Guigal feels that the wines need at least two years before they can absorb so much new oak.

The Guigal which most of us are likely to see in the shops is the Côtes Brune et Blonde, which is made from fruit bought in from contract growers. In a good year, like the 1985, the wine can be enchanting, with lovely violet aromas. The 1984 is not bad either, though slightly more leathery. A 1979 I drank recently in a London restaurant was rather more disappointing; it seemed a shade dilute for great Côte Rôtie.

Guigal makes an extremely good Hermitage from fruit bought and vinified *sur place*. The 1986 seemed rather awkward and tannic the last time I tried it, but it might have been going through a funny stage. The 1985 was a lovely wine with lots of sloe and raspberry character. The 1983 was possibly the best Guigal Hermitage I've had, with a good violets-and-raspberry nose and impressive length.

PAUL JABOULET AÎNÉ

La Roche de Glun, 26600 Tain-l'Hermitage

Production: 1.6 million bottles. Hermitage 50 acres red wine; Crozes-Hermitage 70 acres of red wine. Jaboulet buys grapes or wine for its St-Joseph, Côte Rôtie and Cornas

Quality: 🍇🍇–🍇🍇🍇🍇🍇   Price: ★★–★★★★★

Best vintages: 1961, 1978, 1983, 1985, 1986, 1988, 1989, 1990

For most people in the wine trade the mention of the house of Jaboulet conjures up an image of the genial export director Gérard Jaboulet with his engaging manner and idiosyncratically fluent English. Gérard possesses the considerable knack of making all visitors feel welcome, and he appears never to tire of tasting wines (Jaboulets certainly, but also the best wines from all over the world) and is perpetually ready to pull up some wonder from his own cellar to convince you – if ever you needed convincing – that the great wines of Hermitage are some of the longest-living wines in the world.

Gérard's affability is one of the firm's greatest assets: he makes friends easily. On the other side of the family is cousin Philippe, the president of the AOC and vice-president of Crozes. Philippe is more withdrawn, more reserved. He is in charge of the Jaboulet vines.

Jaboulet owns far fewer vines than Chapoutier. Its Cornas is bought in from growers who make the wine and store it for them until 1 December. In St-Joseph it buys in grapes for its popular, reasonably priced, Le Grand Pompée. There is a cheaper Crozes (Thalabert is made from the firm's own vines) and a Châteauneuf-du-Pape, Les Cèdres, which are both made from bought-in grapes. Besides these there is a huge range of Rhône 'products': Côtes du Ventoux, Côtes du Rhône Villages, Côtes du Rhône Parallèle 45 (half Grenache, half Syrah), Gigondas and Vacqueyras.

It would be ridiculous to imagine that all the wines in such a portfolio should be of great quality; of course there will be lapses. More recently, however, Jaboulet has come under criticism even for its top wines, like the Hermitage La Chapelle. There are complaints about inconsistent bottling which means that one batch doesn't measure up to the last. In recent years some of Jaboulet's firmest supporters have defected to other camps in Hermitage.

The question is, then: does Jaboulet still deserve its five-star rating for wines such as La Chapelle? I think on balance that it does. La Chapelle is still consistently one of the greatest wines of Hermitage, and it has been so for as long as anyone can remember. One hopes, however, that a more consistent bottling policy will reduce the element of uncertainty in the next few years and that some of the grumbling will cease. *On verra!*

So what is La Chapelle? The answer is a brand: La Chapelle is a trade mark for Jaboulet's top Hermitage wine. Grapes come from Bessards, Greffieux, Méal, Diognières, Croix and Maison Blanche. La Chapelle is made from the best vats of the older vines; the rest goes to make straight Hermitage.

Recent vintages of La Chapelle have seen much more new oak than previous ones: I don't know how much was used on the huge, brooding 1990, but the 1989, for example, was housed in 45 per cent new and 55 per cent one-year-old casks. I tasted it in the autumn of 1990. It was a big, tight, concentrated wine which was not showing much of its fruit then. The 1988 had been bottled in March of that year. The wine was an obvious classic, with a pronounced spice-and-gingerbread nose with some fairly powerful new oak. The 1987 was already pleasant drinking at the beginning of 1992. The 1986 was marked by nutmeg, tobacco and cereal. The 1985 was more immediately attractive, with its strawberry/raspberry fruit and tarry palate.

Of the older wines, the 1983 was heading for glory when I tasted it last in 1988; the cereal nose was already giving way to the mature fruit. It should be ready to drink from 1992. The 1978 was mature Hermitage of a great year; there was a slight whiff of caramel with tarry ripe, red fruits on the palate – almost like a roadworks in the sun. The 1973 was not from such a favoured vintage; the bouquet was rather buttery, with a taste reminiscent of tomatoes. The best Hermitage I have ever tasted was the 1961; the colour was still intense in 1988, evidence of yields as low as 11 hl/ha (450 litres per acre). There was a bouquet of game and liquorice, with a feeling of sweetness – almost sweet pastry – on the palate. It was a very fine old wine.

One sees less of Jaboulet's Côte Rôtie Les Jumelles. I have not, for example, tasted any of the three latest vintages. The 1986 I recall as being very closed up in 1988. Gérard himself preferred the 1985, which I have not tasted. More recently I enjoyed a bottle of the 1978 at lunch at J. M. Raynaud (Tain's best restaurant by a long way) with Philippe Jaboulet. It was a lovely old Côte Rôtie with a predominant aroma of ripe black-currants and all the elegance one associates with the appellation.

The Domaine de Thalabert is one of Crozes-Hermitage's best wines. The vines are in one of the best parts of the AOC and the yields, at 30 hl/ha (1,200 litres per acre), are among the most modest. Tasted from the cask, the 1990 and the 1989 were looking very good: lovely colour, excellent violet/raspberry/tar aromas and fine cooling tannins. The 1990 possibly had the edge on the excellent 1989. The 1986 was a big, deep wine which took a long time to come round. The 1983 Thalabert was a classic with its tarry, raspberry fruit; the 1978 had big, sweet fruit and showed no sign of decline after nearly ten years in the bottle. In general, Thalabert outdistances Jaboulet's St-Joseph, though the St-Joseph is more expensive.

The Jaboulet Châteauneuf Les Cèdres is made from 70 per cent Grenache, with the rest Cinsault or Syrah. The 1990 was made in an old-fashioned almond-and-tobacco style. There was rather more Cinsault than Syrah on the 1989, which was pleasantly raisiny with some torrefaction aromas. The 1981 was 30 per cent Syrah with some mature honey/gingerbread charac-ter and a touch of damp autumn leaves. The 1979 was more gamy, with a fairly intense autumnal scent; the Syrah here was as high as 35 per cent.

JOSEPH JAMET

Valin, Ampuis, 69420 Condrieu

Production: 10 acres (12,500 bottles) Côte Rôtie

Quality: 🍇🍇🍇🍇   Price: ★★★★

Best vintages: 1983, 1985, 1987, 1988, 1989

The Jamet vines are tended by two young brothers, Jean-Paul and Jean-Luc Jamet, and situated on the Côte Brune. True to form there is little Viognier – about 2 per cent. The brothers work the musts with a submerged cap, and there have been increasing amounts of new oak used in recent vintages.

The Jamet brothers are currently making some of the best wines in Côte Rôtie. This is amply borne out by the 1988 vintage, where behind the new-oak butteriness there was a dense concentration of tarry, violet-and-raspberry fruit. Their 1987s were also good, picked after a fine September and before the rains, to produce wines rich in plum/violet aromas. Elsewhere in Côte Rôtie the 1986 wines were affected by rot after the rains, but not here; the wine has some of that intensely tarry, almost roadworks-like fruit with a little touch of violets too.

The brothers consider the 1985 to be one of their best years, and it will come round some time after the 1986. Here the accent is on chocolate and raspberries, with an authentic, Syrah pepper finish. The 1984 was ready when I tasted it last, in 1988. It was by no means a poor wine, though the fruit was lacier, more delicate, with some incense character. The 1983 was made from particularly concentrated musts and dominated by animal/liquorice tastes. In 1988 it was nowhere near ready to drink; possibly it will open up from 1992.

ROBERT JASMIN

Le Vagnot, Ampuis, 69420 Condrieu

Production: 10 acres (12,500 bottles) Côte Rôtie

Quality: 🍇🍇🍇   Price: ★★★★

Best vintages: 1979, 1982, 1985, 1987, 1988, 1989, 1990

Robert Jasmin is a big, bluff, Falstaffian figure who clearly enjoys good food and wine. It comes as no surprise to learn that the first Jasmin in Ampuis was a cook who had come from his native Champagne to work in the kitchens of the Château d'Ampuis, just a few hundred yards from where Jasmin's cellars are now. When I first met Jasmin he was gaily rolling a barrel around dressed in a pair of perilously tight, fluorescent blue shorts. On that occasion and since then he has always been ready to share a funny story and to open a few old bottles lodged in the furthest recesses of his cellar.

Jasmin makes traditional Côtes Rôties from vines situated mostly on the Côte Brune. Often dominated by big, chewy tannins, they are rarely among the more charming or aromatic of wines. The 1990 from cask, however, seemed to have all those fruits and flowers which typify good Côte Rôtie, and Jasmin bought a few new barrels in that year which may betoken a change of heart. The 1989 from the more classic vintage was far more tannic, but there were some good things on the nose. Similar was the 1988, which had a pretty, raspberry/black-pepper nose but a dense palate which will need years. It was impressively long.

Jasmin is proud of his 1987, which, like some other growers in Côte Rôtie, he places before the rain-affected 1986. There was not much Viognier in any of these wines, which may account for the lack of that charming *primeur* nose in extreme youth. Jasmin believes you have to have 10 per cent Viognier to make any difference; he has only 2–3 per cent. With all the rot about, the 1986 was noticeably light – a wine to drink up quickly, he thinks. The 1985, on the other hand, was 'a great year': very dense and structured, it was going through a closed patch when I tried it in 1988.

The 1984 was a success here, with its sloe and plum tastes made unfined and unfiltered to preserve all the goodness in the fruit. The 1982 was impressively complex but still not really ready nine years later, although there were interesting notes of rose-petal and cherry, cereal and undergrowth; it struck me as being rather more Hermitage than Côte Rôtie. The same might be said of the 1979, which had the same autumn-leaf and liquorice taste but rather aggressive tannins.

JEAN LIONNET

Rue Pied-la-Vigne, Cornas, 07130 St-Péray

Production: 14.5 acres of Cornas (*c.* 25,000 bottles); 4 acres of Côtes du Rhône

Quality: 🍇🍇🍇   Price: ★★★

Best vintages: 1985, 1987, 1988, 1989, 1990

Jean Lionnet is Jean-Luc Colombo's best pupil in Cornas. Indeed he is pretty well Colombo's only pupil in Cornas, but then, as the French say, no man is a prophet in his own land.

The new thinking has its plus side, which is immediately visible in the cleanliness of Lionnet's cellar and the very modern stainless-steel vinification vats. Downstairs there are rows of small oak barrels, the newest and swankiest in the village. About one-third of the casks are renewed annually, but some of the wine is not put into oak at all, in order to inhibit over-oaky, super-tannic flavours in his wines.

There is no doubt that Lionnet gets good fruit from his vines: a 1990 tasted from the vat was archetypal young Syrah, with lots of pepper and peony aromas. The issue is whether he is right to use so much new oak on an already heavily tannic wine. Not just that, for Lionnet is also keen to add his violet-scented pressings to the brew, making it even more mouth-puckering in its tannins.

The top cuvée here is called Rochepertuis, and this is the only wine exported. The 1989, tasted from the cask, was pleasantly silky, which must show that Lionnet's tannins are not of the aggressive sort. I was only a little put off by the new-oak aromas, which for me appeared to detract from the flavours of the fruit. The same quibble applies to the 1988.

The 1987, from a lighter year, had the same silky tannins but a rather atypical nose which seemed dominated by bananas. The 1985, however, was reassuring: although Lionnet had given it the same treatment, the Old Adam in the wine had clearly decided to reassert itself. Here were the barbarian elements of Cornas: liquorice, leather, herb-covered hillsides,

chocolate, raisins, blackberries and blackcurrants – all under-
pinned by those silky tannins. It was an impressive wine and the
purest Cornas. Nature obviously reverts to type!

ROBERT MICHEL

Grand-Rue, Cornas, 07130 St-Péray

Production: 17 acres (*c.* 25,000 bottles) Cornas

Quality: 🍇🍇🍇🍇🍇   Price: ★★★ (La Geynale: ★★★★)

Best vintages for La Reynarde: 1981, 1985, 1988, 1989, 1990

Best vintages for La Geynale: 1984, 1987, 1988, 1989, 1990

Robert Michel is a quiet, friendly man who put me in mind of a
scoutmaster. He lives in the middle of the village over a series
of ancient cellars which his barrels share with some venerable
mould. With 17 acres, he owns about 10 per cent of the Cornas
AOC and has reasonable quantities to dispose of. About 80 per
cent of these go abroad, principally to Britain and the United
States.

Michel now makes three different cuvées of Cornas: a *pieds de
coteaux* wine using the vines from the flat land; a *cuvée des coteaux*
called La Reynarde using some of the grapes from the high
terraces; and La Geynale, using grapes from his best south-
facing site, the name of which is local dialect for *genêt* or broom,
these vines all having been planted between 1910 and 1930.

I have to admit that I'm not very keen on the *pieds de coteaux*
cuvée, but its advantage is that it allows people to buy a little
Michel at reasonable prices. Most customers who call at his
door go away with a few bottles of the *pieds*, which, in a year like
1990 or 1989 produces a wine with sweet raspberry fruit; but
it's not Cornas and Michel wouldn't pretend it was.

The La Reynarde is generally one of the best wines in Cornas. Deep, with a marked scent of peonies or carnations and a
rich chocolate-and-raisin fruit on the palate, the 1989 is a winner with its apricot aromas; and that white-fruit character is
also detectable on the 1988. Michel is rare in that he actually

dislikes the dry, hot years and revels in the difficult years, which bring all his talents as a wine-maker to the fore. I was not as keen as he was on the La Reynarde 1987 but I liked the 1986, which was shedding its infant fruit for the mature cereal-and-tobacco character of Cornas. This character is even more marked on the generally ill-starred 1984. A 1981 La Reynarde was classic mature Cornas, with a whiff of something feral accompanying the carnations and peonies, blackcurrants, black-berries, leather and violets.

Michel has been making La Geynale since 1984. It is now possibly the top wine in Cornas, although there are years when he is outgunned by Clape. This is his richest wine, with dense, damson fruit. Like the La Reynarde wines, the 1989 was marked by white fruit (peaches and apricots) and was a far more open and aromatic wine than most 1989 Cornases. The 1988 was closed up when I tasted it in the spring of 1991, but should prove a match for any of his wines if left for a decade or so.

It is in the off years that La Geynale really scores, and one need have few reservations in buying it in vintages like 1987 and 1984. The 1987 was full of big red fruits, violets and cream and was superbly balanced. The 1984 was marked by blackcurrants and had fully opened out when I tried it in 1991.

ROBERT MICHELAS

Le Chassis, Mercurol, 26600 Tain-l'Hermitage

Production: 40 acres (30,000 bottles) of Crozes-Hermitage; 2.5 acres (2,500 bottles) of Hermitage Rouge; 6 acres (10,000 bottles) of Cornas; 7 acres of St-Joseph (5,000 bottles of red wine)

Quality: 🍇🍇–🍇🍇🍇   Price: ★★–★★★

Best vintages: 1988, 1989, 1990

This is a very large domaine by Rhône standards, with fingers in a number of pies. I have never had the good fortune to taste Michelas's Hermitage, but production is so minute that I should imagine that it is all mopped up by a handful of local restaurants. Likewise I have never tasted his St-Joseph.

Happily there is a little more Crozes-Hermitage to go round. The 1989 Domaine St-Jemms seemed to me to be a little light for the vintage, especially placed beside blockbusters like Pochon and Graillot. It also seemed heavy-handed on the sulphur. I found the same SO_2 problem on the 1988, which marred much denser, more appealing fruit. Michelas's top Crozes, Domaine des Marinets, spends a year in big oak tuns. The 1988 was toffeed and full; the 1987 was rather lighter; the 1986 rather clumsy and jammy.

Michelas's Cornas, Les Chassis, is more dilute than some. The 1986 had a nice honey-and-bayleaf character with a little touch of raspberry/violet fruit.

ÉTIENNE POCHON
DOMAINE POCHON
CHÂTEAU DE CURSON

26600 Tain-l'Hermitage

Production: 21 acres of Syrah, chiefly around the Château de Curson, producing about 36,000 bottles of red wine annually

Quality: 🍇🍇🍇   Price: ★★

Best vintages: 1988, 1989, 1990

In the past few years Étienne Pochon has emerged as one of the few growers who bring repute to the beleaguered AOC of Crozes-Hermitage. His top wines come out under the Château de Curson label, and the next best are released as Domaine Pochon. Pochon consults Jean-Luc Colombo, so it should come as no surprise to find that he is in favour of a limited use of new oak. Of the straight Crozes, the 1989 has the edge on the 1988, when Pochon got a lot more concentration from his musts. The 1989 had some affinities with the Graillot wine of that year: it is enormous, with masses of prune and chocolate-like fruit. The 1988 Château de Curson was perhaps a little over-oaked when I tasted it at Vinexpo in 1989, but this might have been a *folie de jeunesse* (on the part of both wine and wine-maker): it certainly had plenty of guts, with all that bacon, prune and tar fruit.

RENÉ ROSTAING

Le Port, Ampuis, 69420 Condrieu

Production: *c.* 15,000 bottles Côte Rôtie

Quality: 🍶🍶🍶🍶–🍶🍶🍶🍶🍶   Price: ★★★★

Best vintages: 1987, 1988, 1989, 1990

René Rostaing is a former property-developer with a passion for the wines of Côte Rôtie. He had a little land in the Côte Brune at La Landonne and a clutch of vines in the Côte Blonde before he married Albert Dervieux's daughter. Now he has benefited from the Dervieux vines, which have put him into the big league as far as Côte Rôtie is concerned. His choice of father-in-law was a wise one, for Albert Dervieux always vini-fied his excellent Brunes and Blondes separately as well as put-ting the less distinguished wine into a straight Côte Rôtie. René Rostaing has continued this policy and now bottles a plain Côte Rôtie as well as his Côte Blonde and La Landonne wines.

Rostaing has built a new cellar with all the modern con-veniences. Some new wood is used, but not in order to flavour the wines. His Côte Blonde vines are now all between sixty and eighty years old and give superbly concentrated fruit. Another advantage with vines of this age is that they are more able to cope with drought years such as 1990.

Rostaing made a powerful 1987 from his La Landonne vines. In the autumn of 1991 it was still rather muted, with little touches of raspberry on the nose. The tannins were suitably big, though by no means aggressive. It should make a great Côte Rôtie by 1995.

Rostaing's 1986 Côte Blonde was more closed up than the La Landonne. The fruit is big and tightly knit; it will be a few years yet before it begins to give its best. Drink from 1993.

MARC SORREL

128 avenue Jean-Jaurès, 26600 Tain-l'Hermitage

Production: 5 acres of red Hermitage, making about 8,000 bottles

Quality: 🍇🍇🍇   Price: ★★★—★★★★

Best vintages: 1985, 1988, 1989, 1990

Marc Sorrel is a son of the local *notaire*. When his father died, Sorrel was out of work and he decided to take over the family's vines on the slopes of Hermitage. Another brother (there are four in all) had trained for the law and he became the *notaire* in succession to his father. Such is French life.

Another feature of French life is, of course, the equal distribution of goods among all the children. This has meant that, although Marc has inherited the bulk of the vines, the other three brothers have retained 1.25 acres which they market separately. Marc Sorrel also disposes of 1.7 acres of white grapes from Rocoules and a small plantation in Crozes.

While many of the best palates of the British wine trade speak in terms of hushed respect whenever the name of Sorrel is mentioned, I have always found his wines tough, mouth-puckeringly tannic and hard to love. It may well be that I have never been able to experience the wines when properly mature. Had I had the chance, either in a restaurant or from a shop, I would have leapt at it. Sadly, the opportunity has never come my way and at the estate itself the wines sell out at such an indecent speed that come the spring it is all barren and the only thing you may taste are the wines in cask.

Sorrel makes two different red wines: a younger-vine cuvée, labelled simply Hermitage, and Le Gréal, which is a blend of fruit from Greffieux and Méal. One of the results of Sorrel's popularity has been the chance to invest in some new oak. This is particularly noticeable on the 1990s.

The 1990 *jeunes vignes* was built in true Sorrel style with those massive tannins just behind the flavours of new oak. The straight Hermitage cuvée has the virtue of being a little suppler, which is also true of the honeyed 1985. The 1983, on the other hand, I found a little too feral even for my liking; the cereal/straw note had been affected by strong animal tastes so that my comment reads 'slightly soiled hay – zoo cages'.

The 1988 Gréal was made from yields of 27 hl/ha (1,093 litres per acre). New oak dominates the wine, but there is also good fruit here: smoky raspberries and chocolate. It is one of my favourite Sorrel wines. The 1987 Gréal, which was brought in before the rains, is the usual fierce tannic brew, although a little smokiness was discernible when it was young. The 1986 Gréal I found bunged up and hard. I find it difficult to see how and when this wine will begin to show some form of charm. Yields were once again very low (30 hl/ha; 1,214 litres per acre). I preferred the 1985 to many of Sorrel's wines: here at least is some blackberry/blackcurrant fruit. The tannins are there too, and in profusion. Don't bother to touch it before 1996.

CAVES DE TAIN-L'HERMITAGE

Route de Larnage, 26600 Tain-l'Hermitage

Production: Crozes-Hermitage, 3 million litres (65 per cent of total AOC production); St-Joseph, 200,000 litres (11 per cent of total AOC production); Cornas, 30,000 litres (15 per cent of total AOC production); Hermitage, 145,000 litres (25 per cent of total AOC production)

Quality: 🍇–🍇🍇🍇   Price: ★–★★★

Best vintages: 1978, 1982, 1983, 1985, 1988, 1989, 1990

This vast co-operative is wholly equipped with the very latest technology and vinifies a significant percentage of the production of Syrah wines in the northern Rhône. If you are a wine-buyer looking for your own-label Crozes, St-Joseph, Cornas or Hermitage, here is the place to come; just slap the vat you like and its contents will be bottled up and delivered to your door.

Naturally the wines are technically proficient: there is more modern wizardry here than anywhere else in the area. The quality, however, is necessarily variable. When you are a co-operative cellar you can dictate terms only up to a point. You can give cash incentives for better grapes and penalize those who give you ropy ones, but you end up by taking them all. The trick here, then, is to opt for the better wines produced under the co-op's own label, as it is the less favoured wines which are sold off first to French and British supermarkets.

The top wines from the co-op are not at all bad. The oenologist, Jean-Étienne Guibert, is an intelligent and reasonable man who knows what he is doing. I toured the vats with him in the spring of 1991, sampling from dozens of possible Crozes-Hermitages, Cornases and Hermitages. The Hermitages he separates out, keeping the best old vines from the Cave's own 42 acre domaine on the slope. To his top vat Guibert adds back some of the *vin de presse* to make a proper, concentrated *vin de garde*.

Given the great sea of Crozes-Hermitage which flows through the doors of the Cave at vintage time, it is hard for the wine-makers to isolate the high-quality wines. Guibert thinks that this may ultimately be possible, but for the time being the Crozes and St-Josephs from the co-op are its least exciting products. The co-op is the biggest producer of Cornas, of which it made a nicely packed 1989 and a characteristic 1988 with some *garrigue* aromas and plenty of fruit. The Cave is experimenting a little with new oak, and the Cornas has a touch of vanilla from the casks.

The best wine here is the Hermitage. The Cave not only receives Hermitage grapes from its *coopérateurs*, it also possesses a 42 acre domaine in Hermitage. Some people in Hermitage resent the unconventional role played by the Cave in the AOC, and there is a good deal of finger-waving down at the local equivalent of the Three Stags on a Saturday night. Personally I find the Cave's Hermitage perfectly reliable and, indeed, often better than that made by some of the smaller producers, although I regret the amount of new oak that has been used on wines like the 1989.

The 1988 is rather forward, with plenty of appealing raspberry fruit with authentic herb and violet notes. Interestingly enough, Guibert himself thought he had overdone the oak in the wine.

The 1983 gives a fair indication of how such wines age. Even if they are approachable fairly young, they seem to hold on to their fruit, with added elements of cereals and tobacco creeping in. The 1978 was quite exquisite, with a sweet, raspberry nose, a palate of strawberries and an aristocratic note of damp undergrowth on the finish.

VIDAL-FLEURY

Route Nationale 86, Ampuis, 69420 Condrieu

Production: 25 acres (40,000 bottles) Côte Rôtie

Quality: 🍾🍾🍾🍾–🍾🍾🍾🍾🍾   Price: ★★★–★★★★

Best vintages: 1985, 1986 (La Châtillonne), 1988, 1989, 1990

This, the oldest estate in Côte Rôtie, is now owned by Marcel Guigal, whose cellars are a couple of hundred yards down the road. Guigal allows Vidal-Fleury to carry on independently, but he has insisted that the quality of the wines be improved. Before the mid 1980s, many wines from the estate were frankly disappointing.

Some of Guigal's oaking policy has been taken on by Vidal-Fleury, which now ages its Côtes Brune et Blonde in 50 per cent new oak. The top Côte Blonde wine, La Châtillonne, is housed entirely in new oak. Only 3,000–4,000 bottles of this wonderful wine are made. About 8 per cent of the grapes are Viognier.

The 1987 Brune et Blonde was already showing a little touch of game in the autumn of 1991, with some tar and carnation notes. The wine was soft and approachable, with some blackcurrants on the palate and great length. This wine is drinkable relatively early, from 1992.

La Châtillonne 1986 was a superb wine, despite what was generally a lack-lustre vintage in Côte Rôtie. The bouquet was a heady combination of apricots, violets, carnations and fresh raspberries, giving an impression that the wine was quite ready in 1991. The palate revealed big, silky tannins. The wine is immensely long. This can be drunk from 1992.

Vidal-Fleury is (I think) the only house to make a *marc de Côte Rôtie*. I only discovered this lovely brandy at the Beau Rivage in Condrieu. The next day I was round like a flash to Vidal-Fleury to buy a couple of bottles.

The Rhône Valley: the Southern Rhône

In the southern Rhône the Grenache grape is the mainstay, but it is generally combined with other grapes in order to prevent it from oxidizing and to give it the benefit of more powerful aromatic notes. For the main these additional cultivars are the Syrah and the Mourvèdre, although there is still a considerable amount of Cinsault and Carignan around. In general, these last two grapes do not produce exciting wines.

Châteauneuf-du-Pape

| Production: 9.9 million litres of red wine

Châteauneuf-du-Pape is the greatest of all Grenache wines. At the last count some 77 per cent of the AOC was planted with Grenache, and most of the top estates (the exceptions are Beau-castel and Nerthe) are between 65 and 90 per cent Grenache; one estate (Rayas) is thought to be 100 per cent Grenache. Yet

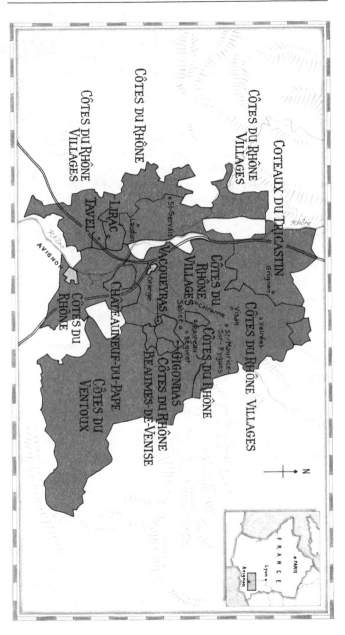

it is funny how few people, even in the wine business, ever think of Châteauneuf as Grenache. There is a good deal more Grenache in the average Châteauneuf than there is Cabernet Sauvignon in a Haut-Médoc wine or indeed Merlot in a St-Émilion.

The confusion originates in history. The connection with the popes of Avignon is at best an exaggeration, at worst a lie. The largely French popes confined their attentions to wines from the Languedoc: Beaucaire, St-Gilles, Nîmes, Uzès and Pont-St-Esprit as well as Muscats from Lunel and Mauguio; 'despite the legend, those of Châteauneuf counted only for a minuscule proportion' (Joseph Girard, *Évocation du vieil Avignon*, Les Éditions de Minuit, 1958). The only firm connections with the papacy are the brief stopover Clement V made in the castle on the night of 5 April 1314 and the rebuilding of the hilltop fortress by order of John XXII from 1317 to 1333.

The confusion extends to the history of the wines. The man who assembled the famous thirteen varieties was a lyrically minded engineer by the name of Joseph Ducos, from Auch in Armagnac. Ducos bought Château La Nerthe for a song in 1879, just after phylloxera had cut a swathe through the vines. Ducos was one of the first men in France to understand the need to replant using American rootstock. Once he had mastered the process, he set about restoring the vineyard by collecting cuttings of the grapes which had formerly existed there from all over the Midi.

A century ago there were a great many more cultivars in France than there are today. Ducos appears to have isolated thirteen which he believed to have thrived in the area: Grenache, Syrah, Mourvèdre, Counoise, Muscardin, Vaccarèse, Cinsault and Terret Noir for the reds; Clairette, Piquepoul Blanc, Bourboulenc, Roussanne and Picardan for the whites. In what proportions they had been mixed before phylloxera is not at all clear, though it seems likely that Grenache dominated even in those days. Ducos's ideas on the right blend for Châteauneuf were actually rather peculiar and were not eventually incorporated in the AOC: he believed that the Grenache and Cinsault should not exceed one-fifth of the wine;

that Syrah, Mourvèdre, Muscardin and Camarèse should make up two-fifths; that three-tenths should come from Counoise and Piquepoul Noir; and that white grapes (Bourboulenc and Clairette) should be used for a tenth part to add brilliance to the wine.

When in 1923 the growers of Châteauneuf appealed to the Norman lawyer Baron Le Roy de Boiseaumarié of Château Fortia to plead on their behalf in the hope of winning a statute to protect the identity of their wines, they envisaged an AOC founded on Ducos's research. Le Roy drew up a model of a statute which was ultimately to be accepted by all of France's AOCs. As such he is the father of the Appellation d'Origine Contrôlée. He is *not*, however, the father of Châteauneuf-du-Pape.

The third factor which is frequently misunderstood in the history of Châteauneuf-du-Pape was the planting of the high plateau of Mont-Redon, with its famous *galets* – pebble-like stones, often the size of an ostrich egg. Before the First World War there were simply no vines on the plateau and Ducos knew absolutely nothing of this quality factor so often associated with Châteauneuf (in fact the *terroir* is geologically varied, and very few estates own a piece of the plateau). This was affirmed to me by M. Abeille of Domaine de Mont-Redon. In 1921 Abeille's grandfather, along with *grandpère* Brunier of Vieux Télégraphe, began clearing the *gros galets* of woods, apricot, cherry and olive trees (the cherries enjoyed some local fame). The process was not finished by the Second World War, when a vital fillip was introduced by Burgundian merchants who were looking for high-strength Grenache to blend into their Burgundies. By the 1950s the plateau was finally planted with 90 per cent Grenache. It is chiefly Grenache from the plateau which gives that aroma which I associate with tobacco, cigarette packets or even Woodbines. The wines from the plateau of Sorgues, for example, are lighter and less aromatic than those from the plateau of Mont-Redon. The mistral also plays its role in Châteauneuf, often drying out the wines in cask and vat to give them a *goût de mistral*.

Many Châteauneuf growers are openly critical of the

Grenache, which they like to believe was in some way imposed on them by the Burgundians. Part of the problem is the alcoholic strength of Grenache vats in warm years. With a good summer, the Grenache can climb to 17° Baumé, making wines which are scorned by the wine writers of French women's magazines, who tell their readers to touch nothing over 11.5° or 12°. On the other hand, realists like M. Abeille at Domaine de Mont-Redon have to admit that Grenache is the *fond de sauce* as far as the wine is concerned. It is also true that Grenache simply isn't good if the degree is too low: the best, according to 100-per-cent-Grenache advocate Jacques Reynaud at Château Rayas, is 15.5°. Good Grenache is also old; as the present Baron Le Roy asserts, only the old vines have sufficient acidity to work as an anti-oxidant, oxidation being the grape's chief drawback.

The most suitable adjuncts to the Grenache are, of course, Syrah and Mourvèdre. The Syrah gives those aromas of violets and plums, raspberries and tar. The Mourvèdre provides tannins and backbone as well as the bilberry/boiled-sweets/wine-gums character. Jacques Reynaud disapproves of Mourvèdre, which he says is to be used only when the wines tend to age too quickly. Paul Avril at Clos des Papes disagrees: for him the Mourvèdre is the Merlot of Châteauneuf. Mourvèdre plantations seem to be on the increase in the AOC.

When I asked the charming Mme Durieu of Domaine Durieu what Châteauneuf should be made of, she replied, 'It's Grenache, Syrah, Mourvèdre. All those other things, that's just folklore.' Some growers, however, set some store by the famous thirteen. Many like the peppery Counoise – or the Muscardin, which gives the wine freshness and length. The Cinsault also has the advantage of lowering the alcoholic degree of the Grenache vats. Rarely, however, do these 'funnies' exceed 5 per cent of the blend.

Like many other AOCs, Châteauneuf-du-Pape now has its reforming oenologist, in this case Noël Rabot. Rabot is Bordeaux-trained and advocates a limited use of new small oak, *pigeage* and bottling of the whole vintage at once (highly important in Châteauneuf, where this is sadly rare); he also appears to advise against high levels of Grenache. Rabot's work may be experienced in recent vintages of the following: Mont-Redon, La Nerthe, La Gardine, Louis Mousset, Vieux Lazaret and Beaurenard.

Lastly there is the famous Châteauneuf bottle, with its embossed crossed keys, which was invented as long ago as 1937. With the exception of Jacques Reynaud's wines (Rayas and Pignan) and those put out by the leading *négociants* of Tain-l'Hermitage, it is fair to say that all the Châteauneuf worth buying is marketed in this bottle. The chances are that any other Châteauneuf will be some Burgundian brew which bears about as much resemblance to Châteauneuf-du-Pape as does a porpoise to a duck-billed platypus. Recently, local Châteauneuf merchants have won the right to use the bottle, but their crest is slightly different, so study it with care: the grower's label has the crossed keys *under* the papal tiara, while the merchant's has Saint Peter's keys crossed *over* the tiara. A subtle distinction, and worth knowing.

Domaine Durieu is a 49 acre estate with cellars in the centre of Châteauneuf. Its wines are 70 per cent Grenache with an unusually high (10 per cent) proportion of Counoise. Its 1989 is particularly successful.

Bosquet des Papes is a traditional house using a blend of 80 per cent Grenache. It made fine, representative wines in 1988, 1986 and 1985, and a superb 1983 which was all violets, figs, chocolate and dried herbs. The 1989 was very closed and dense when I last tried it. No *assemblage* is practised, and quality could vary considerably from bottle to bottle.

Caves St-Pierre is a big merchant house buying wine from all over the AOC. Its 1986 Domaine des Cigales was good, but quality in general is variable.

Domaine Roger Sabon is a 37 acre estate in Châteauneuf. (The Sabons also own a tract of land in Lirac; see the entry for Lirac.) The wine is 80 per cent Grenache and 10 per cent Syrah. The Cuvée Prestige and Cuvée Réserve are generally good wines, especially the 1986 and 1985 of the former. At the estate, I enjoyed a wonderful 1967 wine with masses of complex, spicy aromas.

Château La Nerthe is an old estate which was allowed to run

down until it was acquired by merchants David et Foillard in 1985. The present owners have restored both the cellars and the château and have introduced Rabot-style concepts of Châteauneuf-making. New oak is used here, for which the administration advances some rather spurious-sounding justifications drawn from the history of the estate ('Châteauneuf was traditionally housed in new oak'). For me the wine has lost some of its character by reducing the Grenache to 57 per cent and increasing the Syrah and Mourvèdre to 20 and 17 per cent respectively. A Cuvée des Cadettes has been created for the estate's top wines, of which the 1986 is a fine example. The 1988 Châteauneuf has classic Châteauneuf character. I also liked a liquorice-flavoured 1981 made by the previous owners.

Père Anselme is a large merchant house in Châteauneuf itself, and also contains a museum of wine-making. Its La Fiole comes in a rather peculiar wonky bottle which looks as if it ought to have cobwebs painted on to it; it must be impossible to stack. Two wines from the 1983 vintage were memorable, especially the Médaille d'Or.

Domaine de Nalys is a 130 acre estate where Philippe Dufays introduced carbonic-maceration techniques in the 1950s. The idea was to lighten the wine to make it more popular with an increasingly health-conscious market. Another estate which went over to carbonic maceration was Domaine de Beaurenard. Personally I cannot get on with this Beaujolais style of Châteauneuf, but others might enjoy it. The best wine I have drunk from Nalys was a rather more traditionally inclined 1981.

Lucien Gabriel Barrot is a small estate using 85 per cent Grenache. I have drunk its wines only rarely but have always enjoyed them. It made a superb 1980 and a very fine 1976.

Les Clefs d'Or is a traditional estate, using 80 per cent Grenache, which is popular with Robert Parker. I find the wines rather over-extractive and ever so slightly bitter. The 1986 is a great bruiser of a wine, with blockbuster tannins. The wines tend to be hot and alcoholic, as was borne out by the now mature 1975, which was still aggressive after fifteen years.

Louis Mousset is a big domaine owning five châteaux and

working closely with M. Rabot. The jewel in the crown is the Château des Fines Roches, a superb folly looking out over the whole AOC. The other labels are Clos du Roi, Font du Roi, Clos St-Michel and Fabrice Mousset. The best of these is Fabrice Mousset, which is 90 per cent Grenache. The 1989 is a classic, with its raspberry and Woodbines nose. The other estates are a trifle lack-lustre, unfortunately.

See separate entries for Château de Beaucastel, Henri Bonnot, Domaine Font-de-Michelle, Château Fortia, Domaine du Grand Tinel, Domaine de Mont-Redon, Clos des Papes, Château Rayas and Domaine du Vieux Télégraphe; and for Chapoutier, Delas Frères and Paul Jaboulet Aîné in the northern Rhône.

Côtes du Rhône and southern Rhône Villages

Production: AOC Côtes du Rhône 100,800 acres (210 million litres), AOC Côtes du Rhône Villages 6,900 acres (14.5 million litres), AOC Lirac 2.1 million litres of red and *rosé*, AOC Tavel 2,130 acres (3.6 million litres), AOC Coteaux du Tricastin 4,940 acres (10 million litres), AOC Côtes du Ventoux 15,800 acres (24 million litres), AOC Vacqueyras 2.8 million litres of red and *rosé*

Côtes du Rhone is a vast AOC with one or two pockets in the Syrah-dominated north but otherwise confined to the Grenache-rich south. Some of the *négociants* make good wines here: Guigal's is pricey but fine stuff, likewise Vidal-Fleury's; Jaboulet's best goes into Parallèle 45, and there are reliable wines from Chapoutier. One or two estates deserve mention: the Château du Grand Moulas is always a good bet, and its Cuvée de l'Écu contains a high percentage of Syrah – the 1985 was deep and smoky, with tarry raspberry fruit. The Château de St-Estève is one of the most progressive estates in the region.

For the Château de Fonsalette, see Château Rayas. For Coudoulet de Beaucastel, see Château de Beaucastel.

Côtes du Rhône Villages is an AOC made by the communes of Rochegude, Rousset-les-Vignes, St-Maurice-sur-Eygues,

St-Pantaléon-les-Vignes, Vinsobres, Chusclan, Laudun, St-Gervais, Cairanne, Beaumes-de-Venise, Rasteau, Roaix, Sablet, Séguret, Visan, Valréas.

Quality begins to improve with these basically Grenache wines. In St-Gervais, the Château Ste-Anne made a very classy 1988 with a good whack of Syrah, giving it flesh as well as some distinctly feral aromas. Another estate making good use of Syrah is Domaine Rabasse-Charavin in Cairanne. The basic wine is 70 per cent Grenache and rather creamy and supple. The Syrah cuvée is an aristocratic wine worthy of the northern Rhône; the 1986 was full of deep, gamy Syrah.

In Rasteau is the Domaine de la Soumade, which makes unfortified wines of high quality but also a rare *vin doux naturel*. Rasteau's Grenache-based VDN is the only red fortified wine permitted outside the Pyrénées Orientales. Of La Soumade's unfortified wines there was a nice earthy 1986, but I preferred the freshly-milled-black-pepper aromas of the 1987. The 1988 was obviously improved with some Syrah. The fortified wines are full of big raspberry fruit and are better than those of the co-operative.

Sablet's Domaine des Goubert is part of the same operation as its award-winning Gigondas. I have found the Sablet wines very attractive in the past and, from their leather, raisin and chocolate fruit, I imagine that they must contain a fair amount of Syrah.

In Séguret is Gabriel Meffre's Château de Courançonne, a largely Grenache-based wine. The 1988 vintage, with its cedary fruit, won a Gold Medal at the International Wine Challenge in 1991.

Valréas is the home of the excellent Domaine des Grands Devers, owned by René Suard. The ordinary wine is 40 per cent Syrah, and Suard also makes a pure-Syrah cuvée.

Lirac is an AOC known for both reds and *rosés*, the reds sometimes vying with Châteauneuf and the *rosés* with Tavel. One of the big names here is Jean-Claude Assémat, who owns both the Domaine des Causses and the Domaine des Garrigues. At Causses, Assémat makes a blend of 30 per cent Grenache, 30 per cent Carignan, 15 per cent Mourvèdre and 15 per cent Syrah, with a little Cinsault completing the blend. The 1989 was wonderfully chunky. Assémat makes a 70 per cent Syrah wine which he puts into new oak; both the 1988 and the 1989 were big and peppery.

The Domaine Roger Sabon has a large estate in Lirac (see the entry for Châteauneuf). I remember a delicious 1987 with lots of apricot and tobacco fruit. Another name to remember is the Domaine Duseigneur, which is 40 per cent Grenache with Syrah and Mourvèdre plus a little Carignan and Cinsault. According to the effects of *coulure*, either the Grenache or the Syrah seems to dominate the wine; so Syrah dominates the 1985 and 1983, Grenache the 1986 and 1984.

Tavel wines are 100 per cent *rosé* mostly made from Grenache and a little Mourvèdre. The best-known wines are those of Château d'Aquéria, which are made from five separate *cépages*, with the Grenache making up the best half.

Coteaux du Tricastin used to be written off as a *vin de comptoir* in Parisian cafés, but things have improved a little here. The estate to watch is the Domaine de Grangueneuve.

The Côtes du Ventoux has always produced light wines of little distinction. One exception is Malcolm Swann's at the Domaine des Anges.

Vacqueyras is the Rhône's newest AOC. The best wines here are made by Roger Combe at the Domaine de la Fourmone and by M. Ricard at the Domaine Le Couralou. The latter uses a good deal of Syrah; the 1985 and 1988 vintages were particularly good.

Gigondas

Production: 3.5 million litres, chiefly from Grenache, with small amounts of Syrah, Mourvèdre, Cinsault, etc.

'The poor man's Châteauneuf' is the way that Gigondas is often written off. The grape mix (without the folklore) is generally the same, with a maximum of 80 per cent Grenache and a minimum of 15 per cent Syrah or Mourvèdre. Growers may throw in any of the other red Rhône grapes except the Carignan. Unlike Châteauneuf, Gigondas producers are permitted to make *rosé*, though few good wine-makers seem to avail themselves of the chance.

The vines lie in the shadow of the Dentelles de Montmirail, so the soils are basically limestone or chalky. White wines have been abandoned in Gigondas, the first of the Côtes du Rhône Villages to be upgraded to full AOC status.

While there are a fair number of ropy wines put out under the Gigondas label, there are a handful of estates which make wines which are able to match some of the best in Châteauneuf. As one might expect, the usual battle is being fought between the old-tun/lots-of-Grenache school and the new-oak/lots-more-Syrah-and-Mourvèdre school.

The leading estate in the traditional Gigondas line is the Domaine des Pallières. I tasted a good number of this excellent estate's wines by courtesy of its London agents in 1989, and they proved just how good and long-lasting Gigondas can be. The 1985 was an excellent wine with a nose reminiscent of brown sugar; the 1984, from a rained-out vintage, slightly less exciting, though not without authentic Grenache tobacco aromas; the 1983 was one of the best in the line-up – opulent and long. The 1982 appeared to be drying out, which would mean that it was not destined for a long future; likewise the 1981. The 1979, on the other hand, was still very much on form, with the same burnt-sugar nose as the 1985, allied to some gamy aromas. The 1978 was a little dry, reminding me of rather old Chianti, but the 1976 was still vibrant and appeared to be holding its fruit for a few years longer.

Domaine Raspail-Ay is a 20 acre estate making some of the best Gigondas about. The wines are around 70 per cent Grenache with the rest made up principally of Syrah and Mourvèdre. The 1985 seemed to me to be particularly successful; others have singled out the 1982 for praise.

At the Domaine St-Gayan, Roger Meffre makes wines which have plenty of admirers. I found the 1986 rather ungainly, with its aggressive, huge tannins, and wondered if it would pull round. The 1984, from a poor year, was rather sulphury – evidence that the wine had not been too healthy from the start. I have not tasted recent vintages.

One wine I enjoyed recently was the 1988 Gigondas from Pierre Perrin. This is a product of the *négociant* side of the Perrins of Château de Beaucastel; it is full of proper tobacco, plum and chocolate tastes: a real success.

I don't claim any great knowledge of the *nouvelle-vague* Domaine des Goubert, which uses a percentage of new oak (especially for the top Cuvée Florence): the only wine I've tasted was the 1988 non-wooded wine. This was a poor bottle, and I shall reserve judgement until I have the chance to taste a broader range.

CHÂTEAU DE BEAUCASTEL

84350 Courthézon

Production: 170 acres in Châteauneuf producing around 200,000 bottles of red Châteauneuf; some 75 acres of Côtes du Rhône making Coudoulet de Beaucastel (formerly Cru du Coudoulet)

Quality: 🍇🍇🍇🍇   Price: ★★★

Best vintages: 1970, 1980, 1981, 1983, 1985, 1986, 1988, 1989, 1990

For a period every year, before the Perrins assemble their red Châteauneuf, it is possible to taste nearly half of the famous thirteen grape varieties allowed under the AOC Châteauneuf-du-Pape at Château de Beaucastel: Cinsault, Grenache, Syrah, Mourvèdre, Counoise, and Muscardin. Beaucastel is an atypical Châteauneuf in that it is not mostly Grenache, Perrin senior having taken against the grape; since he took over the wine-making fourteen years ago, François Perrin has not planted a

Grenache vine in Châteauneuf. The current blend is roughly 30 per cent Mourvèdre, 30 per cent Grenache, 20 per cent Syrah and 10 per cent Cinsault with a few of the 'funnies' thrown in – chiefly Counoise.

Beaucastel also differs from other Châteauneufs in that the Perrins flash heat the grapes to 80 °C before pressing them. This process is designed to kill the 'oxidases', meaning that there is no need to use SO_2. It also produces more colour and extract. In general the Perrins try to keep chemicals out of their wine, and Beaucastel is to some degree 'organic'.

The vines, many of them fifty years old, are grown on the clay-soiled plateau of Courthézon in the north of the appellation. This is not the same fruit as that produced under the gruelling heat of the *galets* of the plateau of Mont-Redon, which could have something to do with the decision to play down the Grenache in Beaucastel. The Perrins are carrying out one or two experiments with new oak; so far they have found that it benefits the Syrah but not the Mourvèdre or the Grenache.

Beaucastel wines are assembled before bottling. There are no separate productions.

I tasted both the 1990 and the 1989 Beaucastels before *assemblage*. The basic Grenache for the 1990 wine was a huge, dark, sweet wine heavy with blackberry fruit. The acidity was low, however, and the alcohol high. The Syrah after *pigeage* was deep, with extremely ripe fruit, and the Mourvèdre also was a success, with all the boiled-sweets character of the ripe grape. Everything pointed to a great year at Beaucastel. Similarly for 1989, where I tasted the fruitiest of Cinsaults. The 1989 Grenache was less alcoholic and more typical in its tobacco character, but the Syrah and Mourvèdre seemed somehow less exciting.

When Beaucastel gets mature, it develops a heavy animal nose which is not always appreciated. Recently a reader wrote to the editor of *Decanter* to complain that his 1981 Beaucastel had smelled of manure. If this is something you object to, you won't like the old wines from this estate. When they are young, however, they are full of delicious fruit – like the 1988, which is a summer pudding of a wine. The 1987, from a generally bad year in Châteauneuf, is less successful.

With the 1986, the gamy side of Beaucastel creeps in: my note reads 'hay, with an animal living in it'. The wine is superbly structured, with masses of fruit on the palate. The 1985 had me thinking of burnt brown sugar with raspberries; the 1983 of truffles and gingerbread ('with a wild boar on the finish'); the 1981 of cumin and well-hung game, leather, liquorice and tar. The 1970, which I last tasted with Beaucastel's London agents, had moved on a stage and was giving off super ripe mature aromas of honey, liquorice and quince.

The Perrins of Beaucastel also make one of the best Côtes du Rhônes in their Coudoulet de Beaucastel (formerly called Cru du Coudoulet). On their *négociant* side they make good Gigondas as well as a popular Côtes du Ventoux called La Vieille Ferme.

HENRI BONNOT

35 rue de l'Église, 84230 Châteauneuf-du-Pape

Production: Bonnot admits to 15 acres in Châteauneuf; no other figures are ever likely to come to light

Quality: 🍇🍇🍇   Price: ★★★

Best vintages: 1986, 1988, 1989, 1990

Henri Bonnot is one of the great eccentrics of Châteauneuf, an AOC which seems to breed them in considerable numbers. Bonnot lives in a simple village house and brings in his grapes through the front door then vinifies them in his sink. Rusty tanks are installed on a sort of balcony at the back of the house, and downstairs are the dirtiest set of cellars I've ever set eyes on. Yet, Henri Bonnot is to some degree the darling of Robert Parker (who dines with him *chez lui* when he is in Châteauneuf), and it has to be said that Bonnot can make some remarkable wines.

Bonnot is a man of strong opinions and seems oblivious to

what others think of him or his wine. While I was in his cellars in November 1990, he decided to give an extempore lecture on Dutch cheeses: *'Je ne ferai pas manger à mon chien des choses comme ça'* (I wouldn't give my dog food like that). I looked at his dog, a rickety creature, literally on its last legs, which must have been nearly twenty; it was in the process of gobbling up a piece of its own excrement off the cellar floor. The visit was further enhanced by the behaviour of Bonnot's young son, who mischievously burned sulphur sticks until he managed to drive us out into the open air.

The question has to be: can one still make wonderful wines in such a squalid environment? The answer is: only up to a point. It is not easy to taste *chez* Bonnot, as most of the time he doesn't have any wine ('I'm thinking of bottling some of this; I need some dough,' he says). On this occasion I managed to coax a few samples of the 1989 out of him: huge wines full of the flavours of fig, mulberry, raspberry, coffee and chocolate. Two samples of the 1988 followed, with rather more tobacco character allied to the chocolate and mulberry. Neither of these wines had, however, been bottled. I tasted the 1987 with Bonnot's English agents. It was not such a fine vintage to start with, and the bottle was marred by the flavours of dirty wood: an obvious reference to the Bonnot cellar. The 1986, which Bonnot produced from a bottle with the label of quite another wine, was a return to form: creamy dried figs, like unfortified vintage port. Bonnot doesn't filter his wines: he simply fines with six egg-whites per cask.

Bonnot's wines are 80 per cent Grenache; for the rest he has 'a little bit of everything', but has a preference for Mourvèdre and Counoise ('the pepper'). Cinsault he uses to 'lower the alcoholic degree' of the Grenache. He steers clear of Vaccarèse: 'It rots like Lord knows what,' he says.

CLOS DES PAPES

84230 Châteauneuf-du-Pape

Production: 79 acres of Châteauneuf of which 90 per cent for red wine, about 100,000 bottles of red

Quality: 🍷🍷🍷🍷–🍷🍷🍷🍷🍷   Price: ★★★

Best years: 1966, 1978, 1979, 1981, 1983, 1984, 1988, 1989, 1990

Clos des Papes is small by Châteauneuf standards, but under Paul Avril's guidance it has come to the fore as one of the very best estates in the AOC. The red wine is made from 70 per cent Grenache with 20 per cent Mourvèdre and 10 per cent Syrah; Avril adds a little Vaccarèse, Muscardin and Counoise, but so little as makes no difference. M. Avril is a firm partisan of the Mourvèdre grape, which he calls the Merlot of Châteauneuf. Syrah, he feels, gives off-notes in old wines. The bunches are not destemmed except in unripe years like 1984 and 1987; vineyard yeasts are preferred. After fermentation, the wines spend between twelve and eighteen months in a battery of wooden tuns.

M. Avril has no large tank for *assemblage* and practises up to six bottlings over a period of six months. This must inevitably lead to quality variations, but this is a familiar story in the region.

The 1989 was very much dominated by a Mourvèdre nose when I tasted it in 1990: a beautiful, big, spicy wine. The 1988 had been recently bottled and was returning to form, with masses of strawberry/raspberry fruit, pepper and leather. The 1987 was a good wine from an ill-starred vintage, with some nice Syrah, Mourvèdre notes and a touch of peony on the nose. The 1986 was slightly disappointing, as are many wines of this vintage, although there was some pleasant Grenache tobacco character. The 1985 was much better: Woodbines, cereals, blackcurrants and blackberries. The 1984 was as much as half Syrah and Mourvèdre as the Grenache failed, leaving yields of only 24 hl/ha (970 litres per acre). The nose is rather truffly.

The 1983 vintage produced more classic wines: blackcurrant, cereal and tobacco. The 1981 had a gamy/minty quality. The 1979 was a real blockbuster: full of honey and spices, leather, herbs, liquorice and dark chocolate – one of the best Châteauneufs I've tasted. I drank the 1978 in Sloan's restaurant in Birmingham: its concentrated black olive fruit did much to improve the sad, recessionary atmosphere of January 1992.

As a treat at the property, Avril opened a bottle of his 1966. The honey note had intensified with plenty of damp-leaf aromas. There was even a whiff of buttery coconut before finishing on a rich truffly note.

DOMAINE FONT-DE-MICHELLE

84370 Bédarrides

Production: about 74 acres of Châteauneuf, making around 100,000 bottles

Quality: 🍇🍇🍇🍇   Price: ★★★

Best vintages: 1983, 1985, 1986, 1988, 1989, 1990

It is not hard to imagine that the Gonnet brothers once played serious rugby: they are not the sort of people you'd choose to meet going down a dark alley-way. Originally their estate was part of the Brunier land (see Domaine du Vieux Télégraphe), their mother being a sister of Brunier *père*. When grandfather Brunier died, the Gonnets got a share of the pebbly plateau which is a quality factor in classic Châteauneuf.

The Gonnet blend is 70 per cent Grenache and 10 per cent each of Syrah, Mourvèdre and Cinsault. There has been a slight increase in the amount of Mourvèdre over the last few years. The Gonnets destem about half their bunches, but, apart from this and the new oak they use on their Cuvée Étienne Gonnet, the wines are fairly classically made. No complete *assemblage* is performed, and bottlings take place over a period of months.

The 1989 is considered benchmark Font-de-Michelle, with its aromas of mulberries, blackberries, herbs and tobacco; the

1988 was even fuller, with an added fruit note and a dark chocolate finish. That year they put some 2,000 bottles' worth into new oak, which I did not find wholly convincing (some people will like it). The ill-favoured 1987 was light, with a tell-tale mushroomy nose. The 1986, on the other hand, was superb and easily one of the best Châteauneufs of the vintage: the wine has a glorious aroma of violets, blackberries and Provençal herbs. The 1985 seemed a little coarse after the 1986, although the 1983 showed a return to form, with undergrowth truffle notes and plenty of violet, blackcurrant and even Turkish delight on the palate!

CHÂTEAU FORTIA

84230 Châteauneuf-du-Pape

Production: 69 acres making around 60,000 bottles of Châteauneuf

Quality: 🍇🍇🍇   Price: ★★★

Best vintages: 1979, 1980, 1988, 1989, 1990

The Baron Le Roy de Boiseaumarié is a capricious old gentle-man. The son of the 'inventor' of Châteauneuf, this former soldier uses some interesting tactics to confuse writers who come to taste at his house. With Jacques Reynaud at Château Rayas, he shares an affection for base-less glasses, which have the advantage of not permitting the writer to put down his glass to take up his pen. This is sad, as Le Roy has a good deal to say which is important.

The wines are tradition itself, and it is interesting to record here (once and for all!) that this so-called *fons et origo* of Châteauneuf does not subscribe to the thirteen-varieties school. The wines of Fortia are up to 80 per cent Grenache with a little addition of Syrah and Mourvèdre. When the weather permits, Le Roy lays his grapes out on plastic sheets in the sun to concentrate the juices before pressing. The fermentation is wholly classic; nor does he approve of the Noël Rabot school of new oak: 'I hate that,' he brays.

The wines appear as unpredictable as the man. A 1984 was unusually good for that poor vintage; moreover, he had managed to use 86 per cent Grenache where others had scarcely managed to fill half their vats with the grape. The wine was stylish: full of classic Grenache tobacco notes. A 1980, from another vintage without a huge reputation, was a splendid wine, full of truffle and incense aromas with a back-up of damp leaves, fresh herbs and pepper. The 1979, from a great year, was even slightly lentilly, with lots of liquorice-and-herb notes.

DOMAINE DU GRAND TINEL

84230 Châteauneuf-du-Pape

Production: 160 acres of Châteauneuf in the communes of Courthézon, Sorgues, Orange and Bédarrides

Quality: 🍇🍇🍇🍇🍇   Price: ★★★

Best vintages: 1978, 1981, 1983, 1985, 1988, 1989, 1990

Although comparatively little known on the export market, there is no doubt that Élie Jeune's Domaine du Grand Tinel is one of the best estates in Châteauneuf. The winery is in a cluttered little house in the village itself, but you are instantly struck by the almost obsessive cleanliness. Jeune's blend is 80 per cent Grenache and 10 per cent Syrah, with the rest made up of Muscardin, Counoise, Cinsault and Mourvèdre. He says as long as they were *old* vines he would like all thirteen, but he shows no desire to plant them.

Many of Jeune's vines are between fifty and eighty years old. I tasted some wonderful 100 per cent Grenache from some of these vines in the 1990 vintage, with all that spicy raspberry fruit which only old vines will give. This fruit came from Courthézon. From Bédarrides the fruit was sweeter, more rounded. A Syrah had an enchanting smoky character.

Naturally, Jeune made great wines in both the 1989 and the

1988 vintages. The 1989 seemed rather toffeed; the 1988 was lighter than some, with masses of spice – cloves and mace. The 1985 was benchmark Châteauneuf, with its tobacco, herb and raspberry fruit. The 1984 was slightly anticlimactic but by no means dishonourable with its prematurely old gingerbread, undergrowth and medlar tastes.

The 1983 also tasted of gingerbread, but there was more fresh fruit here: blackcurrants and raspberries. The 1981 was already turning tile-coloured, and here the earthy notes had crept in: truffles, damp leaves, nutmeg and gingerbread. The 1978 was one of the best Châteauneufs I have ever tasted: it seemed to trounce even the lovely 1981 with its aristocratic blackcurrant nose, honeyed palate and wonderful persistence.

DOMAINE DE MONT-REDON

84230 Châteauneuf-du-Pape

Production: 400 acres of Châteauneuf, 235 in production; about 200 acres or 400,000 bottles for the red wine

Quality: 🍇🍇🍇   Price: ★★★

Best vintages: 1978, 1981, 1985, 1988, 1989, 1990

The largest domaine in Châteauneuf is run by the amiable M. Abeille and is owned by him and his cousin M. Fabre. Châteauneuf's new-broom oenologist Noël Rabot is active here, and since 1985 the vinification has been changed so that the Grenache is assembled with the Syrah or with both Syrah and Mourvèdre before it is passed into big tuns or small new-oak *barriques*. In general, only the Syrah and Mourvèdre are thought worthy of new oak. Later all the elements are brought together and an *assemblage* is made before bottling.

As a result of its ownership of 173 acres of the plateau of Mont-Redon, Mont-Redon should be one of the most classic Châteauneufs, although it has to be said that it has occasionally suffered from uncharacteristic lightness. Grenache Noir makes up the lion's share of the blend, with Mourvèdre providing tannins and Syrah the wine's aromatic qualities. Abeille sets some store by Counoise, calling it 'the pepper' of the blend; otherwise the 'funnies' are restricted to only 5 per cent of the mix.

Despite Robert Parker's occasional pleas, M. Abeille still believes in filtering his wine – fearing the wrath of consumers if they were to find a light deposit. I think Abeille protests too much.

In November 1990 I was able to taste elements of both the 1990 and the 1989 vintages, which were not yet in bottle. The 1990 had been an alcoholic vintage, as was proved by an 80/20 per cent blend of Grenache and Syrah which mingled a raspberry fruit from the Grenache with the bacon-and-lentil character of young Syrah. A 1989 blend of 70 per cent Grenache, 10 per cent Syrah and 20 per cent Cinsault was dense with raspberry and cherry fruit; an 80/20 per cent Grenache/Syrah blend was still chewy with its big tannins. A mixture of Grenache with 20 per cent Syrah and 10–15 per cent Mourvèdre from a new-oak cask was quite delicious with all its big red fruits: 1989 should be a year to watch.

The 1988 was full of nutmeggy spice with beautifully rounded raspberry fruit. Both the rained-out 1987 and the light 1986 were disappointing wines; the 1986 had a strong Woodbines aroma from a Grenache year. The 1985 was a return to form, with its leathery, mature fruit. Glorious wines were the slightly earthy 1981 and the near-perfect 1978. The 1981 was full of truffles; the 1978 of damp autumn leaves, raspberries, blackcurrants and violets.

CHÂTEAU RAYAS

84230 Châteauneuf-du-Pape

Production: available figures unlikely to be trustworthy

Quality: 🍇🍇🍇–🍇🍇🍇🍇🍇   Price: ★★★★

Best vintages: 1986, 1988, 1989, 1990

No figure in Châteauneuf is so controversial as the eccentric hermit Jacques Reynaud. The opinions of wine writers also vary, ranging from eulogy (Parker) to condemnation (Livingstone-Learmonth and Master). As far as the writers are concerned, the crux of the matter seems to be whether or not you had the honour of knowing Reynaud's father and the wines he made in the post-war years. Like Parker, I never knew the late Louis Reynaud and have too little experience of older vintages to judge whether his son has erred or not.

Jacques Reynaud is a creature of secrecy. He abuses the AOC regulations with transparent glee. He won't allow the local authorities to pry into what he is doing and he sends his wine to an oenologist a hundred miles away, in Béziers, to prevent anyone in the village from knowing what he is up to. The six Moroccan gentlemen who work for him are selected for the tightness of their lips.

Reynaud is not an easy man to meet, and it must be counted an honour to be ushered into his presence. Many have failed to achieve this. One English wine-merchant-cum-writer actually caught sight of Reynaud hiding in a ditch when he turned up for a meeting; he emerged only once the man had got back into his car and driven away. I tracked Reynaud down to a wood, a few hundred yards from the house. At first he kept his hand firmly in his pocket; but, when his dog, Blackout, offered his paw, Reynaud was eventually coaxed into giving a form of greeting.

Reynaud's cellars are second only to Henri Bonnot's for dirtiness. He also subscribes to the Baron Le Roy school of glasses, offering base-less cracked vessels for tasting. He is not over-anxious to open bottles, either: he is more happy to survey his audience with an impish, satyr-like expression of curiosity mixed with disdain. One never really knows whether what Reynaud tells you is simply said for the hell of it. It was none the less possible to taste one or two barrels of the 1989 vintage and the assembled 1988. Rayas is apparently made from 100 per cent Grenache from ancient vines which allow only minute yields. The 1989 was no disappointment: a great honk of raspberries was followed by a palate with raspberries, spices, tobacco and herbs. The same 10 hl/ha (405 litres per acre) yields were also responsible for the superb 1988, with its creamy raspberry and plum (I noted 'rice-pudding' at the time), Woodbines, herb and liquorice tastes.

Back in London, Reynaud's London agents, O. W. Loeb, were kind enough to let me taste a couple of other vintages: the 1986 and the 1984. The 1986 was no disappointment, the bouquet rich with figs and chocolate; the palate with dried figs, liquorice, blackberries, chocolate cake, cereals and dried herbs: a wonderful wine. The 1984, however, presented problems. Two bottles were off form, betraying an advanced form of volatile acidity. One poor director (who had recently hurt his leg in an accident) had to keep mounting his motor bike and dashing off to the firm's cellars to find a better example. The third time he was lucky, and *that* 1984 was lovely: raspberries and tar, strawberries, figs and tobacco – a remarkable achievement in a year of generally poor quality and one when the Grenache had been decimated by *coulure*. Two dud bottles out of three is a sobering thought, however, and a possible indictment of M. Reynaud.

Pignan is the second wine of Rayas. It is not pure Grenache this time: there is definitely some Syrah in it, and possibly Cinsault too. The 1986 is dominated by a Syrah nose, tar and raspberries, and has a long, peppery finish.

Reynaud makes a number of other wines both in Châteauneuf and in his marvellous Château de Fonsalette estate in the Côtes du Rhône; the wines are marked by the same eccentricity as the Rayas.

At the Château de Fonsalette, Reynaud occasionally makes a pure-Syrah wine, of which the 1989 is the only vintage I have come across. It is good, convincing Syrah, full of violets, raspberries, pepper, cherries, artichokes and wood smoke.

The main Fonsalette wine is 50 per cent Grenache, 35 per cent Cinsault and 15 per cent Syrah. The vines were planted in 1945. In Reynaud's cellar I tasted some of the constituent parts for the 1989: a lovely Cinsault at 14° Baumé and a deep Grenache at something over 15° (Reynaud told me that 'the best Grenache is at 15.5°') with classic raspberry and tobacco tastes. The 1986 had some mature, gingerbread character, with a slightly appley taste allied to truffles, chocolate, apricots and tobacco. Fonsalette is possibly the very best of the straight Côtes du Rhônes.

DOMAINE DU VIEUX TÉLÉGRAPHE

84370 Bédarrides

Production: about 125 acres of Châteauneuf

Quality: 🍷🍷🍷🍷   Price: ★★★

Best vintages: 1981, 1985, 1988, 1989, 1990

This is one of the top estates in Châteauneuf, making chiefly red wine. The grapes here are 70 per cent Grenache, 15 per cent Mourvèdre and 15 per cent Syrah. The Bruniers have none of the 'funnies', though they admit to being tempted by Counoise. They make a little wine from Cinsault, but this is sold to Justerini and Brooks in London and never goes into the Châteauneuf.

The Bruniers marry their grapes in cask, to help the flavours to come together before the final *assemblage*: the vats contain blends of Mourvèdre and Grenache; Syrah and Grenache; and Syrah, Grenache and Mourvèdre. In November 1990 I was able to taste some of these marriages of the young wines in the vats: a straight Grenache/Syrah blend with peppery, plummy fruit; a pure-Grenache vat from forty-year-old vines up on the plateau of Mont-Redon, with lashings of blackberry, blackcurrant and raspberry fruit; and an opaque blend of Grenache and Mourvèdre tasting of boiled sweets. 1990, the younger Brunier told me, was 'the Mourvèdre year'.

That same boiled-sweet character was present on the 1989, which had been in large oak for two months. The tannins were huge, with a very aggressive Mourvèdre character. The 1988 is considered the Bruniers' best wine of the 1980s; it was already showing some leather character, with a palate of brown sugar, strawberry, blackberry and more leather. The tannins were feminine compared to those of the huge 1989; eventually they will evolve into a wine like the classic 1981: liquorice, raspberry, brown sugar, pencil shavings and herbs.

ITALY

The first man to plant Syrah in Italy was Paolo de Marchi (see Isole e Olena), but others have now learnt from his experience and it appears there may be further experiments with the grape, as well as with Mourvèdre in some of the hotter regions.

The only other estate to bottle a Syrah wine has been Villa Banfi in Montalcino, which has been making a wholly *barrique*-aged wine called Collalto since 1989. Villa Banfi has 20 acres of Syrah which was previously used to add character to its *vino novello*.

The Tuscan house of Fontodi has followed de Marchi's example by adding small amounts of Syrah to its Chianti Classico from the 1990 vintage; results are reported to be good. In Piemonte, Cerretto has also planted a little Syrah on an experimental basis.

Grenache probably reached Italy from Spain at the time of Spain's domination of the Mediterranean. It exists under a variety of synonyms, being called Grannaccia or Guarnaccia in the Campagna and Alicante elsewhere. The only part of Italy that makes Grenache wines of any distinction is Sardinia (see below), where it is called Cannonau.

Sardinia

Production: 3,950 acres of Cannonau di Sardegna (Grenache), producing 1 million litres of red wine (fortified and unfortified)

The Spanish brought Grenache to Sardinia some time between the fifteenth and the eighteenth centuries. It is now the island's third most widely planted cultivar, after Nurágus di Cagliari and Monica di Sardegna. The Cannonau wines I have tasted were sampled at a tasting organized at the Italian Trade Centre in London in January 1991; they included normal-strength wines, sweet unfortified reds and fortified reds. The two straight reds were Le Bombarde, from the co-operative at Alghero, and the Cannonau Riserva from the co-op in Jerzu; both had a faint but authentic herby nose.

Some of the Cannonau wines are allowed to stop fermenting naturally, meaning that the strength creeps up to 15° with no problem whatsoever. This was the case with the sweet, ruby dessert wine from Jerzu. The same co-operative's Cannonau Draj 1985 was made in a *rancio* style. One of the best fortified wines at the tasting was a pleasant plum/raspberry/fig-tasting Anghelu Ruju 1977 from the Tenute Sella & Mosca.

The best Grenache I have had from Sardinia was the herb-and-blackcurrant-tasting Cannonau des Parteolla from Dolia. The 1988 vintage was particularly good.

ISOLE E OLENA

Barberino, Val d'Elsa, FI 50021

Production: about 3,600 bottles

Quality: 🍇🍇🍇   Price: ★★★★

Best vintage: 1989

Paolo de Marchi planted Syrah in the early 1980s, on the recommendation of Marcel Guigal in Côte Rôtie. At first the Syrah musts were added to the Chianti Classico, and the wines from the 1986, 1987 and 1988 vintages all contain a very small percentage of Syrah. From 1988 he began producing a pure-Syrah wine, at first experimentally, but in 1989 he released a convincingly dark, concentrated Syrah with a herbs-and-flowers nose and a chocolatey/peppery finish.

Sadly, de Marchi's 1990 Syrah crop was destroyed by wild boars, which particularly admired the quality of the sweet, early-ripening fruit. They left too little on the vines to allow de

Marchi to make commercial quantities of a Syrah wine. It is hoped that de Marchi will have the sense to eat the wild boars in the future, preferably moistening their roast meat with some of his fine Syrah.

NORTH AFRICA

Production:

Morocco: 40 million litres (no specific figures available)

Algeria: *c.* 200 million litres (no specific figures available)

Tunisia: *c.* 60 million litres (no specific figures available)

Before independence, the three westernmost states of North Africa were all well known for their strong, dark-coloured wines. These not only provided excellent material for the blending vat in poor European vintages; they also had devotees who appreciated their powerful, full flavours and high alcohol content. One such was James Bond's boss 'M', who was known to drink a half bottle of 'red infuriator' with his club lunch (a full bottle when annoyed with Bond). The grapes which went to make these wines were not only the big-yielding Carignan, Cinsault, Alicante Bouschet and Aramon, but also Grenache and Mourvèdre. In Algeria's Coteaux de Mascara there is even a little Syrah grown.

Outside North Africa, wines from Morocco, Algeria and Tunisia are easiest to find in the many North African restaurants of France. The names to look out for are the Cuvée du Président and the Coteaux de Mascara from Algeria, the wines of Sidi Larbi in Morocco, and the *vins gris* from Tunisia – above all the Gris de Boulouane. I can't promise an earth-shattering wine-drinking experience, but the *rosé* wines seem well suited to the local spicy foods, especially couscous with its accompanying dollop of harissa or *sauce piquante*.

SOUTH AFRICA

| Production of Shiraz: less than 1 per cent of the vines planted – *c.* 100,000 litres

Shiraz is planted on the following estates: Altydgedacht, Backsberg, Bellingham, Bertrams, Blaauwklippen, Bon Courage, Boschendal, Bottelary, Bovlei, Delheim, Die Krans, Douglas Green, Fairview, Fleur du Cap, Groot Constantia, Hartenberg, Klawer, Klein Constantia, KWV, La Motte, Landskroon, Lievland, L'Ormarins, La Maison du Roi, Meerendal, Muratie, Nederburg, Oude Nektar, Riebeek, Rooiberg, Rust-en-Vrede, Saxenburg, Simonsig, Simonsvlei, Spier, Springlands, Stellenbosch Farmers' Winery, Swartland, Uitkyk, Van Loveren, Vergenoegd, Vriesenhof, Welmoed, Woolworths, Zandvliet, Zevenwacht and Zonnenblum.

Grenache is grown in tiny quantities on the Citrusdal and Lutzville estates.

South Africa is the oldest vine-growing country in the so-called New World, and it can trace a Syrah tradition going back to the first wine-making experiments in the last years of the seventeenth century. Syrah, however, never really caught on; it was susceptible to vineyard diseases and, more recently, wine-makers have complained about its occasionally capricious behaviour in the winery. South Africa's political isolation has not helped either: while Australia and California have leapt ahead in the past decade, South Africa – cut off from vital markets, and with an ever more shaky rand – has not been able to catch up with the technological developments available elsewhere. Provincialism continues to show its hand in South African wines. At a tasting of French and Australian Syrahs organized by wine writer Angela Lloyd of *Wynboer* magazine in 1989, the invited South African wine-makers proved somewhat ignorant of the wines on the table, although they included wines by Delas Frères and Gérard Chave.

Still, the provincialism is not wholly without advantages. Given the universal use of the term 'Shiraz' to denote Syrah wines, the impetus (and possibly the vines too) to make such wines in the post-war years must necessarily have come from the Antipodes. But if South Africa's Shiraz is based on an Australian model, the grape does not seem to suffer from the inferiority complex which affects it in the South Pacific; with only 1 per cent of the vineyard area, Shiraz in South Africa did not perform the work-horse functions of the grape in Australia. The Pinotage (a cross between Cinsault and Pinot Noir) played this role. There was consequently no reaction against the grape when wine-lovers began to clamour for Chardonnay and Cabernet. Most South African Shiraz still develops a typical gamy aroma when old, and wine-makers do not seem to have come round to the Australian way of thinking that these farmyard smells are something to be eliminated at all costs.

Until the post-war years Shiraz served one or two incongruous functions in South African vineyards, notably for some wine-makers using Shiraz to make a *blanc de noirs* wine. Naturally other estates use Shiraz in order to top up a blend of Cabernet or Pinotage. The man credited with having introduced straight Shiraz wines is Bernard Podlashuk at Bellingham.

Coastal Region

Coastal Region wines contain fruit from the vineyards around Cape Town. If the wine comes wholly from one of the regions named below then there is no need for it to be called Coastal Region. The biggest name here is of course the KWV (Kooperatieve Wynbouwers Vereeniging van Zuid Afrika), which is based in Paarl. The KWV represents 5,000 members with a total of 247,000 acres making 900 million litres of wine. The wines have the virtue of being temptingly cheap, but the 1989 Shiraz was tired and flabby and certainly not the best wine I've had from this source.

Bellingham uses fruit from two separate regions, and the wines are therefore issued as 'Coastal Region' brews. Syrah bottling in South Africa began here, back in 1948. The wines now spend two years in oak (some of it new) before release. The 1986 Shiraz was an honest, earthy, gamy Syrah.

Constantia

This is the heartland of South African wine-making, with the Groot Constantia estate dating back to 1685. In the eighteenth and nineteenth centuries, Constantia was world-famous for its liqueur wines. In the present century the vineyard was allowed to go into decline and the vines have only comparatively recently been replanted. There are now 250 acres. I have only tasted the 1986 Shiraz from Groot Constantia and cannot honestly say that I was impressed: a nose of chestnuts was followed by a palate of horse manure. This may have been a bad bottle, but, given the historical importance of the estate, Groot Constantia needs to be among South Africa's finest.

Neighbouring Klein Constantia was only replanted in 1980, although it too had a fine reputation before 1819. There are now 346 acres of vines, with the first wines bottled only in 1986. I tasted that first Shiraz and must confess that I was amazed by the quality of the fruit: a bouquet of rose petals, dense raspberry and violet on the palate, with a slight touch of game. The 1986 Shiraz from Klein Constantia is the best South African Shiraz I have tasted, and I'm not at all surprised to learn that the wine-maker Ross Gower was made the *South African Wine Guide*'s Wine-maker of the Year for 1991.

*

Paarl

The 655 acre Landskroon estate is one of South Africa's oldest, lying in full view of the Table Mountain and still owned by the Huguenot de Villiers family. I found its 1989 Shiraz marred by rather stewed, jammy fruit.

Sydney Back's Backsberg estate has been going since just after the war. The Shiraz from the 1988 vintage had very pleasant fruit, with touches of incense. My only criticism is that the wine seemed unduly light for a Shiraz and that Back should work the tannins a little more.

Fairview is also owned by a Back (Charles). Its 1985 was classic old Syrah with its old farmyard nose with a pleasant touch of violet. The Reserve wine from the 1983 vintage seemed to have done a spell in American oak and was far more like an Australian Shiraz than any other South African wine I've tasted.

Robertson

There is less Syrah in the torrid region of Robertson than in Paarl or Stellenbosch. Bon Courage has been making wine since 1983 but it seems to have achieved some style in that short time. The 1989 Shiraz had nice almond-and-peony aromas.

The Zandvliet estate contains 2,500 acres of which 250 acres are given over to vines. The wine-maker here has gone over to using some new oak, but he retains some large oak tuns too and passes the wines through both. The 1986 Shiraz has an oaky nose with some interesting tobacco-enhanced fruit; all in all a good, tightly made wine which will carry on improving for a few years.

*

Stellenbosch

Though only planted in 1979, Rust-en-Vrede has rapidly moved to the forefront of South African wineries. Some Shiraz goes into its Stellenbosch blend, which is principally Cabernet/Merlot. A straight Shiraz is also made: the 1988 was full and chunky, with lots of clean, plummy fruit; the 1986 was full of coffee/leather aromas – a very good wine.

The 1988 Lievland Shiraz impressed me less, perhaps because I'm not so keen on the flavours of American oak. In fact the American oak does not make up even the majority of the wood used (which is mainly Nevers), but the fact that I detected it must show that a little goes a long way. The Lievland had some spicy rhubarb-and-plum fruit. The Delheim wine from the same vintage also had good upfront Syrah tastes – violets and raspberries – even though it seemed to lack spark.

Another 1988 Stellenbosch is the Welmoed Koop Wynkelder, which was aged for fourteen months in big tuns. It has rather more traditional toast and animal characters and is not squeaky clean: I noted 'like the smell of the inside of a dirty ear'.

The 1987 Zonnenbloem from the Stellenbosch Farmers' Winery had a strong Woodbines character which had me thinking of Grenache.

The 1983 Vergenoegd was past its best in 1991, although it still had clean rose-petal and blackberry-pastille fruit without any game/farmyard aromas.

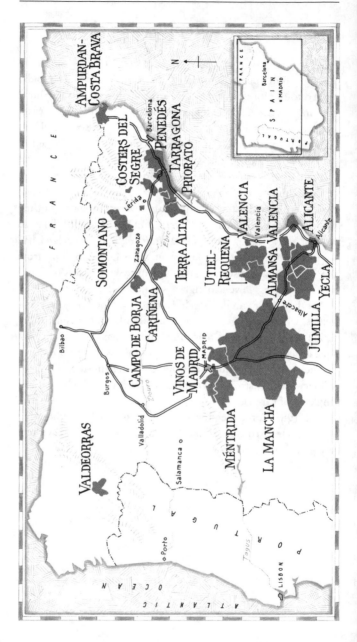

SPAIN

> Production of Grenache (Garnacha): 422,000 acres
>
> Production of Mourvèdre (Monastrell or Mataró): 267,000 acres

Spain is the sleeping giant of European wine, and in no respect is this more true than in the potential realization of great wines from the country's huge acreage of Grenache and Mourvèdre. Garnacha is one of the dominant grape varieties in Ampurdán-Costa Brava (i.e. just down the coast from Banyuls and Collioure), Campo de Borja, Cariñena, Costers del Segre, La Mancha, Méntrida, Penedès, Priorato, Somontano, Tarragona, Terra Alta, Utiel-Requena and Valdeorras as well in the lesser-quality region of Madrid. As for Monastrell, this is one of the most important cultivars in Murcia, Alicante, Albacete and Valencia as well as being the principal variety in Almansa, Costers del Segre, Jumilla, Valencia and Yecla.

Where there are signs of life in the great Iberian hulk, it is neither the Garnacha nor the Monastrell that is providing the vital force; the renaissance of Spanish viti/viniculture in red wines has been most noticeable in the planting of Tempranillo and also to some degree Cabernet Sauvignon. Garnacha and Monastrell are rather dirty words, and yet quite stunning results might easily be achieved from them with a little forward planning.

I have an undated cutting from the French *Courrier Agricole* given to me by Lucien Peyraud – the man who created the post-war glories of Bandol. The article is entitled '*Un grand vignoble de mourvèdre en Espagne!*' and recounts the story of a visit to Spain by, among others, Pierre Torrès and Anne Seguin of the research station at Tresserre in the Pyrénées Orientales. Their aim was to examine the Monastrell or Mataró to see if it really was the same grape which is now being seen as the great hope all along the Mediterranean seaboard of France.

The oenologists returned to France with no doubts whatsoever that they were dealing with the same animal – and in unheard-of quantities compared to the plantations in France. Much of what they saw perplexed them: in many cases the vineyards were far from the sea, planted in shallow dips between rugged hills; in the majority of cases the vines were ungrafted, as the soil was composed of large quantities of sand, in which the phylloxera aphis cannot operate; the domaines were far larger than their equivalents across the border and the yields were surprisingly low.

That Pierre Torrès and Anne Seguin should have returned to France aghast at what they had seen should come as no surprise: Mourvèdre is a cult grape in France, yet here, in Jumilla, was an unloved corner of Spain where there was more Mourvèdre than anyone knew what to do with. It should also be recalled that in the Pyrénées Orientales, where Torrès and Anne Seguin had come from, the Grenache was also seen as a regenerator only twenty years ago; but there is actually more of this Spanish grape in Spain than there is even in France.

It would be an interesting experiment to send some Spanish wine-makers to France for a few days to show them the way Mourvèdre is used in Bandol, and then take them up to Châteauneuf-du-Pape, Lirac or Gigondas to show them how to combine the Mourvèdre with a majority of Grenache. Maybe this will happen one day, but for the time being most go-ahead Spanish estates are not looking to enhance the palette of flavours they already have but to offer something in the form of international flavours which will earn them considerably more money on the export market.

If Garnacha is respectable in the more up-market wine regions of Spain, it is only for the production of *rosados*. Both in Rioja and in Navarra, Garnacha plays a subsidiary role in the red wines but the increasing tendency is to try to eliminate it altogether from all but the cheaper *crianzas*: pure Garnacha you will only meet in the pink wine. Some of these *rosados* are actually very good. In Navarra the house of Julian Chivite claims that it makes the best *rosado* in Spain; it is certainly good (but then so is that from the rival house of Ochoa!). Another worthwhile *rosado* is Las Campanas from Vinicola Navarra.

The most interesting province of Spain as far as Garnacha is concerned must be Catalonia (see the separate entry for Miguel Torres), and within Catalonia the star Garnachas in my experience have all come from the tiny enclave of Priorato in Tarragona. There are only five companies in Priorato producing wine on any scale: Scala Dei, De Muller, Masia Barril, Societat Cooperative Priorat, and the Unión Agraria Cooperativa. Only the first three are known outside Spain, and De Muller is only really known for its fortified wines made in a style reminiscent of Banyuls up the coast.

Of the two companies whose wines are most frequently encountered in the export markets, Scala Dei produces the lighter, more elegant wines. Its reds are 80 per cent Garnacha and 20 per cent Cariñena (Carignan) with a little Cabernet Sauvignon. The top wine is the Cartoixa Scala Dei, which is slightly oaky but otherwise rather well mannered compared to the wines of Masia Barril.

Masia Barril tries to retain some of those old leathery, *rancio* flavours which were once the hallmark of wines up and down the Catalonian coast. The Extra comes at a hefty 14°, with real gamy notes. The best wine of all in my opinion is the Especial which, at nearly 17°, is about the strongest wine you are ever likely to find on the market. The strange thing is that it has extremely attractive *rancio*-style fruit. The Especial is (in a rather polished way) a chunk of Mediterranean history.

The straight wines from De Muller have never attracted me so much. The Legítimo Priorato de Muller is very black and tannic, with toffee and bitter-chocolate flavours.

Priorato is essentially a blend of 70 per cent or more Grenache wth Carignan acting as an anti-oxidant as well as providing some aromas for the bouquet.

Once you cross from the old province of Catalonia into Murcia or Valencia, the basic grape shifts from Garnacha to Monastrell.

Very few estates in regions such as Jumilla, Yecla or Costers del Segre merit individual mention for the time being, even if the potential is there. One Jumilla which is reliable is the Bodega Señorio de Condestable, which makes fruity reds from 100 per cent Monastrell called Condestable, Señorio de Robles and Vilamar. The 1986 Condestable I recall being attractively priced above all.

Also in Jumilla is the experimental Bodegas Vitivino, which is French-owned. It makes just one 100 per cent Monastrell wine called Altos del Pio. The 1988 was still quite light for pure Mourvèdre, but it had some classy chocolatey fruit for all that.

Away in Yecla is the Bodegas Castaño which makes a 100 per cent Monastrell wine called Castaño from carbonic maceration. I'm not mad about this wine, preferring the Viña Las Gruesas, which is 20 per cent Garnacha and has a pleasant raspberry/fig and almond taste. The Pozuelo is clearly put into new American oak barrels.

Throughout the Murcia region producers make a *doble pasta* Monastrell by feeding back the skins after a *rosé saignée*. Naturally the wines are intensely tannic and dark; they also rise to quite prodigious levels of alcohol.

MIGUEL TORRES

Commercio 22, 08720 Vilafranca del Penedès

Production: 2,000 acres of Garnacha vines as well as bought-in grapes equivalent to 4.2 million litres; an experimental plantation of 15 acres of Syrah

Quality: 🍇🍇🍇   Price: ★★

Best vintages: 1986, 1988, 1989, 1990

Despite his tireless experimentation with French grape varieties, Miguel Torres has never stopped production of his traditional Penedès reds made from a blend of Garnacha and Cariñena. Naturally it is Garnacha which forms the mainstay and the Cariñena is there to provide fresh fruit aromas and to protect the sensitive Grenache from light and oxygen. The basic wine here is Tres Torres, which is something of a bargain. The 1988 was a particularly successful wine, with plenty of truffly, raspberry fruit.

The better wine is the Gran Sangredetoro, which is a *reserva* wine. I went through a period of disliking Gran Sangredetoro in the mid 1980s, when I thought Miguel Torres had stripped down the wine in the interests of 'elegance'. The 1986, however, was certainly a return to form with its palate of liquorice, truffles, tobacco, almond and dried herbs: it is almost cut in the mould of a good Châteauneuf-du-Pape.

Torres has planted a 15 acre Syrah vineyard, but at the time of writing (October 1991) there have been no firm plans as to what to do with the grapes. It is certain that when Torres does decide to use the fruit he will do something exciting – at least if his Chardonnay, Merlot, Pinot Noir and Cabernet Sauvignon wines are anything to go by.

SWITZERLAND

Minute quantities of Syrah are grown in Switzerland. In the Valais, a Dr Wuilloud has achieved some fame for his Syrah wines at his domaine in Diolly. I am sorry to say that I have never had the opportunity to taste them.

In May 1992 two Swiss Syrah wines were shown at the *journée prestige* in Tain l'Hermitage. Both came from the village of Chamosan in the Valais and both were 1989s. That from Simon Maye was a decent wine with a touch too much oak; the wine from Pierre-Luc Remondeulaz-Michellod was a real eye-opener, however, with a bouquet of buckwheat and an excellent, big, black-fruity palate.

USA

California

> Production of Syrah: 120 acres – about 37 acres in Mendo-
> cino County and some 30 acres in the Napa Valley; most
> of the rest in San-Luis Obispo (and more plantings are on
> the way)
>
> Production of Grenache: about 16,000 acres, mostly in the
> San Joaquin Valley; there is a source of better Grenache in
> Washington State
>
> Production of Mourvèdre: 456 acres, the largest acreage
> being in Contra Costa County

Syrah, Grenache and Mourvèdre are, along with grapes like
Italy's Nebbiolo and Sangiovese, California's version of the
emperor's new clothes – the darlings of the post-Cabernet/
Chardonnay generation. One has to admire the inventiveness
of these Californians who refuse to rest on their laurels; once
they have mastered one branch of viticultural style they simply
press on and try their hands at another. I wonder what it will be
next: *vin jaune* made from pure Petit Manseng? Oak-aged
Grüner Veltliner? I wouldn't put either past them.

Syrah began with Joseph Phelps in the Napa Valley. Phelps
planted in 1974 and made his first wine in 1980. He was followed by Santino and R. H. Phillips in the late 1970s. The
Rhône craze gained momentum in the early to mid 1980s.
Sometime towards the end of the decade, a bright spark coined
the phrase 'Rhône Rangers' to describe wine-makers practising
a Rhône style. There is no formal club as such.

Though the first emphasis was on Syrah – a variety which did not exist before Phelps (although some people, including Gérard Jaboulet, have said that the Petite Syrah at Ridge is in fact Syrah and not Durif) – the Californians have since discovered Mourvèdre, which they quite wrongly believe to exist nowhere else in any profusion. Perhaps Bandol remains unknown to them, or possibly they are thrown by the fact that Spaniards call it 'Monastrell' and Australians 'Mataró'.

The Californian Mourvèdre (which was also called 'Mataró' until recently) was planted by Italians at around the time of the First World War. The best vines are therefore as much as seventy years old. Somehow they survived Prohibition, to be discovered by Fred Cline in the early 1980s. Cline now controls access to these old Mourvèdre vines which are the backbone of his Côtes d'Oakley wines. Cline was a classmate of Randall Grahm at the University of Davis in California, and to some extent these fanatical Rhône Rangers work in tandem.

Grenache has existed in California for donkey's years. It was almost certainly originally planted by the Spaniards. Rhône-Ranger wine-makers, however, are less than happy with the Grenache clones available from the state and say that better fruit is available from Washington State. Bringing in Washington Grenache leads to considerable problems, however, as the Californian wine-makers forgo their right to territorial appellations and vintage dates.

Currently the most noticeable card in the Rhône Ranger pack is the youthful Randall Grahm of Bonny Doon. Grahm attracts a good deal of publicity through his childish puns. Some people may be annoyed by puns, but they should not be put off Grahm's wines, which are genuinely interesting.

We are going to see a lot more Syrah, Grenache and Mourvèdre wines over the next few years. For the time being the leading Rhône Rangers are Berkeley Red, Bonny Doon, Domaine de la Terre Rouge, Duxoup Dry Creek, Edmunds St John, Estrella River, Frey Mendocino, Kendall Jackson, McDowell Valley, Ojai, Orion (Sean Thackery), Paso Robles (planted as early as 1978), Phelps, Preston, Qupé, Russian River, Sierra Vista, Sotoyome, Trumpet View and Zaca Mesa.

At the time of writing, the most interesting new venture to

reach California has been the planting of 250 acres of vines at Tablas Creek near Paso Robles by Robert Haas in conjunction with the Perrin brothers of Châteauneuf-du-Pape. The land was specially selected for its ability to produce a Châteauneuf-style blend, and Haas and the Perrins have planted Syrah, Grenache, Mourvèdre and Counoise. Possibly a little Vaccarèse will also be put down. No wine will be made until the vines are bearing properly. The Perrins intend to use the Beaucastel method of vinification.

In October 1990, barrel-broker Mel Knox and wine-maker Dick Ward very kindly put on a tasting of wines made by the Rhône Rangers for the Octagon group of wine writers in London. Forty-one wines were shown: five whites, a *rosé*, seventeen Syrah-based wines and eighteen wines made in a 'southern-Rhône' style. The tasting was an eye-opener. Most of us had no idea of the number of wines currently being made in Rhône styles. The overall impression, however, was one of slight clumsiness and extremely high alcohol levels; but these are teething problems and with time (and if they do not decide to T-graft their vines to something else next winter) the wine-makers should be making very fine reds and *rosés*. Some already are.

There were two wines in the tasting from Zaca Mesa in Santa Barbara: a pleasant, light 1989 Syrah was rather more impress-ive than an earlier 1987 attempt. The Preston Vineyard in Sonoma had managed to combine 75 per cent Syrah with 25 per cent Petite Syrah (Durif) to good effect, although it oc-curred to me that it might have gone a little overboard on the oak. Some good wines came from Sean Thackery at Orion: the 1988 was strange – pork sausages and herbs – but I found the 1987 more convincing, with its chocolate and raspberry tastes. There was a good, juicy reserve wine from R. H. Phillips' winery in the Dunnigan Hills west of Sacramento, which also makes a Night Harvest Cuvée from Syrah fruit. I was far less impressed by the wines of Kendall Jackson and Sierra Vista.

See also entries for Bonny Doon, Ojai, Joseph Phelps and Qupé.

Of the southern-Rhône-style wines, the Cline Oakley Cuvée

and Côtes d'Oakley occasionally erred in the direction of fiery alcohol. The Côtes is 51 per cent Carignan with 35 per cent Mourvèdre and small amounts of Cabernet and Zinfandel. The Cuvée is 51 per cent Mourvèdre with the rest made from Zinfandel and Carignan. The Cuvée is by far the better wine: with its cigarette aromas, I was convinced that the 1988 was Grenache.

Of the straight Mourvèdres, the wines from Jade Mountain in Sonoma (1988), Taurus and R. H. Phillips were all impressive – especially the Phillips, with its tobacco character of the 1988 vintage. Some of the best wines in this flight came from the Edmunds St John winery in Alameda: a straight Mourvèdre from the 1986 vintage, which was rather peppery, and, from the same year, a blend of Syrah, Grenache and Mourvèdre called Les Côtes Sauvages, which had authentic earthy notes. The two wines which impressed me least here were the Santino Barbara and the Domaine de la Terre Rouge.

BONNY DOON VINEYARD

10 Pine Flat Road, Santa Cruz, CA 95060

Production: 32 acres (96,000 bottles)

Quality: 🍇🍇🍇   Price: ★★★★

Best vintages: 1987, 1988

Randall Grahm made his first vintage in 1981. At that time, this Davis graduate was making the usual Californian stand-bys of Cabernet and Chardonnay. In the past few years, however, Grahm has become passionate about the Rhône Valley and has therefore T-grafted all his vines over to red and white Rhône cultivars. His own small vineyard is not big enough to satisfy all his needs, and he has to look elsewhere for most of his fruit. The bulk of his Mourvèdre is obtained from Fred Cline.

Grahm has a joky style which brings him plenty of publicity. His wines all have funny names, the top wine being called Cigare Volant – both a play on the Châteauneuf estate of La

Cigale Volante and a reference to a brief scare in Châteauneuf in the 1950s when flying 'cigars' (i.e. flying saucers) were seen overhead. Grahm has also made an Old Telegram as a tribute to Vieux Télégraphe in Châteauneuf. I asked one of the younger Bruniers whether he had tasted the wine. He was rather sniffy, saying that Grahm needed to work his tannins better. A good Grenache/Mourvèdre *rosé* is called Vin Gris de Cigare and has authentic tobacco (cigars again!) aromas. It is perhaps a shade too alcoholic.

I have yet to taste Grahm's Côtes de Gilroy, which is billed as 'a fruity Grenache'. A straight 1988 Syrah I found impressive with its upfront, raspberry/strawberry fruit. The 1988 Cigare Volant (54 per cent Mourvèdre, 39 per cent Grenache, 7 per cent Syrah) has a big raspberry and tobacco taste, but is perhaps a little too 'hot' from its alcohol. The 1987 was more peppery, with a raspberry-and-lentil taste.

OJAI WINERY

P.O. Box 952, Oakview, CA 93022
Production: 17,000 bottles
Quality: 🍇🍇🍇   Price: ★★★
Best vintages: 1987, 1988, 1989

This small estate, run by Adam Tolmach, has been making Rhône-style wines since its first vintage in 1983. Tolmach has planted Syrah, Mourvèdre, Viognier and Marsanne.

I have only tasted Tolmach's Syrah, which is made in a low-Baumé, lentils-and-raspberries style. Both the 1988 and the 1987 vintages were successful, with the 1987 having some wood-smoke, even smoky-bacon, aromas often associated with the northern Rhône.

JOSEPH PHELPS VINEYARDS

> P.O. Box 1031, St Helena, CA 94574
>
> Production: 720,000 bottles
>
> Quality: 🍇🍇🍇   Price: ★★★★
>
> Best vintages: 1981, 1986, 1989

Joseph Phelps's winery dates from the early 1970s and he was putting out Syrah wines some time before the rest of the Rhône Ranger pack. His earliest Syrah I've tasted was from the 1980 vintage, and the 1981 is still available at the time of writing. The wine began life with a lot of deep blackberry aromas but now, in its mature state, is marked by some of those rather sewery notes which I associate with ripe Cornas. This is clearly intentional as far as Phelps is concerned, as the 1986 has a similar – Provençal-drains – character.

Phelps also makes a *rosé* called Vin du Mistral from 35 per cent Mourvèdre, 35 per cent Grenache and 30 per cent Syrah. It is a good wine and rather serious for a *rosé*, with lots of lentil/pepper aromas.

QUPÉ WINERY

> P.O. Box 113, Los Olivos, CA 93441
>
> Production: 54,000 bottles
>
> Quality: 🍇🍇🍇🍇   Price: ★★★★
>
> Best vintages: 1987, 1988, 1989

Qupé, which means 'poppy' in a local Indian dialect, is owned by Bob Lindquist, another Californian with a passion for the Rhône. The vineyard was created in 1982 but took a while to find a home. Lindquist vinifies his different Syrahs separately to make Los Olivos and Bien Nacido wines as well as a rather more reasonable straight Syrah made from Paso Robles and

Santa Barbara grapes. He is now making a 'southern-Rhône' Los Olivos Cuvée as well.

The straight 1989 Syrah was good stuff, dominated by some exotic fruit aromas. The ordinary wine in the 1988 vintage had a smoky, tarry nose, built in a very convincing northern-Rhône style. The Bien Nacido Syrah from the same vintage was marred by some clumsy use of sulphur. The Bien Nacido 1989 was much better, with enchanting mango, blackberry and raspberry aromas.

GLOSSARY

AOC

Appellation d'Origine Contrôlée. French legally defined wine region. The statutes of AOCs define the grapes to be used, yields and permitted soil types.

ASSEMBLAGE

The putting together of the elements which will make up the finished blend. Theoretically this should all be done at the same time and not in several instalments. In some properties, however, the wine-makers do not possess a large enough vat to perform this operation and consequently blend for bottling over a period of anything up to eighteen months. In many cases this leads to variations in quality.

BARRIQUE

French word for a small oak cask containing around 200 litres. Outside France it has come to have other implications: *barriques* are invariably new or almost new and are used to add oaky flavourings to the wine.

BAUMÉ

A scale measuring potential alcohol in grape juice or must. The Baumé scale is used here in preference to the Brix, Öchsle or KMW scales because it translates more readily into the alcohol level which is likely to be achieved after fermentation.

CAP
: The cake of skins and pips which settles on the surface of the fermenting must. As the cap contains flavour, colour and tannin, it needs to be 'worked' in order to achieve the maximum extraction if a *vin de garde* is foreseen.

CARBON DIOXIDE (CO₂)
: A natural by-product of fermentation, CO_2 is none the less disagreeable in wine. It can be removed by racking the wine from one receptacle to another.

CARBONIC MACERATION
: *Macération carbonique* in French or 'cab mac' in Australian: the process of stewing ripe, whole berries in carbon dioxide gas to provoke fermentation within the grape itself. It produces wines which are strong on aromas and short on body. Ideally wines made by carbonic maceration should be blended with wines made from traditional ferments: this gives the best of both worlds.

CÉPAGE
: French word for grape variety, varietal or cultivar; Syrah, Grenache and Mourvèdre are all *cépages*.

CÉPAGES ACCESSOIRES
: Grapes of a different variety to the main *cépage* in the blend which are added to give nuances of flavour or to provide structure to the wine. In the Midi, for example, the light, fragrant Cinsault is often used as a *cépage accessoire*, though on its own it is a rather boring grape.

CÉPAGES AMÉLIORATEURS
: Grape varieties used to improve the overall quality of the blend or of a region as a whole. In the Midi, Syrah, Grenache

and Mourvèdre are all seen as *cépages améliorateurs* gradually displacing the Alicante Bouschet, Aramon, Cinsault and Carignan which used to dominate the region twenty years ago.

CÉPAGES NOBLES   Grape varieties which are seen to have noble qualities. Naturally authorities disagree about which varieties deserve this epithet: in Australia neither Grenache nor Mourvèdre (Mataró) is seen as 'noble', whereas in France they are included in that category. Certain grapes are seen as very definitely 'ignoble' – Alicante Bouschet and Aramon, for example.

CHAPTALIZATION   The process of sugaring musts to increase the alcohol level in the finished wine. Chaptalization is very common in France, where the climate is relatively cool and grapes have occasional problems reaching full maturity. In very hot countries such as Australia and California, chaptalization is not only scorned, it is forbidden.

CO_2 See CARBON DIOXIDE.

COTEAUX   French word for slopes. In France it is believed that the best Syrah is grown on steep slopes. Australians tend to poohpooh this.

COULURE   A sickness affecting vines during flowering. If the weather is cold or damp, the flowers fall off, leading to uneven bunches and low yields.

CRU
French word for 'growth' – used to denote a wine of particular quality.

CUVAISON
The time the wine spends in the fermenting vat. In general, the longer the *cuvaison* the bigger the wine; but long fermentation engenders problems of its own, such as volatile acidity.

CUVÉE
In France, a blend of different vats or vineyards; in Austria, misinterpreted to mean an eccentric cocktail of grapes.

ENCÉPAGEMENT
The grape varieties going into a blend or grown on an estate.

GARRIGUE
A word common in the French Midi for the scrubby hillsides which are often covered with wild thyme. Some wines (notably Grenache-based wines) are said to smell of the *garrigue*: they have a bouquet of Provençal herbs or Virginia tobacco.

GRAND VIN
In the opinion of its maker, the top wine from an estate.

H₂S
See HYDROGEN SULPHIDE.

HYDROGEN SULPHIDE (H₂S)
A chemical compound present in wine which smells of stink bombs or rotten eggs. H₂S develops in wine either as a result of sprays in the vineyards (generally against rot in humid regions like the Hunter Valley) or through sulphur sticks being burnt inside barrels to disinfect them. If detected early, H₂S can be removed by passing the wine over

copper. Copper (a small coin will do) is also the test for H_2S: place the coin in the glass; if the eggy smell goes then H_2S was at fault.

INAO — *Institut National des Appellations d'Origine* – the body regulating AOCs in France.

LIEU-DIT — The local name denoting a particular vineyard, exposition or hillside. The *lieu-dit* is often used to signify that the wine is a superior one which hails from some particularly well-favoured site; occasionally it is used to pull the wool over the consumer's eyes. Australians tend to take a dim view of this sort of territorial paraphernalia.

MACERATION — The process of steeping the *marc* in the fermenting must to obtain colour, flavour and tannin.

MACÉRATION SOUS ALCOOL — In VDNs, the process of steeping the grapes or must in rectified spirit.

MARC — The solid part of the grape – pips, husks etc. This is sometimes moistened and distilled to make brandy, which is then called *eau-de-vie de marc*, or just plain *marc*.

MERCAPTAN — A compound of hydrogen sulphide.

MILLERANDAGE — Similar to *coulure*, only this time it is the infant berries which fall off. The result is much the same.

MUST — The juice of freshly crushed grapes, not yet wine.

MUTAGE SUR MARC	In VDNs, the process of steeping the cap in rectified spirit before pressing, rather than cutting the fermenting wine with alcohol as is the case in port-making.
NÉGOCIANT	A wholesale (wine) merchant.
pH	A scale used to measure acidity. A balanced wine is thought to have a pH of around 3.5. A high pH (above 3.5) sometimes causes poor resistance to bacteria; too low a pH (below 3.2, say) makes for characterless wines.
PHYLLOXERA	An American aphis which devastated (hence its full name of *phylloxera vastatrix*) the vineyards of Europe in the nineteenth century and savaged those of Australia not long after.
PIEDS DE COTEAUX	French for the feet of hillsides. As a rule, vines planted on such sites produce indifferent wine.
PIGEAGE	The breaking up of the cap by use of a pole or *pige*.
PLC	*Plafond limité de classement* – the maximum yield stipulated for a particular French AOC. In most years, however, the maxima are stretched upwards by 20 per cent or so, to placate potentially angry French farmers. Quality is rarely if ever taken into consideration.
PRIMEUR	A French name given to very fresh wine, Beaujolais *primeur* being another name for Beaujolais *nouveau*. The term

'primeur' is also used in tasting to denote a particularly youthful character in the wine: *'Il est très primeur votre Hermitage'* etc.

RANCIO

A reductive, oxidized character in old Grenache wines which is much appreciated in traditional Banyuls or Rivesaltes. The wines with a *rancio* taste are faintly reminiscent of Madeira.

RÉGISSEUR

A vineyard manager.

SAIGNÉE

A light 'bleeding' of black grapes to make a *rosé* wine. The advantage is that the hulls can be fed back into the *grand vin* to make it all the denser.

SO$_2$

See SULPHUR DIOXIDE.

SOLERA SYSTEM

A system practised in Spain of constantly replenishing old wines in cask with younger wines after a quantity has been drawn off and bottled.

SULPHIDIC

Over-sulphured or stinking of H_2S – it can mean both.

SULPHUR DIOXIDE (SO$_2$)

A chemical used as a disinfectant in wine-making and also as a preservative. Virtually all wine contains SO_2, but it shouldn't be noticeable or make you cough; if this occurs the wine-maker may be said to have 'overdone it'.

TERRA ROSA

The name given to the limestone soils of Australia. Coonawarra is the most famous of these.

TERROIR

A French concept much vilified by Australians. The French insist that the quality of a wine comes about as a combination of soil, exposition, climate and wine-making. Australians will insist that soil is far less important than the skill of the wine-maker.

VDN

Vin doux naturel – a fortified wine of the Banyuls, Rivesaltes, Maury or Rasteau type. Muscat de Beaumes-de-Venise is also a VDN, but falls outside the scope of this book.

VIN DE COMPTOIR

A dismissive term used to designate the sort of rot-gut you are likely to be served in a French bar or bistro.

VIN DE GARDE

A wine which is likely to benefit from long ageing in a cellar.

VIN GRIS

A wine with a slight pinky-grey colour. This occurs either because the grape is slightly tinted (as in Pinot Gris) or because circumstances like a sandy soil inhibit pigmentation in the grape.

VIN MÉDECIN

A strongly alcoholic and deep-coloured wine formerly used to beef up some less favoured brew. The practice is illegal now.

VIN DE PAYS

The lowest grade of French wine above *vin de table*. Theoretically there should now be some quite interesting *vins de pays* where the wine-maker tries to experiment with grape varieties not tolerated by the local AOC. In practice this is rarely the case.

VIN DE PRESSE

The first-run juice of wine is called the *vin de goutte*. This is the best must. The *vin de presse* is the last squeezings from the grape, and tends to be bitter and tannic, taking many years to soften. *Vin de presse* is generally used only in wines destined for long ageing.

VINO NOVELLO

The Italian version of '*nouveau*'.

VOLATILE ACIDITY

A chemical imbalance in wine caused by bacteria and producing acetic acid. It is not wise to keep wines which are overly volatile, lest they end up in the salad dressing.

INDEX